Values and Opportunities in Social Entrepreneurship

Edited by

Kai Hockerts
Associate Professor, Copenhagen Business School, Denmark

Johanna Mair
Associate Professor, Department of General Management, IESE Business School, Universidad de Navarra, Spain

and

Jeffrey Robinson
Assistant Professor of Management and Global Business, Rutgers Business School, New Jersey, USA

First published 2010 by
PALGRAVE MACMILLAN

Palgrave Macmillan in the UK is an imprint of Macmillan Publishers Limited,
registered in England, company number 785998, of Houndmills, Basingstoke,
Hampshire RG21 6XS.

Palgrave Macmillan in the US is a division of St Martin's Press LLC,
175 Fifth Avenue, New York, NY 10010.

Palgrave Macmillan is the global academic imprint of the above companies
and has companies and representatives throughout the world.

Palgrave® and Macmillan® are registered trademarks in the United States,
the United Kingdom, Europe and other countries.

ISBN 978–0–230–21668–6 hardback

This book is printed on paper suitable for recycling and made from fully
managed and sustained forest sources. Logging, pulping and manufacturing
processes are expected to conform to the environmental regulations of the
country of origin.

A catalogue record for this book is available from the British Library.

A catalog record for this book is available from the Library of Congress.

10   9   8   7   6   5   4   3   2   1
19 18 17 16 15 14 13 12 11 10

Printed and bound in Great Britain by
CPI Antony Rowe, Chippenham and Eastbourne

Contents

List of Figures

List of Tables

List of Appendix

Acknowledgements

The production of this volume was aided immensely by a large number of people. We first thank the participants of the 3rd International Social Entrepreneurship Research Conference (ISERC) in Copenhagen. In particular, we would like to thank the members of the ISERC blind review panel, which made possible a selection of high quality papers. We furthermore appreciate the work of the authors of the contributions included here who have taken the reviewers' feedback very constructively, in many cases revising their papers substantially. We believe that the result is reflected in the high quality of the work presented here.

Furthermore, we would like to thank the Copenhagen Business School (CBS) as well as the Asia Link programme for their financial support of the ISERC conference. At CBS we are also deeply indebted to the team at the Centre for Corporate Social responsibility (cbsCSR) which houses the Social Entrepreneurship research stream here and which has been the primary host of the ISERC conference.

Particular thanks are due to Anne Hanusch who has helped to pull together this volume at CBS as well as the editors at Palgrave who have made possible both this book and the series in which it features.

Notes on Contributors

Geoff Desa is Assistant Professor of Management at San Francisco State University. His research interests lies at the intersection of technology and social entrepreneurship: to understand how entrepreneurs use new technologies in resource-limited environments. Geoff completed his PhD in Technology Entrepreneurship and Strategic Management with a minor in Public Affairs from the University of Washington in Seattle. He also holds a BS in Electrical Engineering from the Georgia Institute of Technology, an MS in Electrical Engineering from Stanford University, and an MS in Business Administration from the University of Washington. His industry background includes founding-team experience at Novera Optics, a Silicon Valley optical start-up, and research and development at Hewlett Packard and Agilent Research Laboratories. Geoff has also consulted with the University of Washington Technology Transfer Office, the Center for Innovation and Entrepreneurship and the Global Business Center. He is on the consulting board of the Common Data Project, a technology social venture engaged in information technology privacy.

MariaLaura Di Domenico is Lecturer in Organizational Behaviour at the Open University Business School in the UK. Her research interests include social and community enterprises and the 'third' sector, social entrepreneurship, and small and medium-sized enterprises (SMEs). Her work has been published in journals including Human Relations; Entrepreneurship, Theory and Practice; and Organization Studies.

Kees Dorst is Professor of Design and Associate Dean Research at the Faculty of Design, Architecture and Building of the University of Technology, Sydney. He is also senior researcher in Design Studies at the Department of Industrial Design of Eindhoven University of Technology. Kees Dorst studied Industrial Design Engineering at Delft University of Technology, and Philosophy at the Erasmus University in Rotterdam. He has worked as product designer, consultant and design researcher. He has written many papers and several books, most recently *Understanding Design* (2006). His research now focuses on the development of design expertise, and on the uses of design expertise and design thinking in problem arenas that are not associated with the 'traditional' design professions.

Heather Douglas is a doctoral candidate at Griffith University in Brisbane, Australia. After completing a Master of Social Welfare Administration and Planning from University of Queensland and has an MBA, Heather's PhD investigates theories underpinning social entrepreneurship start-up processes. Her interests are entrepreneurship and organization theory, business ethics, civil society and social innovation. She teaches management, marketing and sociology. Following extensive experience establishing innovative health and disability services, Heather worked as a researcher, advised the Australian and Queensland Governments on developing and delivering supportive social systems, and established a consultancy business. In response to unmet community needs she founded and facilitated the development of numerous voluntary civil society organizations. She sits on several community enterprise committees, and is a member of the governing board of Griffith University.

Paola Grenier has researched and written on social entrepreneurship since 1997. She gained a PhD from the London School of Economics and Political Science on the role and significance of social entrepreneurship in UK social policy. She has a BA in psychology from Cambridge University, and an MSc in Organizational Psychology from Birkbeck College, London University. She has specialized in non-profit sector studies, and has published articles on social capital, social movements, venture philanthropy and social entrepreneurship. She lives in Hungary and has also written on the Hungarian non-profit sector. Prior to her role in academia, for more than a decade Paola worked in the UK charity sector and the Hungarian non-profit sector.

Helen Haugh is Senior Lecturer in Community Enterprise at Judge Business School (University of Cambridge). Her research interests focus on the establishment, growth and impact of social and community enterprise, corporate social responsibility and business ethics. Her work has been published in *Entrepreneurship Theory and Practice*, the *Journal of Small Business Management* and the *Journal of Business Ethics*.

Kai Hockerts is Associate Professor at the Copenhagen Business School (CBS) where he coordinates the Minor in Social Entrepreneurship. His research has been published in journals such as the *Journal of Business*

Venturing, Journal of Business Ethics, and Business Strategy and the Environment. He has also written a number of case studies including the award winning "Mobility CarSharing – From Ecopreneurial Start-up to Commercial Venture".

Jill R. Kickul is the Director of the Stewart Satter Program in Social Entrepreneurship in New York University Stern's Berkley Center for Entrepreneurial Studies. Prior to joining NYU Stern, Professor Kickul was the Richard A. Forsythe Chair in Entrepreneurship at Miami University, Ohio. Her primary research areas of interest include innovation and strategic processes within new ventures, micro-financing practices and wealth creation in transitioning economies, and social entrepreneurship. She is the author of *Entrepreneurship Strategy: Changing Patterns in New Venture Creation, Growth, and Reinvention* and more than 50 other publications in entrepreneurship and management journals. Professor Kickul's work on entrepreneurship education development has been nationally recognized and was named by Fortune Small Business as one of the Top 10 Innovative Programs in Entrepreneurship Education.

Andrea Larson is Associate Professor at the Darden Graduate School of Business where she teaches courses on entrepreneurship, innovation and sustainability in the MBA program and the MBA for Executives program. Her work on alliances and entrepreneurial innovation has been published in journals including Administrative Science Quarterly, Journal of Business Venturing, Entrepreneurship Theory and Practice, and Interfaces (special issue on sustainable business innovation/practices). Co-founder of The Ingenuity Project to integrate theory and practice on entrepreneurship/innovation and sustainability issues, author of multiple book chapters, and visiting faculty at Stanford Business School (2007 and 2010), in 2009 she provided Congressional testimony on U.S. competitiveness in "green" technology in world markets. She holds a PhD from Harvard University.

Woodrow Lucas is a Ph.D. student in organization studies, Owen Graduate School of Management, Vanderbilt University (degree expected 2011). He is the recipient of Provost Merit Fellowship for PHD scholarship. Lucas received both a Master of Business Administration degree and a Master of Theological Studies degree from Vanderbilt University. Lucas earned a Bachelor of Arts degree from Northwestern

University with honors in Mathematical Methods in the Social Sciences. His current research interests include organizational forms, corporate social responsibility, social entrepreneurship, positive organizational scholarship.

Johanna Mair is Associate Professor of Strategic Management at IESE, the Business School of the University of Navarra in Barcelona, Spain. She teaches strategy and social entrepreneurship in the MBA program, executive programs and the PhD program at IESE. Her current research lies at the intersection of traditional strategy and entrepreneurship. She has received numerous awards for her research and publications. In 2007 she was recognized as a 'Faculty Pioneer' by the Aspen Institute and received the 'Ashoka Award for Social Entrepreneurship Education'. In addition she has received the 2007 Strategic Management Society Best Paper for Practice Implications Award.

Simone Maase is a consultant for emerging social entrepreneurship at GreenWish, a Dutch not-for-profit organization aimed at supporting grassroots initiatives for social and sustainable development. She holds a MS in Industrial Design Engineering from Delft University of Technology. She has worked as product designer and taught design students about social awareness and sustainable development at the Academy of Arts and Design, Bolzano, the Utrecht School of the Arts and the Eindhoven University of Technology. She started her PhD while still teaching at the department of Industrial Design, Eindhoven University of Technology; the subject is partnerships for social entrepreneurship. Her research interests include the partnership process, its inhibiting factors and how to facilitate the partnership process applying a co-design approach. Her supervisor is Kees Dorst.

Javier Monllor is an Assistant Professor of Management and Entrepreneurship at DePaul University's Kellstadt Graduate School of Business in Chicago. His research interests include social entrepreneurship, opportunity recognition, creativity and entrepreneurial cognition. He has presented at various research conferences including the Babson Frontiers of Entrepreneurship Research Conference, the Ethics and Entrepreneurship Research Conference and the Allied Sciences Research Conference and has published papers in the International Journal of Entrepreneurship and Small Business, in Advances in Entrepreneurship: Firm Emergence and Growth and the Journal of Small Business Management.

Nathalie Moray is Assistant Professor in Management at University College Ghent. She obtained a PhD in Management Science (2004) in the field of industry–science relations and academic entrepreneurship and published her work in several journals such as *Research Policy* and *Journal of Business Venturing*. In 2001–2002 she was a visiting doctoral fellow at Sloan School of Management, MIT, USA. Currently, she is constructing a database of social entrepreneurs in Flanders (Belgium), geared towards the development of a panel data set. The overall goal of this research effort is to investigate the process through which social purpose business ventures build and develop business models to create value. She teaches general management and strategic management to bachelor and master students in business administration.

Alex Nicholls is the University Lecturer in Social Entrepreneurship at the Skoll Centre for Social Entrepreneurship, University of Oxford. Nicholls' research interests range across several key areas within social entrepreneurship, including: the interface between the public and social sectors; organizational legitimacy and governance; the development of social finance markets; and impact measurement and innovation. Nicholls is widely published in peer-reviewed journals and is the co-author of a major research book; *Fair Trade: Market-Driven Ethical Consumption* (with Charlotte Opal, Sage, 2005). His best-selling edition of a collection of key academic papers on the state of the art of social entrepreneurship globally was published by Oxford University Press in 2006 and went into paperback (with a new introduction) in 2008. Nicholls has held lectureships at academic institutions including University of Toronto, Canada; Leeds Metropolitan University; University of Surrey; and Aston Business School. He has been a Fellow of the Academy of Marketing Science and Member of the Institute of Learning and Teaching. He also sat on the regional social enterprise expert group for the South East of England and is a non-executive director of a major fair trade company.

Francesco Perrini is Professor of Management & CSR and SIF Chair of Social Entrepreneurship at the Institute of Strategy, Department of Management of Bocconi University, Milan, Italy. He is also Senior Professor of Corporate Finance at the SDA Bocconi School of Management. Professor Perrini is Head of the CSR Unit at SDA Bocconi and the Business Ethics and Social Issue in Management Unit at Bocconi University; he is also Director of the Bachelor of Business Administration and Management (CLEAM), member of the Advisory Board of the SPACE Bocconi,

Research Centre for Studies on Security and Protection against Crime and Emergencies and of the Board of Directors of the Italian Centre for Social Responsibility (I-CSR), Milan. Since 1990 he has been a researcher at Bocconi, focusing on Strategic and Financial Management: Management of Corporate Development Processes (strategy implementation, acquisitions management; financial strategies and valuation; innovation, SMEs) and Social Issues in Management (Corporate Governance, Sustainability, Social Responsibility, CSR, SRI, Sustainable Innovation and Social Entrepreneurship).

Jeffrey Robinson is Assistant Professor of Management and Global Business at Rutgers Business School, New Jersey, USA, where he leads the school's urban entrepreneurship research and economic development initiatives. Prior to joining Rutgers, he was on the faculty of NYU's Stern School of Business. He is the recipient of a 2007 Faculty Pioneer award from the Aspen Institute for his path-breaking research, teaching and service activities at the intersection of business and society.

Saras D. Sarasvathy is a member of the Strategy, Entrepreneurship and Ethics area and teaches courses in entrepreneurship and ethics in Darden's MBA program. In addition, she teaches in the doctoral program and the research seminar on Markets in Human Hope. In 2007, Saras was named one of the top 18 entrepreneurship professors by Fortune Small Business Magazine. A leading scholar on the cognitive basis for high-performance entrepreneurship, Saras serves as Associate Editor of the *Journal of Business Venturing* as well as advisor to entrepreneurship education and doctoral programs in Europe and Asia. Her scholarly work has won several awards including the 2001 William H. Newman Award from the Academy of Management, the 2009 Gerald E. Hills Best Paper Award from the American Marketing Association, and her book *Effectuation: Elements of Entrepreneurial Expertise* was nominated for the 2009 Terry Book Award by the Academy of Management. In addition to a master's degree in Industrial Administration, Saras received her Ph.D. in Information Systems from Carnegie Mellon University. Her thesis on entrepreneurial expertise was supervised by Herbert Simon, 1978 Nobel Laureate in Economics.

Brett R. Smith is Ph.D. and the Founding Director, Center for Social Entrepreneurship at Miami University in Oxford, Ohio. His research interests focus on social entrepreneurship with specific emphases on scaling of social impact, new development models and social entrepreneurship education. His research has been featured in a number of leading academic journals including *Entrepreneurship & Regional Development, Journal of Small Business Management, Journal of Social Entrepreneurship, Leadership Quarterly,* and *M.I.T. Innovations.* He won the *ASHOKA Award for Pedagogical Innovation* at the Skoll World Forum on Social Entrepreneurship for the partnership he developed with Bono's company to found Edun Live on Campus. He has been invited to speak on social entrepreneurship at the United Nations, Nelson Mandela Foundation and many leading international universities. He has also been awarded two national grants related to social entrepreneurship by Learn and Serve American and U.S. Department of State. His work in social entrepreneurship has been highlighted in *Time, Business Week, Financial Times,* CNN, MSNBC and more than 100+ other media outlets.

Roger Spear has played a major role in the development of international research on co-operatives, social enterprise, and the social economy through his work with three international research networks. As chair of the International Co-operative Alliance (ICA) research committee he strengthened global research on co-operatives through two new networks in Asia Pacific and Latin America. Work with the Ciriec network of researchers on the European social economy led to a major publication with considerable influence over European policy. Work with EMES (European research network on social enterprise) on three major international comparative studies has pioneered research in this rapidly emerging field, influencing EC policy, and through books and journal articles helped establish its theoretical foundations. His most recent project has been as part of a team on two UNDP-funded projects about social enterprise in Eastern Europe and former CIS countries.

Robin Stevens is a doctoral student at the University College Ghent, faculty of Business and Policy Administration, Ghent, Belgium. He also teaches courses in organizational behavior and CSR. His primary research interest lies within the relative new field of social entrepreneurship. His research endeavors focus on the process of value creation within social entrepreneurial firms and more specific on the role of the social mission. The interplay between this social mission and the economic reality challenges social entrepreneurs and nurtures his academic research. Robin Stevens holds a master degree in political sciences and obtained an advanced master in public management from Ghent University.

Paul Tracey is Reader in Organizational Behaviour at Judge Business School (University of Cambridge). His research interests include social entrepreneurship, regional innovation and institutional change. His work has been published in the *Academy of Management Journal*, the *Academy of Management Review*, and *Organization Science*.

Bart Victor holds the Cal Turner Chair in Moral Leadership at The Owen Graduate School of Management at Vanderbilt University. Professor Bart Victor joined the Owen faculty from the Institute for Management Development International (IMD), in Lausanne Switzerland where he was Professor of Management and Director of the Program for Management Development. Prior to IMD, Bart Victor was on the faculties of the University of North Carolina and the University of Nebraska. His research focus includes strategy making processes and organizational design. In particular he has recently turned to the impact of social entrepreneurial initiatives on the strategy and organizing problem. In addition to his academic experience, Bart Victor has significant experience as a manager: From 1970 to 1979, he founded and operated Child Day Care Centers in California, Illinois, and New York. He then spent several years as a management consultant based in Washington D.C. Bart Victor is a member of several professional organizations, including the Academy of Management and the International Association for Business and Society.

Clodia Vurro is a PhD candidate of Business Administration and Management at Bocconi University, Milan, Italy, where she is also research fellow of the CSR Unit, Department of Management. She is member of the SPACE Bocconi Research Centre for Studies on Security and Protection against Crime and Emergencies and of the FINDUSTRIA Centre. Her primary research interest is in learning processes of organizational change applied to social and sustainable entrepreneurship and socially responsible behaviour.

Fiona Wilson is an Instructor at Simmons College School of Management in Boston. Fiona has over 15 years' experience as a practitioner in England, Spain and the US, including serving as VP of Marketing for CMGI (the Internet Investment & Development company), and working for Ogilvy & Mather Advertising in various senior roles. She has also consulted to many venture-funded companies. She has undertaken extensive work, as a volunteer and board member with not-for-profit organizations, and was co-founder and Director of the Team With a

Vision, an international team of blind athletes competing in the Boston Marathon. Fiona graduated with highest honours from the Simmons School of Management MBA program. She is currently completing her doctoral work at Boston University School of Management, writing her dissertation on the topic of social ventures.

Jeffrey G. York is an Assistant Professor of Management and Entrepreneurship at the University of Colorado at Boulder. His research is focused on studying the entrepreneurial creation of public goods, particularly in the green building and renewable energy industries. He was the winner of the 2009 Society for Business Ethics Best Dissertation Award and his work has been published in the *Journal of Business Venturing, Journal of Management* and *Journal of Business Ethics*. He received his Ph.D. from the Darden School of Business, at the University of Virginia.

1
Introduction

Kai Hockerts, Johanna Mair and Jeffrey Robinson

The conference series that inspired this book was launched in 2005, in Barcelona, with the first International Social Entrepreneurship Research Conference (ISERC) hosted by IESE Business School. This event was followed in 2006 by ISERC2 at New York University (NYU), and then led to ISERC3 at the Copenhagen Business School in 2007. When planning the first ISERC conference we faced a situation in which hardly any academic research into social entrepreneurship was available. Our motivation was to 'stimulate scholarly discourse [and] demonstrate that rigorous research can be done in this field' (Mair et al., 2006: 3) as well as 'foster collaboration between a group of scholars with common interests' (Robinson et al., 2009: 1).

The situation has changed dramatically since 2005. The number of academic conferences, as well as the number of edited volumes, has multiplied considerably. We are pleased that the ISERC series has contributed in a small way towards this coming of age of the social entrepreneurship research area. Geoffrey Desa provides a glancing view of this development in his chapter 'Social Entrepreneurship: Snapshots as a Research Field in Emergence' (Chapter 2).

Drawing on papers presented at the ISERC3 conference in Copenhagen, this volume focuses on four essential parts of the social entrepreneurship process. These are the role of values in social entrepreneurship, the discovery and exploitation of social opportunities, the modelling of the social venturing process, and strategic perspectives in social entrepreneurship. Such a focus allows the debate about social entrepreneurship to move beyond the general discussion about definitions, emerging general theories and first empirical insights. Instead, we have singled out here four phenomena that we consider to

1

be both insufficiently researched and critical to our understanding of social entrepreneurship.

Values in social entrepreneurship

Values are at the heart of social entrepreneurship. However, much of the early research into social entrepreneurship has simply taken values for granted. Social entrepreneurship was implicitly defined as a force for good requiring individuals with a strong set of values. However, it was rarely questioned where these values come from or how social entrepreneurial behaviour differs according to the set values it is based upon.

In his chapter 'Religion and Social Entrepreneurship' (Chapter 3) Roger Spears takes an institutional perspective and examines the way religious institutions and actors have supported social entrepreneurship. He studies the role of Protestant and Jewish religion in motivating people to take entrepreneurial activity for both economic and social ends. He examines in particular three dimensions of religious institutions (ideological discourse, networks and leadership) that he finds to be critical elements of social entrepreneurship.

This first theoretical paper on values in social entrepreneurship is neatly supplemented by an empirical study by Paola Grenier. In her discussion 'Vision and Values: the Relationship between the Visions and Actions of Social Entrepreneurs' (Chapter 4) she studies in depth the assumption that social entrepreneurs are driven by a specific vision which they hope to fulfill. Her exploratory study analyses how social entrepreneurs express their visions, and how their visions guide and shape their actions.

The first part of the book closes with the contribution 'Divergent Orientations of Social Entrepreneurship Organizations' (Chapter 5), in which Heather Douglas aims to create a clearer understanding of how variations in orientations affect the functioning of different kinds of social entrepreneurship organizations. Drawing on interviews with founders of two nascent organizations, she describes some of the differences in values, intentions and operational processes within these organizations.

Discovery and exploitation of social opportunities

The academic debate about the discovery and exploitation of social opportunities is currently probably one of the most engaged substreams of the social entrepreneurship research field. In this volume we approach this question from three angles. In his conceptual study 'Social Entrepreneurship: A Study on the Source and Discovery of Social Opportunities' (Chapter 6) Javier Monllor analyses where social opportunities come from and how the concept and study of the discovery, evaluation and exploitation of social entrepreneurial opportunities can have a positive impact on the social entrepreneurship field. He develops a set of nine propositions which lend themselves to testing in future research.

Brett Smith, Jill Kickul and Fiona Wilson complement this section with an empirical contribution, 'Entrepreneurial Opportunity Evaluation: A Discrete Choice Analysis of Financial and Social Entrepreneurial Opportunity Attributes' (Chapter 7). They find that prospective entrepreneurs value both financial and social opportunity attributes. Social value creation attributes of an opportunity were second only to growth considerations, and superseded even financial considerations in the evaluation of an opportunity.

The section closes with 'Inchoate Demand in Social Entrepreneurship' (Chapter 8) in which Jeffrey York, Saras Sarasvathy and Andrea Larson study the emerging demand for social products in three business areas (television, the automotive industry and home products).

Modelling of the social venturing process

In Part 3 we combine two contributions that take a process perspective on social entrepreneurship. The first, by Clodia Vurro and Francesco Perrini, entitled 'Developing an Interactive Model of Social Entrepreneurship' (Chapter 9) proposes a multi-dimensional framework. Their model is intended as a template for systematically studying social entrepreneurial processes.

Simone Maase and Kees Dorst study seven cases of social innovation start-ups in the Netherlands in their chapter 'Emerging Social Entrepreneurship: Exploring the Development Process' (Chapter 10). They explore the development processes in these organizations and seek to identify patterns and phases. The chapter distinguishes four phases in the development of the solution: development phase, pilot phase, improvement phase and growth phase.

Strategic perspectives in social entrepreneurship

In Part 4, our final section, we take a strategic management perspective towards the social entrepreneurship debate. In their chapter 'Strategic

Partnerships: Results from a Survey of Development Trusts in the UK' (Chapter 11), Helen Haugh, MariaLaura Di Domenico and Paul Tracey present results from a survey of development trusts and their partnerships. They discuss partnership activities as well as the disbenefits of these partnerships.

Nathalie Moray and Robin Stevens draw on one of the theoretical foundations of strategic management theory in their contribution, 'A Resource-based View of Value Creation in Social Purpose Business Ventures' (Chapter 12). They discuss how social mission and choice of business model impact on the social performance of social ventures.

Social performance is also at the heart of Alex Nicholls' chapter, 'The Functions of Performance Measurement in Social Entrepreneurship: Control, Planning and Accountability' (Chapter 13). He explores the use of metrics in a sample of 41 socially entrepreneurial organizations.

The volume closes with a contribution by Bart Victor and Woodrow Lucas entitled 'Is It Ever Better to Lend than to Give? A Social Embeddedness View of Alternative Approaches to Poverty Alleviation' (Chapter 14) in which they take a close up look at the growing practice of micro-lending, asking the question whether business models can be used to directly and effectively alleviate poverty.

Social entrepreneurship – between field and fascination

Like many other academic disciplines, management research is subject to fashions. Undoubtedly, social entrepreneurship research has become fashionable in the past five years. The days in which leading management journals return submissions without a review 'because no suitable reviewer could be found' are over. If anything, the field risks overexposure. The result could be a quick boom followed by a similar quick bust.

Looking at the circle of scholars we have engaged with over the past three ISERC conferences and the subsequent edited volumes, we see, however, fascination with and real passion for the topic. We are thus confident that the momentum which has motivated us to create the ISERC series will continue to drive scholarly interest in this emerging research area. At the same time, we are happy to note that both young scholars and established academics are approaching this field, thus bringing fresh perspectives and allowing us to continually expand our understanding of social entrepreneurship.

References

Mair, J., Robinson, J. and Hockerts, K. (eds) 2006. *Social Entrepreneurship.* New York: Palgrave Macmillan.
Robinson, J., Mair, J. and Hockerts, K. (eds) 2009. *International Perspectives on Social Entrepreneurship Research.* New York: Palgrave Macmillan.

2

Social Entrepreneurship: Snapshots of a Research Field in Emergence

Geoff Desa

Introduction

Social entrepreneurship is a term used to describe innovative approaches to address social problems. Over the past ten years, the subject has gained increasing interest on the lecture circuits of public administration and business schools. As Paul Light, a professor of public administration wryly stated, 'There appears to be plenty of evidence that social entrepreneurship exists, particularly when measured by the rapidly increasing number of conferences, case studies, and funders interested in the topic' (Light, 2005: 1).

However as a topic of research social entrepreneurship appears to be non-existent in mainstream management literature. A search of leading management journals revealed no articles on social entrepreneurship.[1] This raised the question, if not in leading journals, then where? Is social entrepreneurship more than a catchphrase in the popular press? More than a set of incommensurate approaches that share a common name? This chapter provides a snapshot of research in emergence and has three objectives:

- to review the definitions and early conceptualizations of social entrepreneurship;
- to highlight the emergent streams of social entrepreneurship research; and
- to suggest pathways to link social entrepreneurship to existing fields of research.

The following sections describe current streams of research in social entrepreneurship. I review the literature in each stream and suggest avenues to build upon extant research. I conclude with future research avenues and thoughts on the perils and triumphs that characterize an emerging field. Particularly encouraging is Arthur Stinchcombe's (1982) suggestion to carefully link emerging research to its intellectual heritage to preserve the richness and depth of the field.

Current streams of social entrepreneurship research

A review of the emerging literature on social entrepreneurship suggests four broad streams. First, there is literature that attempts to define the field of social entrepreneurship and differentiate it as a unique phenomenon of study. Definitions of the field draw on arguments found in the management, entrepreneurship and organizational theory literatures. Social entrepreneurship is described as a set of innovative approaches that are used to address social issues (Wry, 2006). Frameworks are presented to capture the different types of social ventures. The individual social entrepreneur and the nature of the opportunity play a prominent role in this literature. A second stream focuses on the resource-constrained environments within which social enterprises operate. The literature is largely descriptive and focuses on how social enterprises acquire and utilize resources to serve their social mission. A third stream addresses the constraining and enabling role of institutions on social enterprise. Literature in this stream focuses on internal governance mechanisms and external regulatory actions that influence social entrepreneurship at the level of individuals ventures and communities. A recent addition to this stream focuses on how social entrepreneurship may occur despite existing institutions, thereby changing public perceptions, and creating new markets in the process. A fourth stream focuses on performance metrics for social entrepreneurship. Philanthropic and investment perspectives are used to describe venture sustainability and social performance. The literature suggests that a measure of social return on investment is necessary to include with the traditional financial accounting measures in order to accurately describe the performance of social enterprises.

Defining and differentiating social entrepreneurship as a distinct field of study

The term 'social entrepreneurship' has two different sources of origin in the 1980s, with two different meanings. Edward Skloot of the Surdna Foundation used the term to highlight the possibility of income generation by a non-profit venture[2] (Light, 2005). Bill Drayton, the founder of the Ashoka organization, looked beyond the non-profit organization and described social entrepreneurship as a process that involved identifying, addressing and solving societal problems (Ashoka, 2006). Consequent definitions of social entrepreneurship have highlighted the role of the individual or the opportunity, and have ranged from the non-profit definition to the broader definition of social change (Table 2.1 lists the definitions).

In the former, social entrepreneurship typically refers to the phenomenon of applying business expertise and market based skills to the non-profit sector (Frumkin, 2002; Reis, 1999; Thompson et al., 2000). As a category of non-profit research, this stream has followed the shifts in managerial competencies and market based attitudes of non-profit executives who try to improve the operational efficiency

Table 2.1 Definitions of social entrepreneurship, the unit of analysis and the research focus

Author(s)	Definition	Unit of analysis	Research focus
Young (1986)	Non-profit entrepreneurs are the innovators who found new organizations, develop and implement new programs and methods, organize and expand new services, and redirect the activities of faltering organizations (p. 162).	non-profit entrepreneur	Individual
Waddock and Post (1991)	Private sector leaders who play critical roles in bringing about 'catalytic changes' in the public sector agenda and the perception of certain social issues (p. 393).	private sector	Individual
Thompson, Alvy and Lees (2000)	People who realize where there is an opportunity to satisfy some unmet need that the state welfare will not or cannot meet, and who gather together the necessary resources (generally people, often volunteers, money and premises) and use these to 'make a difference' (p. 328).	subset of business entrepreneurship	Opportunity

Thompson (2002)	People with the qualities and behaviors we associate with the business entrepreneur but who operate in the community and are more concerned with caring and helping than 'making money' (p. 413).	social entrepreneur	Individual
Frumkin (2002)	Social entrepreneurs have a combination of the supply-side orientation and the instrumental rational, providing a vehicle for entrepreneurship that creates enterprises that combine commercial and charitable goals (p. 130).	social entrepreneurship	Opportunity
Alvord et al. (2004)	Social entrepreneurs are individuals who are catalysts for social transformation. They are leaders who need two types of skills: (1) the capacity to bridge diverse stakeholder communities, and (2) long-term adaptive skills and response to changing circumstances.	social entrepreneur	Individual
Barendsen and Gardner (2004)	Social entrepreneurs are unusual 'in terms of their compelling personal histories, their distinctive profile of beliefs and their impressive accomplishments in the face of odds' (p. 50). The social entrepreneur is a new version of the long-existing term 'changemaker'.	social entrepreneur	Individual

10

Table 2.1   (Continued)

Author(s)	Definition	Unit of analysis	Research focus
Light (2006)	A social entrepreneur is an individual, group, network, organization, or alliance of organizations that seeks sustainable, large-scale change through pattern-breaking ideas in what and/or how governments, nonprofits, and businesses do to address significant social problems.	social entrepreneur	Opportunity
Dart (2004)	Social entrepreneurship is an encompassing set of strategic responses to many of the varieties of environmental turbulence and situational challenges that non-profit organizations face today (p. 13).	non-profit innovation	Opportunity
Perrini and Vurro (2006)	Only those innovators who are able to actively contribute to social change with creativity and innovation, typical of the classical entrepreneurial process, can be called social entrepreneurs, regardless of their specific organizational form (for-profit or non-profit).	social entrepreneur	Individual
Mair and Martí (2004)	Social entrepreneurship is defined as the innovative use of resources to explore and exploit opportunities that meet a social need in a sustainable manner	social entrepreneurship	Opportunity

Dees (1998)	Social entrepreneurs possess five criteria: (1) adopting a mission to create and sustain social value; (2) recognizing and relentlessly pursuing new opportunities to serve that mission; (3) engaging in a process of continuous innovation, adaptation and learning; (4) acting boldly without being limited by resources currently in hand; and (5) exhibiting a heightened sense of accountability to the constituencies served and to the outcomes created (p. 4).	social entrepreneur	Individual

and effectiveness of their organizations (e.g. Dart, 2004; Young, 1986). Social entrepreneurs are described as individuals in non-profit organizations who start social transformations by bringing about changes in the public perception of social issues (Alvord et al., 2004; Waddock and Post, 1991).

The latter interpretation extends the scope of social entrepreneurship to initiatives that may not fall within the non-profit sector, but yet have a prominent social mission and social purpose (Perrini and Vurro, 2006). In this interpretation, social entrepreneurship refers to an innovative activity with a social objective in either the for-profit sector, such as in social purpose commercial ventures (e.g. Dees and Anderson, 2003; Emerson and Twersky, 1996), in the non-profit sector, or as a hybrid across sectors which mix for-profit and non-profit approaches (Austin, 2006; Dees, 1998). In this broader interpretation, social entrepreneurship may include entrepreneurship in emerging markets that serves to enhance the social, cultural or economic conditions of impoverished communities (Prahalad, 2005). Social entrepreneurship can include enterprises which have exclusively social goals and no commercial exchange (e.g. non-governmental organizations), and enterprises that feature social goals subordinate to financial goals (e.g. social cause branding undertaken by corporations) (Peredo et al., 2006). Social entrepreneurship may also include cross-sector collaborations between for-profit and non-profit ventures that address the sustainability of financial and social missions (Austin, 2000). The distinction between social and commercial entrepreneurship is not dichotomous, but rather a continuum ranging from purely social to purely economic. Even at the extremes, there are still elements of both. That is, charitable activity must still reflect economic realities, while economic activity must still generate social value. In its broadest sense, social entrepreneurship is defined as the innovative use of resources to explore and exploit opportunities that meet a *social* need in a *sustainable* manner (Mair and Martí, 2004). In this definition, the primary emphasis is on meeting a 'social need' that market forces have failed to address or ignored. Social entrepreneurship is exercised where some person or persons (1) aim either exclusively or in some prominent way to create social value of some kind, and pursue that goal through some combination of (2) recognizing and exploiting opportunities to create this value, (3) employing innovation, (4) tolerating risk and (5) declining to accept limitations in available resources (Peredo et al., 2006).

The next sections highlight the three research streams that much of social entrepreneurship literature seeks to address: the acquisition and utilization of resources, institutional effects on social entrepreneurship and performance evaluation.

Resource-mobilizing actions that sustain or grow a social venture

The second stream of social entrepreneurship research focuses on the resource-constrained environments within which social enterprises operate. The literature is largely case-based and focuses on the processes by which individuals and social ventures acquire and utilize resources to serve their social mission. At the individual level, the literature focuses on highlighting the characteristics and actions of enterprising individuals at the core of a social venture. Scholars have explored how past experiences (Barendsen and Gardner, 2004), social identity (Simms and Robinson, 2006 and current environments (Astad, 1998; Thompson, 2002) can determine the choice of venture, and the resource-seeking actions pursued. At the venture level, scholars have looked at how venture orientation (for-profit or non-profit) affects the resource-seeking behaviors and the consequent sustainability of the venture (Lasprogata and Cotten, 2003; Shaw and Carter, 2004).

Past experiences: Specific experiences, many of them early in life, may help explain social venture formation. Barendsen and Gardner (2004) conducted a qualitative study based on small matched-samples and in-depth interviews, which suggested that social entrepreneurs have a much higher incidence of childhood trauma and parents with high levels of social and/or political engagement. 'Priorities suddenly become clear when life seems short or when one faces a stark choice. Under such circumstances, a calling may be discovered' (Barendsen and Gardner, 2004: 44). Social entrepreneurs also have past experience working with social issues. Social entrepreneurs are 'energetic, persistent, and unusually confident, with an ability to inspire others to join them in their work' (45). They are also deeply committed to their cause, very independent, and able to explain the link between their specific goals and a broader picture of an alternative world. Almost all are also spiritual or religious, and 'believe in human potential, or the possibility of change' (47).

Social Identity: Social identity may predict the type of social venture and the consequent resource seeking actions (Simms and Robinson, 2006). Social entrepreneurs often have two identities: the entrepreneur and the activist. Although the two identities can and do co-exist (e.g. Barendsen and Gardner, 2004), social entrepreneurs must decide which comes first. Simms and Robinson hypothesize that founders with a primary activist identity will be more likely to create non-profit organizations, while those with a primary entrepreneurial activity are more likely to create for-profit entities. However, the perceptions of benefits and risk are driven by very different goals; income and financial independence or social impact and recognition. Social entrepreneurs who view themselves as activists first may miss important opportunities for change. They may ignore resource-seeking actions that involve financial gains and market tools that they deem as secondary or unimportant. In contrast, social entrepreneurs who pursue the entrepreneurial identity may risk losing the legitimacy of the social cause (Dart, 2004).

In addition, social entrepreneurs often take specific actions to gain access to resources for their social ventures. In doing so, they draw on personal credibility, framing and reputation effects.

Personal Credibility: Social entrepreneurs may have significant personal credibility (past records of success) which they use to tap into critical resources and build the necessary network of participating organizations (Sharir and Lerner, 2006; Thompson, 2002; Waddock and Post, 1991).

Framing & Reputation Effects: Social entrepreneurs take different legitimating actions to gain access to resources (Astad, 1998; Waddock and Post, 1991). First, they frame the project in terms of important social values, rather than in purely economic terms. This results in a sense of collective purpose among the social entrepreneur and those who join the effort. Second, social entrepreneurs focus on reputation effects by leveraging media coverage rather than through direct action.

Social Network: In an exploratory qualitative study of 33 Israeli social ventures, Sharir and Lerner (2006) concluded that the ability of a social venture to acquire the resources necessary to maintain program service and continuity depended upon the entrepreneur's social network, the ties established with other voluntary and public sector organizations. The entrepreneur either depended upon the resources of the network to which he belonged; or, the entrepreneur proactively created the network and invested time and effort in constructing it. In either case, venture performance depended upon mobilizing others to allocate capital, labor and effort to a venture that had an uncertain future. The measure of performance was the quantity of resources available for the venture's growth and development, and whether the venture met its initial goals. Other variables that affected the performance of social ventures included founder commitment, the initial capital base, venture legitimacy in the public discourse, team composition, private and public sector alliances, market tests and previous managerial experience.

Notably, the literature on resource mobilization has focused on the role of the individual entrepreneur and has left out the role of the collective. The founding social entrepreneur seeks resources based upon personal credibility, past experiences and social ties. The roles played by the stakeholder communities of investors, volunteers and partners is largely absent in explaining how social ventures acquire resources, serve customers and grow. For example, the economics of a social entrepreneurial venture often make it difficult to compensate staff as competitively as in commercial markets. In fact, many employees in social entrepreneurial organizations place considerable value on nonpecuniary compensation from their work (Austin et al., 2006). Yet these stakeholder communities are vital to nascent ventures in resource-constrained environments. There remains much interesting research to be done on the role played by the collective, investors, volunteers and other stakeholders in acquiring and utilizing resources.

Institutional effects on social enterprise

A third stream of research focuses on the effect of institutions on social enterprise. Institutions are defined here as the humanly derived constraints that structure human interaction. They are made up of formal constraints (rules, laws, constitutions), informal constraints (norms of behavior, conventions and self-imposed codes of conduct) and their enforcement characteristics (North, 1997). This stream looks at whether social entrepreneurship happens through or against existing institutions

(Antal, 2006). When social entrepreneurship happens *through* existing institutions, scholars look at how institutions facilitate and create boundaries of practice for social ventures (e.g. Lasprogata and Cotton, 2003). Social entrepreneurship often takes place at the intersection of multiple institutions and may be influenced concurrently by the government, the market and the community (Shaw and Carter, 2004). The predominant research focus has been on policy, governance and regulatory effects that enable or constrain the community development efforts of social entrepreneurs (Bayliss, 2004; Korosec and Berman, 2006; Wallace, 1999).

When social entrepreneurship happens *against* existing institutional arrangements, the creation of a venture may in itself cause a change in that existing institutional arrangement (Mair and Martí, 2004). For example, environmental degradation may be seen as the result of a market failure caused by existing institutional arrangements. Dean and McMullen (2007) provide an example of how entrepreneurs resolve environmentally relevant market failures by seizing upon potentially profitable opportunities. As these entrepreneurs succeed in creating sustainable businesses, public perception is changed and institutions are reconfigured to accommodate the new market.

Social entrepreneurship through existing institutions: community
development and social enterprise

This section looks at how social enterprises may help institutions meet the needs of communities, and vice versa. Social enterprises may serve as the bridge between disadvantaged communities and existing institutions (Bayliss, 2004; Wallace, 1999). As a complement, existing regulatory institutions may serve as an important resource to social entrepreneurs dedicated to helping the community (Korosec and Berman, 2006).

Porter (1995) made the case for inner-city development through existing free-market institutions. His model for rejuvenating the inner city argued for the operation of profitable businesses with an export orientation within a regional economy, built upon the talents of local entrepreneurs and mainstream private organizations to confront issues of poverty and unemployment. However, inner city markets pose a challenge for business managers and entrepreneurs because many do not understand how to address the significant social and institutional factors that restrict market entry (Robinson, 2004). Porter's model was also criticized by Emerson and Twersky (1996) as being unrealistic for the inner city community. For example, getting a job was often not as significant a milestone as keeping it. Many residents lacked the basic skills regarding how to act and/or contribute to a work setting.

In such cases, social enterprises may help lower entry barriers to business by forming a link between the social issues relevant to the local context and the economic benefits of the market. Wallace (1999) examined the role of social enterprises in facilitating inner-city community development in the US. She suggested that in contrast to traditional businesses and volunteer agencies, social enterprises formed an effective social, political and economic link between the government and free-market enterprise. Social enterprises such as affirmative businesses and direct-service agencies played a large part in revitalizing the local community by providing self-help, development of local jobs, businesses, and human resources by and for communities. These enterprises provided viable alternatives for transitional employment into the mainstream business community.

Korosec and Berman (2006) examined how existing institutions helped social entrepreneurship, here defined as the activity of private individuals and organizations taking initiatives to address social challenges in their communities. Based on a national survey and in-depth interviews among jurisdictions with populations over 50,000, the authors found that municipal governments helped social entrepreneurs by (1) increasing awareness of social problems, (2) helping them to acquire resources, (3) coordinating with other organizations, and (4) implementing programs. Nearly three-quarters of cities provided active or moderate support, which was positively associated with the perceived effectiveness of non-profit organizations in their communities. Specific efforts included the development of new programs and services that brought counseling, awareness and support for teenage truancy, substance abuse, public health, environmental protection, and public safety. The authors concluded that municipal government support for social entrepreneurship is an important approach for strengthening communities.

Social entrepreneurship against existing institutions: market failures and institutional entrepreneurship

When social entrepreneurship happens *against* existing institutional arrangements, the creation of a venture may in itself cause a change in the existing institutional arrangement (Mair and Martí, 2004; Sarasvathy, 2006). There is a limited emerging literature that looks at social entrepreneurship from the perspective of institutions (Antal, 2006; Mair and Martí, 2004). In this literature, the realization of new ideas requires combining the energies and resources from different institutions and often involves pushing conventions aside or creating new space between existing institutions. The literature follows from work in institutional entrepreneurship that attempts to explain how institutions arise or change (DiMaggio, 1988; Fligstein, 1997). The literature also draws upon theories of new institutional economics (North, 1997) and critiques of the same (Olson, 1996; Simon, 1991).

An example of social entrepreneurship against existing institutions is put forward by Sarasvathy (2006) who argues that in contrast to current separations (for-profit vs. non-profit) in business and society, equity markets should be opened up to all social ventures that invest in human potential, whether they be for-profit or non-profit. Existing institutional arrangements are often designed to achieve a variety of organizational goals through collective action. For-profit organizations, for example, achieve goals through the specific institutional arrangement we call the 'market'. Non-profit organizations achieve goals through non-market mechanisms that include charity and philanthropy. Sarasvathy (2006) points out that there are problems with market and non-market mechanisms. Social enterprises that are able to survive under these conditions are forced to go against existing institutions, and come up with creative mechanisms that incorporate the best of both market and non-market solutions. For example, Dean and McMullen (2007) describe how entrepreneurs resolve environmentally relevant market failures by seizing upon potentially profitable opportunities. As these entrepreneurs succeed in creating sustainable businesses, public perception is changed, and institutions are reconfigured to accommodate the new market.

Mair and Martí (2006) argue that the institutional entrepreneurship perspective is a promising way to understand the role of social entrepreneurship in changing or giving birth to norms, institutions and structure. It may be an interesting lens through which to study the emergence of social entrepreneurship, for example, by examining the conflict between the values of social entrepreneurs and their perceptions of reality or, in institutional entrepreneurship terminology, between social entrepreneurs' beliefs and their shared norms (i.e. institutions).

Mair and Martí (2006) propose that social entrepreneurship can also inform theory on institutional entrepreneurship. Neither DiMaggio's (1988) nor Fligstein's (1997) theory of institutional entrepreneurship are explicit about the paradox of embedded agency. Highly embedded actors may be conditioned by the very institution and therefore not consider changing existing rules. Embeddedness might reflect both an enabling and a constraining condition at the same time. Although it is easier for highly embedded social entrepreneurs to ensure access to resources and win legitimacy, less embedded actors are more likely to engage in social ventures that challenge rules and norms, as they are not 'locked' into the existing structure.

Performance and metrics of social ventures (funding, philanthropy, measures)

The fourth stream of literature addresses funding sources, performance and performance metrics of social ventures. The non-distributive restriction on surpluses generated by non-profit organizations and the embedded social purpose of for-profit or hybrid forms of social enterprise limits social entrepreneurs from tapping into the same capital markets as commercial entrepreneurs. Funding sources typically fall into two categories, philanthropy and investment. Ventures that fall towards the non-profit, non-governmental end of the social enterprise spectrum typical receive funding from philanthropic sources (Austin et al., 2006; Pepin, 2005). Ventures that have earned income strategies that fall towards the for-profit end of the spectrum, receive funding from socially responsible investors, or social venture funds (Harrington, 2003; Pepin, 2005). Such commercial ventures often seek financial return on investment by creating an earned income enterprise operated by charities and their trading/holding companies alone or in partnership with the corporate sector (Austin, 2000; Lasprogata and Cotten, 2003; Ott, 2001).

Social Venture Investing: Socially conscious investors make decisions by screening for positive and negative issues, shareholder advocacy, community investing and providing social venture capital (Harrington, 2003; Hillman and Keim, 2001; Orlitzky, Schmidt and Rynes, 2003). Screening is usually the first step to make sure companies do not produce objectionable products or engage in practices such as discrimination or environmental pollution. Harrington (2003) suggested that investors with more customized social screens bought individual stocks, as opposed to mutual funds. Investors with a social focus also found opportunities to buy into new or growing companies before they sold shares to the public. Socially responsible venture funds often provided lists of companies that produced socially responsible products, who sought investment capital. Social venture capital is also used to fund commercial ventures, but rather than seeking a complete return on investment the investor may off set some or all of the investment against social outcomes (Pepin, 2005).

Venture philanthropy: Within the context of venture philanthropy, charities, venture capitalists and entrepreneurs often work together in strategic alliances (Austin, 2000; Pepin, 2005). Human resources and funding are invested as donation in the charity by entrepreneurs, venture capitalists, trusts and corporations in search of a social return on their investment. Venture philanthropy involves high engagement over many years with fixed milestones and tangible returns and exit achieved by developing alternative, sustainable income (Brainerd, 1999). Venture philanthropists may also invest without establishing an equity position in the commercial enterprise. Any profits are redirected to mission-related activity, although the business activity may or may not be mission related (Pepin, 2005).

Funding and performance metrics are closely related. Scholars have called for the inclusion of social return performance metrics in addition to financial performance metrics (Margolis and Walsh, 2003; Paton, 2003). Performance metrics used by practicing social ventures include social return on investment (SROI) developed by the Robert's Enterprise Development Fund in the US (Gair, 2005), best-practice benchmarking (Darby and Jenkins, 2006) and adaptations of the Kaplan and Norton's Balanced Score Card (Paton, 2003). However, there are few journal articles on social entrepreneurship that have included any measure of performance (Light, 2005). The field has tended towards case-based research, with small in-depth descriptive studies that are biased towards successful social ventures. The literature search detected 24 case study-based articles (number of cases in each sample varied from 1 to 33), and only one large sample study (n = 70, Sharir and Lerner, 2006).

One particularly in-depth study provided a comparative analysis of seven cases of social entrepreneurship from Asia, Latin America, North America and Africa (Alvord et al., 2004). The authors detected certain patterns associated with successful social entrepreneurship that led to significant changes in the social, political, and economic contexts for poor and marginalized groups. There appeared to be similarities in the core innovation, the leadership and organization, and in scaling up that produced societal transformation. First, the innovation characteristic common across social ventures was an ability to mobilize the existing assets of marginalized groups. Second, successful social entrepreneurship initiatives were often founded by leaders with the capacity to work with and build bridges among very diverse stakeholders. Leaders also emphasized systematic learning within the organization. Third, scaling the social enterprise occurred in three ways. Social entrepreneurship initiatives built local capacities to solve problems. Capacity-building strengthened local capacities for self-help and then scaled up to a wider range of clients. Social ventures also provided product 'packages' to solve problems. These initiatives scaled up coverage with services that could be delivered by low-skill staff to individuals or small groups. Finally, ventures often built social movements to deal with other powerful actors. Social movement building expanded influence by alliances and campaigns to shape the activities of decision-makers.

Conclusion and future research paths

Social entrepreneurship research is at a very early stage, yet draws from distinguished antecedent literatures. Table 2.2 provides a summary of the four main streams of social entrepreneurship research and its antecedents. The challenge for researchers in an early-stage field such as social entrepreneurship is how to judiciously apply theories from other domains to answer questions relevant to the situations in which social entrepreneurs may find themselves (Mair et al., 2006). Social entrepreneurship research can succumb to the liability of newness (Stinchcombe, 1965), staying fragmented and widely dispersed, making it difficult for scholars to build upon and contribute to the emerging stream of knowledge. How then might scholars link social entrepreneurship to mainstream management and entrepreneurship literature, yet take advantage of its rich and varied relationships to a diaspora of domains?

In 1982, Arthur Stinchcombe delivered an address to the American Sociological Association on the use of classics in contemporary research that remains relevant today. He suggested that established scholarly works – the 'mothers and fathers' of emergent research, served six different functions:

a) as *touchstones*, examples of beautiful and possible ways of doing scientific work;
b) as *developmental tasks*, to induce complexity of mind and replace the clichés of rote research;
c) as *sources of fundamental ideas* and root concerns about social entrepreneurship;
d) as *routine science*, as sources of puzzles and hypotheses for empirical work;
e) as *rituals* to express the solidarity and common concerns of social entrepreneurship as a discipline; and
f) as *intellectual badges* for the first footnotes of a paper to identify a style of work.

Table 2.2 Summary of social entrepreneurship literature review

Literature category	Research question	Sub-category	Antecedent literature	Representative articles	Theoretical Lenses
Social entrepreneurship definition	What is social entrepreneurship?	Innovative approaches to solve social problems	Entrepreneurship	Drayton (2002), Peredo et al. (2006), Mair and Martí (2006)	
		Earned income activity of non-profits	Non-profit	Thompson et al. (2000), Reis (1999), Frumkin (2002)	
		Initiatives with a prominent social mission and supporting financial mission	Emerging markets (management)	Perrini and Vurro (2006), Prahalad (2005)	
			CSR, Ethics	Hemingway (2005), Harding (2005)	
Performance and metrics of social ventures	How can the performance of social ventures be measured?	Venture Philanthropy	Best practice benchmarking	Darby and Jenkins (2003), Pepin (2005)	
		Socially responsible investing	Balanced score-card	Paton (2005), Harrington (2003)	
			Social Return on Investment	Gair (2003)	

Table 2.2 (Continued)

Literature category	Research question	Sub-category	Antecedent literature	Representative articles	Theoretical Lenses
Resource mobilization	How do social ventures acquire and mobilize resources?	Case-based descriptions of SE process	Exploratory (no antecedent)	Sharir and Lerner (2006), Thompson (2002), Astad (1998), Barendsen and Gardner (2004), Prahalad (2005)	Resource Based View, Resource Dependence, Social Movements
Literature category	Research question	Sub-category	Antecedent literature	Representative articles	Theoretical Lenses
Institutional effects	What role does internal and external governance play in enabling and constraining social ventures?	SE through existing institutions (governance, regulation)		Wallace (1999), Bayliss (2004), Korosec and Berman (2004)	IO Economics, Social Capital, Embeddedness
	How does social entrepreneurship occur in the absence of supporting institutional structures?	SE against existing institutions (market failures, non-market failures, market creation)		Dean and McMullen (2005), Antal (2006), Sarasvathy (2006)	Institutional Entrepreneurship, Effectuation

Prof. Stinchombe's thoughts help us put emergent research in social entrepreneurship in perspective, which has indeed already benefited from links to established areas in management, public administration and entrepreneurship. The definitions of social entrepreneurship may be traced back to writings on non-profit organizations (Hansmann, 1980; Young, 1984), corporate social responsibility (Kanter, 1999; Wartick and Cochran, 1985) and entrepreneurship (Gartner, 1985; Shane and Venkatraman, 2000). Research on the acquisition and utilization of resources by social entrepreneurs has largely been case-based but is starting to draw upon theories of resource-dependence (Pfeffer and Salancik, 1978), the resource-based view (Barney, 1991; Peteraf, 1993) and social capital (Burt, 1997; Putnam, 2000). Theories of competitive advantage (Porter, 1995) and institutional entrepreneurship (DiMaggio, 1988) inform how social entrepreneurs may navigate social and institutional barriers (Robinson, 2004; Wallace, 1999).

Austin et al. (2006) and Mair and Martí (2006) posed a series of research questions that, while relevant to social entrepreneurship, may also deepen our understanding of the role of new ventures in society. Adding to that series I conclude with a list of research questions (Table 2.3) drawn from the review within this chapter. The exciting domain of social entrepreneurship has great potential to serve as an empirical test-bed that extends our current theories and broadens our conception of entrepreneurial activity across the board.

Table 2.3 Future research questions for social entrepreneurship

---

The founding of social ventures
Where do ideas for social enterprises come from?
How are opportunities for social entrepreneurship identified and evaluated?
How does the community play a role in the founding of the venture?
What affects the extent and form of competition and collaboration among social enterprises?

Acquisition and utilization of resources
How does for-profit/non-profit orientation affect resource mobilization in a social venture?
To what extent is social entrepreneurship a collective effort? What role does the community play in the acquisition and utilization of resources?
What are the most effective ways for a social entrepreneur to mobilize and manage stakeholders?
How does innovation (technological, service or organizational) occur within a social enterprise?

Table 2.3   (Continued)

How does a social entrepreneur determine the optimum mix of financing sources for the social enterprise? To what extent do these activities create tension with mission or organizational values?

What role do incentives play in the mobilization of stakeholders in social enterprises?

Institutional effects (through and against institutions)

How do contextual forces shape opportunity creation for social entrepreneurship?

How do country or community contextual differences change these forces?

What are the effects of market forces on the formation and behavior of social enterprises?

To what extent do social enterprises correct market failure?

Do social enterprises perform the function of early-stage risk assumption and market development?

What new financial instruments may be designed to overcome some of the current deficiencies in the philanthropic capital markets?

Funding and performance effects

What are the key drivers of the philanthropic capital markets?

How can one measure social-value creation? How can entrepreneurs best communicate the social value proposition to different stakeholders?

To what extent are earned-income strategies successful?

To what extent can pecuniary incentive systems of businesses be effectively utilized in social enterprises and, vice versa, to what extent can nonpecuniary incentive systems in social enterprises be deployed in businesses?

Source: From the literature review and Austin et al., 2006; Mair et al., 2006; Desa and Kotha, 2005.

Notes

1. Using the ABI-Inform database, I searched for articles that met three criteria (cf. Busenitz et al., 2003): (1) publication in one of seven major academic journals in the field of business management: *Academy of Management Journal, Academy of Management Review, Strategic Management Journal, Journal of Management (JOM), Organization Science (OS), Management Science (MS)*, and *Administrative Science Quarterly* (2) use of one or more keywords related to social entrepreneurship in the article title or abstract (i.e. social entrepreneurship, social entrepreneurial, social entrepreneur, social venture, social enterprise) and (3) publication between 1985 and 2006, inclusive. All editor notes, book reviews, review articles on the entrepreneurship domain, and replies to published articles were omitted so that the data would contain only articles and research notes that were non-invited and peer reviewed.

2. A non-profit venture is defined as a tax-exempt organization that carries out activities described by the US Internal Revenue Service tax code as charitable, religious, educational, scientific, literary, testing for public safety, fostering national or international amateur sports competition and the prevention of

cruelty to children or animals. The term charitable is used in its generally accepted legal sense and includes relief of the poor, the distressed or the underprivileged; advancement of religion; advancement of education or science; erection or maintenance of public buildings, monuments or works; lessening the burdens of government; lessening of neighborhood tensions; elimination of prejudice and discrimination; defense of human and civil rights secured by law; and combating community deterioration and juvenile delinquency (http://www.IRS.gov/charities).

References

Alvord, S. H. B., David and Letts, Christine. 2004. Social Entrepreneurship and Societal Transformation: An Exploratory Study. *The Journal of Applied Behavioral Science*, **40**(3): 260–82.

Antal, A. B. 2006. Reflections on the Need for 'Between Times' and 'Between Places'. *Journal of Management Inquiry*, **15**(2): 154–66.

Ashoka 2006: Ashoka, Innovators for the Public. Available at: http://www.ashoka. org/social_entrepreneur Last accessed: July 5 2010.

Astad, P. 1998. Grassroots Entrepreneurs: Change Agents for a Sustainable Society. *Journal of Organizational Change Management*, **11**(2): 157–73.

Austin, J., Stevenson, H. and Wei-Skillern, J. 2006. Social and Commercial Entrepreneurship: Same, Different, or Both? *Entrepreneurship Theory and Practice*, **30**(1): 1–22.

Austin, J. E. 2000. *The Collaboration Challenge: How Nonprofits and Businesses Succeed through Strategic Alliances*, foreword by Frances Hesselbein and John C. Whitehead (ed.), 1st edn. San Francisco, CA: Jossey-Bass.

Barendsen, L. and Gardener, H. 2004. Is the Social Entrepreneur a New Type of Leader? *Leader to Leader*, **34**: 43–50.

Barney, J. 1991. Firm Resources and Sustained Competitive Advantage. *Journal of Management*, **17**(1): 99–120.

Bayliss, D. 2004. Ireland's Creative Development: Local Authority Strategies for Culture-led Development. *Regional Studies*, **38**(7): 817–31.

Brainerd, P. 1999. Social Venture Partners: Engaging a New Generation of Givers. *Nonprofit and Voluntary Sector Quarterly*, **28**(4): 502–7.

Burt, R. S. 1997. The Contingent Value of Social Capital. *Administrative Science Quarterly*, **42**(2): 339–65.

Busenitz, L. W., West, G. P., Shepherd, D., Nelson, T., Chandler, G. N. and Zacharakis, A. 2003. Entrepreneurship Research in Emergence: Past Trends and Future Directions. *Journal of Management*, **29**(3): 285–308.

Darby, L. and Jenkins, H. 2006. Applying sustainability indicators to the social enterprise business model: The development and application of an indicator set for Newport Wastesavers, Wales. *International Journal of Social Economics*, **33**(5/6): 411.

Dart, R. 2004. Being 'Business-like' in a Nonprofit Organization: A Grounded and Inductive Typology. *Nonprofit and Voluntary Sector Quarterly*, **33**(2): 290–310.

Dean, T. and McMullen, J. 2007. Toward a Theory of Sustainable Entrepreneurship: Reducing Environmental Degradation through Entrepreneurial Action. *Journal of Business Venturing*, **22**(1): 50–76.

Dees, G. 1998. *The Meaning of Social Entrepreneurship*. Available at http://www.caseatduke.org/documents/dees_sedef.pdf. Last accessed: July 5 2010.

Dees, J. G. and Anderson, B. B. 2003. Sector-Bending: Blurring Lines between Nonprofit and For-Profit. *Society*, 40(4): 16–27.

DiMaggio, P. J. 1988. Interest and Agency in Institutional Theory. In Zucker, L. G. (ed.), *Institutional Patterns and Organizations: Culture and Environment*: 3–22. Cambridge, MA: Ballinger.

Emerson, J. and Twersky, F. 1996. *New Social Entrepreneurs: The Success, Challenge and Lessons of Non-Profit Enterprise Creation*. San Francisco: Roberts Foundation, Homeless Economic Development Fund.

Fligstein, N. 1997. Social Skill and Institutional Theory. *American Behavioral Scientist*, 40(4): 397–405.

Frumkin, P. 2002. *On Being Nonprofit: A Conceptual and Policy Primer*. Cambridge, MA: Harvard University Press.

Gair, C. 2005. If The Shoe Fits: Non-Profit or For-Profit? The Choice Matters: Roberts Enterprise Development Fund. San Francisco.

Gartner, W. B. 1985. A Conceptual Framework for Describing the Phenomenon of New Venture Creation. *Academy of Management Review*, 10(4): 696–706.

Hansmann, H. B. 1980. The Role of Nonprofit Enterprise. *Yale Law Journal*, 89(5): 835–901.

Harrington, C. 2003. Special Section: Investment Planning: Socially Responsible Investing: Balancing Financial Need with a Concern for Others *Journal of Accountancy*, 195(1): 52–61.

Hillman, A. J. and Keim, G. D. 2001. Shareholder Value, Stakeholder Management, and Social Issues: What's the Bottom Line? *Strategic Management Journal*, 22(2): 125–39.

Kanter, R. M. 1999. From Spare Change to Real Change – The Social Sector as Beta Site for Business Innovation. *Harvard Business Review*, 77(3): 122–132.

Korosec, R. L. and Berman, E. M. 2006. Municipal Support for Social Entrepreneurship. *Public Administration Review*, 66(3): 448–62.

Lasprogata, G. A. and Cotten, M. N. 2003. Contemplating 'Enterprise': The Business and Legal Challenges of Social Entrepreneurship. *American Business Law Journal*, 41(1): 67–113.

Light, P. 2005. *Searching for Social Entrepreneurs: Who might they be, where they might be found, what they do*. Paper presented at the Association for Research on Nonprofit and Voluntary Associations.

Mair, J., Robinson, J. and Hockerts, K. 2006. *Social Entrepreneurship*. New York, Palgrave Macmillan.

Mair, J. and Martí, I. 2004. *Social Entrepreneurship: What Are We Talking about? A Framework for Future Research*. Barcelona: IESE, University of Navarra.

Margolis, J. D. and Walsh, J. P. 2003. Misery Loves Companies: Rethinking Social Initiatives by Business. *Administrative Science Quarterly*, 48(2): 268–305.

North, D. C. 1997. Economic Performance through Time. In Persson, T. (ed.), *Nobel Lectures, Economics 1991–1995*. Singapore, 1997: World Scientific Publishing Co.

Olson, M. 1996. Distinguished Lecture on Economics in Government – Big Bills Left on the Sidewalk: Why Some Nations are Rich, and Others Poor. *Journal of Economic Perspectives*, 10(2): 3–24.

Orlitzky, M., Schmidt, F. L. and Rynes, S. L. 2003. Corporate Social and Financial Performance: A Meta-Analysis. *Organization Studies*, **24**(3): 403–41.
Ott, J. S. 2001. *The Nature of the Nonprofit Sector*. Boulder, CO: Westview Press.
Paton, R. 2003. *Managing and Measuring Social Enterprises by Rob Paton*. London and Thousand Oaks, CA: Sage.
Pepin, J. 2005. Venture Capitalists and Entrepreneurs become Venture Philanthropists. *International Journal of Nonprofit and Voluntary Sector Marketing*, **10**(3): 165–73.
Peredo, A. M. and McLean, M. 2006. Social Entrepreneurship: A Critical Review of the Concept. *Journal of World Business*, **41**(1): 56–65.
Perrini, F. and Vurro, C. 2006. *Developing a Conceptual Framework for Social Entrepreneurial Research, Minnesota Conference for Ethics and Entrepreneurship*. Carlson School of Management, University of Minnesota.
Peteraf, M. A. 1993. The Cornerstones of Competitive Advantage – a Resource-Based View. *Strategic Management Journal*, **14**(3): 179–91.
Pfeffer, J. and Salancik, G. R. 1978. *The External Control of Organizations: A Resource Dependence Perspective*. New York: Harper & Row.
Porter, M. E. 1995. The Competitive Advantage of the Inner City. Harvard Business Review May-June 1995: 53–72.
Prahalad, C. K. 2005. *The Fortune at the Bottom of the Pyramid*. Upper Saddle River, NJ: Wharton School Publishing.
Putnam, R. D. 2000. *Bowling Alone: The Collapse and Revival of American Community*. New York: Simon & Schuster.
Reis, T. 1999. *Unleashing the New Resources and Entrepreneurship for the Common Good: A Scan, Synthesis and Scenario for Action*. Battle Creek, MI: W. K. Kellogg Foundation.
Robinson, J. 2004. *An Economic Sociology of Entry Barriers: Social and Institutional Entry Barriers to Inner City Markets*. Columbia Univeristy, Graduate School of Business – Management.
Sarasvathy, S. D. 2006. Markets in Human Hope. In Sarasvathy, D. K. (ed.), *Effectuation: Elements of Entrepreneurial Expertise*. Edward Elgar Publishing, Cornwall, Great Britain.
Shane, S. and Venkataraman, S. 2000. The Promise of Entrepreneurship as a Field of Research. Academy of Management Review, 25(1): 217–26.
Sharir, M. and Lerner, M. 2006. Gauging the success of social ventures initiated by individual social entrepreneurs. *Journal of World Business*, 41(1): 6–20.
Shaw, E. and Carter, S. 2004. *Social Entrepreneurship: Theoretical Antecedents and Empirical Analysis of Entrepreneurial Processes and Outcomes*. Paper presented at the 24th Babson-Kauffman Entrepreneurship Conference, Glasgow Scotland.
Simms, S. and Robinson, J. 2006. *Activist or Entrepreneur? An Identity-Based Model of Social Entrepreneurship*. Paper presented at the USASBE / SBI, Tucson, Arizona.
Simon, H. A. 1991. Organizations and Markets. *Journal of Economic Perspectives*, **5**(2): 25–44.
Stinchcombe, A. L. 1965. Social Structure and Organizations. In March, J. G. (ed.), *Handbook of Organizations*. Chicago: Rand McNally.
Stinchcombe, A. L. 1982. Should Sociologists Forget Their Mothers and Fathers? *American Sociologist*, **17**(February): 2–11.
Thompson, J. 2002. The World of the Social Entrepreneur. *The International Journal of Public Sector Management*, **15**(4/5): 412–31.

Thompson, J., Alvy, G. and Lees, A. 2000. Social Entrepreneurship – A New Look at the People and Potential. *Management Decision*, **38**(5): 328–38.

Waddock, S. A. and Post, J. E. 1991. Social Entrepreneurs And Catalytic Change. *Public Administration Review*, **51**(5): 393–401.

Wallace, S. L. 1999. Social Entrepreneurship: The Role of Social Purpose Enterprises in Facilitating Community Economic Development. *Journal of Developmental Entrepreneurship*, **4**(2): 153.

Wartick, S. L. and Cochran, P. L. 1985. The Evolution of the Corporate Social Performance Model. *The Academy of Management Review*, **10**(4): 758–69.

Wry, T. 2006. *An Integrative Framework to Understand Social Entrepreneurship*. Paper presented at the 2nd International Social Entrepreneurship Research Conference, New York, NY.

Young, D. R. 1984. Performance and Reward in Nonprofit Organizations: Evaluations, Compensation and Personnel Incentives: Case Western Reserve University.

Young, D. R. 1986. Entrepreneurship and the Behavior of Nonprofit Organizations: Elements of a Theory. In Rose-Ackerman, S. (ed.), *The Economics of Nonprofit Insitutions: Studies in Structure and Policy*. New York: Oxford University Press.

Part I
Values in Social Entrepreneurship

3
Religion and Social Entrepreneurship[1]

Roger Spear

Introduction

This chapter is concerned with the role of religion in social entrepreneurship. It takes an institutional perspective and examines the way religious institutions and actors have supported social entrepreneurship. Max Weber has argued for the role of (Protestant) religion in motivating people to take entrepreneurial activity, leading to the rise of capitalism in the West. It has often been observed that religious groups, especially sects or minority religious groups such as Quakers or Jews, have strong links with entrepreneurial activity – there are a range of factors in the literature which help us explain this. These include in particular the place of high trust networks in facilitating entrepreneurial activity. In addition, religious institutions (through leadership discourse and institutional networks) have historically played important roles in shaping the activities of religious members and priests as well as philanthropists. This has operated through religious leadership discourse, for example papal encyclicals orienting priests to support economic solutions to poverty and social problems in their communities, and the direct action of individual priests, institutional development (networks/organizations) and local religious leaders to catalyse entrepreneurial activity. Thus these three dimensions of religious institutions (ideological discourse, networks and leadership) will be examined in relation to *social* entrepreneurship. For the sake of simplifying the empirical base of this study, the field of social entrepreneurship will be limited to social enterprise which are co-operatives, mutuals and trading voluntary organizations (or non-profits), since there is a good evidence base of religious involvement in entrepreneurship in this sector, from which a number of cases will

31

be drawn using secondary sources. However, the theoretical framework developed will be based on the broader field of literature linking religion and entrepreneurship; thus this theoretical framework should have applicability to broader definitions of the social entrepreneurship field. The chapter covers three religious institutional dimensions underlying social entrepreneurship:

- institutions and high trust religious networks;
- ideology and religious leadership discourse;
- local religious leaders.

Note that it does not deal with the important area of the role of religion in the entrepreneurial development of non-profit organizations – a substantial area which will be the subject of a later paper. The following sections develop an institutional framework, and then examine each of these themes in cases of social entrepreneurship.

Preliminary comments

Value-driven social entrepreneurship

One could consider all social entrepreneurship as value-driven, but in this chapter the emphasis is on key ideologies that inform social entrepreneurship. There are a number of ideologies that seem to play important roles in social entrepreneurship: religion is just one major theme in value-driven entrepreneurship – another major thematic ideology which has informed social entrepreneurship through the ages is socialism; there are also more specific ideological themes like social justice through fair-trade which seem influential in social entrepreneurship. The same theoretical framework (ideology, leadership and institutions) is relevant to each of these ideological themes in social entrepreneurship.

Definitions of social entrepreneurship

One approach to social entrepreneurship is to define it as the creation of new social enterprise as well as entrepreneurial activity by established social enterprise. This is the approach of the EMES network[2] (Borgaza and Defourny, 2001). This EMES approach may be contrasted with a broader US approach which sees social entrepreneurship as covering a wide range of types of enterprise (from voluntary activism to corporate social innovation – see Nicholls, 2006: 12).

As a research field the narrower EMES approach has advantages of much clearer boundaries, while the US approach has a fascinating breadth, encompassing social innovation, NGO activity and profit-oriented business, but this breadth is a challenge for the empirical researcher attempting to define a field. As Hockerts (2006) argues in particular, there may be a transitional character to social enterprise forms around the early phases of entrepreneurship.

This chapter takes the EMES approach to defining the field of interest, but develops a theoretical framework which should be applicable to the broader US definition.

Social entrepreneurship: an institutional perspective

This section uses Weber, Portes and others to develop a theoretical framework that links ideas (ideology) as support for value-based social entrepreneurship processes, both through institutions (as organizations/networks) and through religious leadership in the form of higher level discourse and local entrepreneurial development.

Weber's thesis was that Protestant religion influenced the rise of capitalism because certain elements of religious belief and practice helped shape people's motivations towards business development. Certain forms of Protestantism gave religious value to economic endeavour: first, through the pursuit of economic gain, and, secondly (since luxury and conspicuous consumption was disdained), through investment of these gains. Although in the conclusions to this work, Weber noted the decline of the Protestant ethic in the spirit of capitalism, nonetheless this ideological root of entrepreneurship provides an important theme for altruistic values underlying social entrepreneurship.

Weber's conceptual framework for explaining social action also contained important social dimensions which are very relevant to the analysis here of another aspect of social dimensions of entrepreneurship – its social context.

Weber (1922) argued that there are three types of action:

- action guided by habit;
- action guided by emotion; and
- rational action, guided by the deliberate pursuit of goals.

This chapter is primarily concerned with the latter category of rational action, which can have a means–end structure oriented to individual goals, or towards some transcendental value. But Weber assumed that rational (instrumental) action is socially oriented since 'it takes into account the behaviour of other'. Portes (1995: 4) links with this perspective, exploring the nature of the social context for economic activity; he argues that Weber's view 'implies substantive expectations linked to sociability. By virtue of membership in human groups – from family to churches to associations – individuals acquire a set of privileges and associated obligations that simultaneously further and constrain their selfish pursuits'.

Portes (1995) argues that there are several types of social influence on economic activity, these are (4):

- value introjection (including altruism) arising from socialization, i.e. any action guided by moral considerations; 'Morality or the acting out of collectively held values may influence both the character of personal goals and the selection of means to attain them';
- action guided by moral considerations (altruistic) which derives from group membership and solidarity;
- pursuit of gain is constrained by expectations of reciprocity, developed during social interactions. The acquisition of social capital[3] oils the wheels of economic exchange, and this modifies the behaviour of economic actors;
- interaction (of materialistic action) with other self-centred goals like quest for approval, status and power – which depends on and is sanctioned through the opinions of others (for example linked to group membership). Thus economic power (and wealth) may exert influence, but only authority confers legitimacy.

Economic sociology has elaborated the process whereby types of social influence are promoted; this has led to a focus on the concept of embeddedness (Polanyi 1944, and Granovetter 1995), differentiating between 'relational embeddedness' and 'structural embeddedness'. The former refers to the nature of personal relations between economic actors, and the latter to the broader network of social relations to which they belong. Social networks (with widely different characteristics of density, centrality, size and clustering), provide one of the most important contexts for trust, norms and expectations influencing the interactions to be established and thus for social capital to be developed and reproduced. Portes (1995: 14) argues that several different types of social capital may be operable, informed by the sources and motivations seen in Table 3.1.

Table 3.1 Four types of social capital, Portes (1995: 14)

Source	Values	Bounded solidarity	Reciprocity	Enforceable trust
Donor's Motivation	Altruistic	Altruistic	Instrumental	Instrumental

This provides a framework which shows the different social and economic dimensions underlying rational action, and which recognizes the different sources and motivations, and the fact that they can have negative as well as positive impacts on entrepreneurship. This approach helps to elaborate the perspective (argued by Swedberg [2006] referring to the early Schumpeter, and Steyaert and Hjorth [2006]) that the social dimension of entrepreneurship (a central form of economic activity) is underemphasized. The approach also provides a useful typology for differentiating between the different religious themes underlying (social) entrepreneurship – in particular how they help sustain the role of institutions, religious networks, ideology and religious leadership discourse, and local religious leaders.

These different types of social and economic interacting factors are embedded, as can be seen in an example from the Philippines described by Granovetter (1995: 133):

> Estancia residents are predominantly Catholic, live in a small city where there are elaborate networks of non-economic relations overlaid on the economic ones, and have well-developed personalized ties between clients and customers and among vendors. A sense of 'moral economy' operates in Estancia among subsistence vendors, so this is a setting where at least within a well-defined local group people have a feeling of responsibility for one another.

Granovetter notes: (150)

> in modern settings we also see numerous instances where discrimination against a group served as a double edged sword, preventing them from entering most occupations but pushing them into a niche that they were able to dominate, in part by virtue of the enforced ethnic cohesion within that niche. The general point is that conditions 'that raise the salience of group boundaries and identity, leading persons to form new social ties and action-sets, increase the likelihood

of entrepreneurial attempts by persons within that group and raise
the probability of success'

(Aldrich and Zimmer, 1985)

But he also notes that there is a balance required between insufficient
trust and solidarity, and too much solidarity, resulting in excessive non-
economic claims on economic activity.

Thus in general terms, as Granovetter (145) argues:

> what we must look for then, in understanding successful entrepre-
> neurial activity, is some combination of social cohesions sufficient to
> enforce standards of fair business dealing and an atmosphere of trust,
> along with circumstances that limit the non-economic claims on a
> business that prevents its rationalisation. The relatively small size and
> cohesive social structure of groups that are minorities in their loca-
> tion (and if they are beleaguered and despised minorities, they are
> much more likely to pull together socially and culturally) may often
> provided just the right combination of these factors, and thus helping
> to explain the often noted economic success of expatriate minority
> groups. In settings were hardly any integrated enterprises exist we
> may expect that those that do exist have such origins – for exam-
> ple, the very few integrated craft-commercial enterprises reported by
> Geertz in Sefrou, Morocco, are Jewish in origin.

In addition, an important feature of such social networks supporting
entrepreneurship is the inter-local dimension, for example the capacity
to extend linkages beyond the local area and thereby bringing access to
resources within other localities.

Many authors discussing institutional approaches to social entrepreneurship and social enterprise, for instance Nicholls (2006), Dart (2004)
and Nyssens (2006), argue that legitimacy is a central resource in the
social entrepreneurship process. The first two authors discuss pragmatic,
moral and cognitive legitimacy – and clearly (as Portes notes above)
authority confers legitimacy, and religious institutions and networks
are readily able to provide such resources for entrepreneurs; indeed,
legitimacy is frequently conferred on entrepreneurs through their close
involvement with the church in the phase after entrepreneurial success. This is not to argue that legitimacy derived from religious roots
supports only conventional economic activity – on the contrary, it
could be argued that both moral and cognitive legitimacy, deriving

from the mainstream religions, can give support for distinctive difference, especially if the entrepreneurial responses embody some critique
of unrestrained capitalist society. This then provides support for a social
entrepreneurship and may counter isomorphic tendencies towards conventional business entrepreneurship.

Summary: Weber and the economic sociologists have provided a basis
for understanding that economic activity is inextricably linked to social
context, and how social ties help shape a wide range of instrumental, reciprocal and altruistic exchanges. Religious identity provides one
important basis for constructing a social network in which economic
activity is embedded, and in which social exchanges (of social capital) take place. In terms of mainstream and minority religious networks
there appear to be some strong arguments in favour of minority networks; however, mainstream religious networks can allow access to a
wide range of people with resources. Both can allow access to legitimacy resources, and can help strengthen trust relations. And both can
have some influence over 'value introjection' where 'morality or the
acting out of collectively held values may influence both the character of personal goals and the selection of means to attain them' (Portes
1995:4).

The above discussion has helped developed the institutional perspective on social entrepreneurship being developed here. The following
sections cover the three other religious institutional dimensions underlying social entrepreneurship; first, ideology and religious leadership
discourse, which provides general background to entrepreneurship, and
as we shall see informs social entrepreneurship by local religious leaders; then, institutions and high trust religious networks, which support
conventional entrepreneurship, but which provide a model for institutions and networks in social entrepreneurship; and lastly, the role of
local religious leaders in social entrepreneurship.

Ideology and religious leadership discourse: Catholic and Protestant

Since 1891, when Pope Leo XIII released his hugely influential encyclical
Rerum Novarum (*On the Condition of Labour*), the Catholic Church has
held that unrestrained capitalism is not good for society and that people
have wider social responsibilities.

This position has been modified and developed in later encyclicals,
such as Pius XI's *Quadragesimo Anno* (*On the Reconstruction of the Social
Order*, 1931), written largely in response to the Great Depression, and

similarly for later ones: such as Pope John XX III, in 1961 with an encyclical (Mater and Magistra) on Christianity and social progress; and Pope John Paul II Encyclical, *Centesimus Annus* commemorating the hundredth anniversary of the 1891 publication of Leo XIII's first encyclical. And institutional leaders at national levels promote similar concerns, as can be seen for example in more recent pronouncements by certain Catholic bishops (1996):

> The distinction has always to be kept in mind between a technical economic method and a total ideology or world view. Catholic Social Teaching has constantly been aware of the tendency of free market economic theory to claim more for itself than is warranted. In particular, an economic creed that insists the greater good of society is best served by each individual pursuing his or her own self-interest is likely to find itself encouraging individual selfishness, for the sake of the economy. Christian teaching that the service of others is of greater value than the service of self is sure to seem at odds with the ethos of a capitalist economy.

And:

> ... Those who advocate unlimited free-market capitalism and at the same time lament the decline in public and private morality, to which the encouragement of selfishness is a prime contributing factor, must ask themselves whether the messages they are sending are in fact mutually contradictory. People tend to need more encouragement to be unselfish than to be selfish, so it is not difficult to imagine which of these two messages will have most influence. A wealthy society, if it is a greedy society, is not a good society. [Statement of the Catholic Bishops' Conference of England and Wales, October 1996]

Similar commitments can be seen from religious leaders in many other churches.

Apart from the regular community involvement of churchgoers[4], more recently we have seen examples of church ministers giving more than palliative support to their communities, but taking more active, entrepreneurial stances.

Protestant leadership

Similar developments can be seen here through pronouncements by archbishops on church statements on regeneration (urban/rural). Thus the *Faith in the City* publication in 1985 (Archbishop of Canterbury's Commission on Urban Priority Areas), which addressed spiritual and economic poverty in inner cities, and was highly critical of Thatcherite policies, and *Faith in the Countryside* in 1990 by Archbishops Commissions on Rural Areas have proved extremely influential.

Entrepreneurship: religious institutions and networks

This section covers a range of different religions, from mainstream to smaller groups/sects; the latter appear to be particularly important in supporting the use and reproduction of social capital and high trust networks. The section has had to be rather selective about the wide range of institutions that might be examined in relation to social entrepreneurship (as noted earlier, religious charities clearly have an important place but would require much more extensive coverage than can be provided here).

Case: Quakers and nineteenth-century industrial entrepreneurship in the UK

Kirby (1993), through an examination of a specific period and location of the industrial revolution in northern England in the nineteenth century, attempts to explain the over-representation of Quakers in entrepreneurship at that time. The story is about the history of the development of one of the first railways in the UK: the Stockton and Darlington Railway, which has its origins in the industrial development of the region, in particular the ports, the coal and iron producing industries. By 1870 this railway had played a major role in establishing Teesside as one of the most important industrial regions for iron production in the world. Quaker financial networks were essential to the early development of this railway, a very uncertain new technology, as well as its subsequent expansion. In the eighteenth century the land-locked coalfields of Darlington, West Auckland and Piercebridge, which until then had relied on mules and overland transport, began the search for alternatives. Expensive canal construction for such isolated areas proved unattractive to financiers, despite considerable efforts of canal promoters. In the early nineteenth century a combined canal and railway scheme got some measure of support, but the post-Napoleonic war depression put paid to that. Yet the plan resurfaced a few years later in 1818. However, the route of this canal, while serving Piercebridge well, was not convenient for Yarm or Darlington, and this led to a competing and cheaper rail proposal. Both schemes were highly attractive, giving the coalfields access to ports and thus the London coal trade. Eventually the canal scheme failed to get the necessary backers, while the rail tramway scheme got sufficient financial backing. Local Quakers were major investors, and the extensive Quaker network from outside the region (London, Norwich and Whitby) provided about one-third of the initial investment required. That such a risky venture such as a new railway[5] managed to secure funding is down to the trust and kinship ties of the Quaker network. Of the 19 major shareholders (owning > 5 shares) at the end of 1822, a good majority (12) were Quakers. The risks of this new technology venture subsequently proved problematic, expenses outrunning estimates. This led to several negotiations for additional finance: a large loan from a Quaker banking partnership was secured; increasing numbers of shares were issued, a Quaker guaranteeing the bond of the company; and one of the original promoters of the enterprise advanced the workmens' wages. The Quakers continued to dominate the financial support for the enterprise, but it proved an outstanding success, and they were eventually well rewarded. This success may have played a role in the willingness of Quakers to continue support for further developments linked to this railway, and the exploitation of the coalfields. This included Quaker finance for the purchase of land for additional shipping facilities in Middlesbrough (another part of Teesside), and the development of housing and other social facilities 'with the aim of creating a "model" industrial community' (Kirby, 1993:117). Extending the railway to this new port was financed by the company itself. Similar Quaker financing of enterprise was subsequently seen in the increasing development of iron production facilities, which were closely linked to the coal production, and rail networks already established. Thus this industrial complex of closely linked enterprises was firmly based on a network of Quaker finance, involving kinship ties, which were extended through their religious network to other non-kin Quakers outside the local region.

Kirby argues that the key factors behind this development were multifaceted: they were not so much that the religious beliefs of Quakerism led directly to entrepreneurialism (a Weberian type argument) – though such beliefs seemed to have encouraged entrepreneurship more than other nonconformist or mainstream religions – but, rather, that the institutional features of the Quaker community helped create a high trust financial network which considerably enhanced the capacity for entrepreneurship. Other factors included: a reasonable density of Quakers in this northern industrial region, a degree of exclusion for Quakers which oriented them more to the 'politically neutral' world of business. The other key institutional factors were: the close knit nature of Quaker relationships, strengthened by intermarriage (there were strong sanctions against marrying out) and strong kinship links – all helping to generate a 'web of credit' for entrepreneurship. In addition, the Quaker leadership (the London Yearly Meeting) established norms of good business conduct, documented in 11 pages of the Rules of Discipline and Advice (1834), and bankruptcy could be grounds for disownment by the Society of Friends.

Comments: while this is not a case of social entrepreneurship, there were social dimensions to this entrepreneurial venture (indeed the Quakers were early exemplars of socially responsible business), and the experiences perfectly exemplify the theoretical framework developed for explaining the role played by religious networks in developing high trust relations for 'enforceable trust' in support of entrepreneurship.

Protestant networks in Latin America

The development of entrepreneurial action from within sects and minority religious groups is not something confined to history: indeed, we are seeing their continuing growth in evangelical Protestantism, in separatist churches, in new age cults, neo-Buddhist, neo-Islamist (for example the substantial growth of co-operatives in modern-day Iran, which has a strong church–state theme), and neo-Hindu movements. David Martin (1991) reviews several studies to examine one such development: the growth of Protestantism (mainly Pentecostalism) in Catholic Latin America, exploring the parallels with the role played by eighteenth-century Methodism in being the midwife of economic initiative. He notes the difficulties researching the diverse contexts from which converts are drawn, and indeed the different types of poor that are drawn to this religious option, and he argues that

> basically Protestantism in Latin America is a movement of withdrawal from all that was, on the part of people who are on the move or who have been forced to move. That withdrawal includes the rejection of personal violence and social violence. Those who become Protestants reject the machismo of the male personality and equally reject the path of political rebellion. Bitter experience has taught them they have little to hope for from political action or from the political violence of the left or right. Rather they engage in a personal and peaceable reform which may yield them some tangible 'betterment'.... The betterment is in the first place moral, but it is also in the second place medical and economic.
>
> (Martin, D. 1991:82)

He recognizes we cannot know whether conversion to the new religion facilitates their change, or whether those drawn to conversion are ready for change. Whilst recognizing diverse and sometimes conflicting evidence, Martin concludes:

> what is required is an imaginative response to the way in which over a minimum of two generations, and possibly over several, a religion which encourages sobriety and personal discipline, and which is lay and participatory in style, which abolishes the hierarchy of mediation between man and God and which is created by and helps create a competitive milieu, may also create useful and potent congruencies with an entrepreneurial culture.
>
> (Martin, D. 1991:83)

Thus while there may be evidence of some improvement in the nexus between membership of a religious sect (or minority religious group) and entrepreneurial activity, this relationship needs to be related to context and membership of these religious groups. There is a world of difference between, for example, the economically poor modern-day Pentecostals in South America and the relatively more developed economic status of members of nineteenth-century Quaker and Jewish groups.

A similar framework seems to apply, looking more broadly at diverse religious groups: Amish, Shaker and other religious communities have demonstrated a high level of entrepreneurship in developing economically independent lives. The growth of faith communities has seen a parallel development of a desire for self-sufficiency, with resulting entrepreneurial activity.

Social entrepreneurship: institutions and networks

The first part of this section is concerned with major examples of social entrepreneurship that have large-scale initiatives over extended periods of time. The section ends with more local examples of religious involvement in social entrepreneurship. Key elements in the difference of scale appear to be in the institutional components of development. The first two (larger-scale) examples also appear to draw on more altruistic dimensions of social capital – the bounded solidarity of being a forgotten underclass, reinforced by Basque ethnicity in the Spanish example; together with elements of religious value introjection supported by charismatic leadership in both cases.

North American credit unions

In MacPherson's analysis (2005) of the formative development during the early twentieth century of three movements of North American credit unions[6] – Quebec, America and anglophone Canada – he reveals that two had strong links to religious thinking or religious institutions. Alphonse Desjardins, the founder of the Quebec Desjardins Caisses Populaires, had carefully studied Catholic thought on social problems, including the Papal encyclical *Rerum Novarum* of 1891 which was concerned about rising poverty, and emphasized responses based on the right to organize societies for mutual help and relief. Desjardins was concerned to help local communities with such responses. He aimed to develop credit unions (CUs) where the bond between members was based on social or religious links, with the Roman Catholic priest having an influential role. This religious theme led to a moral bias towards supporting savings for the necessities of life rather than the luxuries. In the early stages of development, and with new federal legislation repeatedly obstructed by mercantile interests, Desjardins was forced to focus on local entrepreneurial support, making use of his local religious connections as well as his influential links with those higher up in the church, and with Conservative and Liberal politicians. His achievements were considerable – with the first Caisse being established in 1900. By 1920, when Desjardins died, there were 140 Caisses, with 31,000 members.

Meanwhile in America, with interest aroused by the first Quebec Caisse, particularly amongst the French Canadians in New England, the first credit union[7] was opened in New Hampshire by Desjardins in 1909 through the work of Father Pierre Hevey. However, the centre of entrepreneurial activity was in Boston, where Edward Filene, a merchant who was socially concerned about poverty and partly driven by his Jewish family history, and with the support of other Liberals from his class, pushed for Massachusetts legislation for CUs to be passed in 1909. The First World War slowed progress, but Filene and others made a major step forward by establishing in 1920 the Credit Union Extension Bureau. The aim of this important new institution was to develop CUs right across the US. For 20 years it was managed by Roy Bergengren, a lawyer, businessman and religious person who in his speeches described the credit union movement as a way of becoming ' "my brother's keeper"; a way of encouraging ethical behaviour in the market place; and a way of promoting democratic practice' (MacPherson:178). In the US the common bond was typically via work, religion or ethnicity; in addition, priests often played informal pressuring roles to help ensure loans were repaid.

Turning now to the anglophone Canadian experience of credit unions (MacPherson, 2005): these like Desjardins were influenced by *Rerum Novarum* (the papal encyclical of 1891), which the priests 'Jimmy' Tomkins and Moses Coady had studied in Italy in the early part of the twentieth century. Their readiness to engage with economic issues can be seen in the following:

> Voluntary poverty, by all means! A certain amount of poverty under any system, yes! But God never intended that the masses of men should live a drab, unenlightened and uncultured life in this world. For these reasons we do not hesitate to invade the economic field: we are convinced that in helping men to live decently we are helping them to save their souls; we think it is our duty to lend a helping hand, an active leadership to the truth we preach from our platforms and pulpits. We wish the people to enjoy the decent living we enjoy, a living which we regard as our fundamental right.
>
> (From the writings and speeches of the Rev. Moses Coady, in Laidlaw, and Coady [1971:57])

Concerned about the sharp declines in agriculture and fishing trade in Atlantic Canada (especially Nova Scotia), they organised a series of Diocesan Rural Conferences. They continued to be very active in both religious networks and through political linkages, to ensure that severe community hardship and discontent was recognized by the authorities. Aside from using their networks in this way, they were distinctively innovative in their use of educational study circle techniques, which grounded study in the everyday problems and realities people faced. This had roots in Owenite practices, the co-operative movement, worker education movements, and the Danish Folk Schools movement. The development of the Atlantic CUs, was also informed by the American CU experience (rather than that of Quebec). Their work also benefited from the institutional support of the Catholic, St. Francis Xavier University, which established an extension department, of which Coady was the first director, and it is noteworthy that he successfully broadened its religious base to include other Christian denominations in its staff and field workers. With the support of staff in that department over 200 credit unions were formed during the 1930s; and further work extended the entrepreneurial developments from Nova Scotia to other provinces in Atlantic Canada.

There are many other examples one could draw on, for example, the post-war development of the Irish Credit Union Movement in the 1950s (McCarthy, 1998). This was founded through the entrepreneurial efforts of one dynamic, pioneering woman, Nora Herlihy, originally from Cork, with many women subsequently playing entrepreneurial roles; but it was also driven substantially by the clergy, and its development was facilitated by the Catholic Church giving time for CU promotion at the end of church services, and space for administration using church facilities. (Note that study groups were also key to their entrepreneurial process.)

Mondragon and Father Jose Maria Arizmendiarrieta

The Mondragon co-operatives are one of the wonders of the social enterprise world. From unlikely beginnings in economically ravaged post-civil war Basque country of Spain, they have grown to become a major economic force in Europe, and the seventh largest 'corporation' in Spain, with over 100 worker co-operatives, a polytechnic university, a high technology innovation facility, a bank and a national supermarket chain.

The social entrepreneur behind the foundations of this inspiring group of social enterprises was Father Jose Maria Arizmendiarrieta, who arrived in the town of Mondragon in 1941. Recognizing the need for economic development to help the community with its large numbers of unemployed, he got the community to raise money and establish in 1943 a technical school (which subsequently developed into a polytechnic and university). He then helped the newly trained apprentices found a new co-operative business, Ulgor, in 1956. And then in 1959, he helped set up the bank Caja Laboral Popular, which became the entrepreneurial force behind subsequent developments of the co-operatives.

Nothing differentiates people as much as their respective attitudes to the circumstances in which they live. Those who opt to make history and change the course of events themselves have an advantage over those who decide to wait passively for the results of the change (Jose Maria Arizmendiarrieta, ideologist and driving force behind the Mondragon Co-operative Experience).

(From MCC website: http://www.mondragon-corporation.com/ENG/ Co-operativism/Co-operative-Experience/Jose-M%C2%AA-Arizmen diarrieta.aspx)

Danish folk schools and Grundtvig

Nikolaj Frederik Severin Grundtvig was a Danish pastor, poet and philosopher. He believed in the wisdom of ordinary people, and was concerned to develop a collective learning experience for poor country folk. His thoughts and writings were very influential, and he developed the idea of self-governing residential schools providing spiritual, cultural and intellectual development of young adolescents, but which in contrast to bookish classical university education would focus on discussion, folk culture, and pragmatic issues to prepare people for the whole life (rather than exams) and their role in democratic citizenship. His ideas inspired the founding of the first folk high school in 1844. This tradition still continues today but with many non-residential folk high schools and part-time classes. Again, religious value introjection supported by charismatic leadership appears to be a key factor in the entrepreneurship.

Local religious leadership – UK

In the UK there have been institutional developments such as industrial missions represented by the Industrial Mission Association. These missions began during the Second World War, for example the South London Industrial Mission (SLIM) began in 1943 and since 1967 has been based at the Christ Church Industrial Centre, Southwark. Since the 1960s the SLIM has broadened to become an ecumenical organization, involving all major Christian denominations, as well as Jews and Muslims. It plans to join with the more recently formed (2005) Mission in London's economy, which has set itself the following objectives:

- to co-ordinate the churches' interventions in discussion of London's economy;
- to respond on behalf of the churches to consultation exercises on London's economy;
- to recruit, train, support, insure and supervise workplace chaplains;
- to support Christians working in the institutions of London's economy;
- to educate churches in the issues facing London's economy so that they might be able to respond appropriately;
- to work with other faith communities in order to create co-ordinated faith-community responses to the issues facing London's economy

There have been about 20 such missions in the UK, but while the economic orientation is clear, it is not known the extent to which this has translated into direct or indirect support for (social) entrepreneurship.

More generally, a large proportion of church ministers and priests are involved in practical ways to help their communities – this ranges from coffee mornings and other social events to different kinds of social support such as giving space in church halls for crèches/nurseries. This section is concerned with addressing higher levels of entrepreneurship: either in terms of economic and social development or social innovation.

Clearly, local contextual factors (linked to inner city deprivation) are more likely to provoke such a response than more comfortable suburban middle-class contexts, but wider socio-economic trends and religious discourse (as noted above) periodically play important roles also. As Foster (2006) argues the mid-1980s in the UK saw some religious reaction to Thatcherism (the rolling back of welfare state and the rise of entrepreneurial culture) in church proposals for urban regeneration. Foster grounds this general reaction by examining the changing roles of ministers in one municipal area. He notes that development of an entrepreneurial role by ministers can be difficult due to contested roles: especially the traditional one of the 'old-fashioned valued priest', or integration with managerial elites; while he recognizes that some are good at scanning for opportunities, but less good at following these up with innovative action, 'there remains a sense of "opportunity lost" in many respects, even where opportunities literally come knocking at the door' (Foster, 2006:199). Nonetheless the institutionally supportive context and the closeness to opportunities provide the basis for more extensive entrepreneurial activity, as can be seen in the next two examples:

Case: Andrew (now Lord) Mawson and the Bromley-by-Bow Centre in London

From a poorly attended inner city church with a leaking roof in 1984, the newly appointed Church of England minister Andrew Mawson with a small team have developed a multi-faceted community resource: a crèche/nursery, a dance school (now floated off as a separate business), a café, a local authority funded disability care service, a development trust and health centre, a commercially sponsored project to reduce youth crime, and so forth. They have done this by being socially entrepreneurial themselves and facilitating or catalysing others into be enterprising, often with the help of under-used church or other local resources (Leadbetter, 1997).

Case: Eric Blakeborough, Baptist minister in Kingston, South London

From a similar starting point in 1968, with a small congregation of 25, Eric Blakeborough wanted to find something for young people to do, and started a youth club which stayed open late. This led inevitably to a recognition of health and drug problems, and a need for treatment. This, in turn, led to Kaleidoscope, a project for the treatment of young people on hard drugs – treating up to 300 people a day with methadone. It became one of the most innovative drug treatment programmes in the country. An additional resource was developed, a residential home for continuing support of young people was established through several churchgoers remortgaging their homes to provide finance (Leadbetter, 1997).

Conclusion

The chapter has attempted to examine the relevance of three religious institutional dimensions underlying social entrepreneurship:

- institutions and high trust religious networks;
- ideology and religious leadership discourse;
- local religious leaders.

It has developed a conceptual framework for elaborating these dimensions and has shown that there is substantial evidence for high trust religious networks supporting entrepreneurship amongst smaller religious groups and sects, although there is not so much evidence of *social* entrepreneurship here. The chapter has argued that, with more mainstream religions, the advantages accessed by entrepreneurs are: motivating discourse by religious leaders, networks that allow access to diverse actors with resources; and access to legitimation resources. In addition, though not dealt with in depth, this chapter has noted institutional (organizational) developments that can be central to social entrepreneurship especially religious charities and intermediary structures like industrial missions. Portes's typology of social capital has added to the analysis by providing a framework for differentiating between altruistic/instrumental motivations and solidarisitic, reciprocal and enforceable trust characteristics of the structure of embedded relations between actors in the entrepreneurial endeavour.

Many cases are in the distant past, so it is relevant to raise questions about the continuing relevance of religion in social entrepreneurship: Grenier (2006) suggests secularization has reduced the influence of mainstream religions on entrepreneurship, when she argues that in a context of globalization and individualism, social entrepreneurship may be one way individuals find spiritual expression, athough she also notes that 'moral individualism' can also encompass spiritual beliefs strongly linked to religion. In addition, it is clear that many modern-day social entrepreneurs make great use of business corporate social responsibility networks and other networks such as those associated with various social movements like fair-trade or environmental sustainability. This suggests an alternative source of social entrepreneurship where the growth of new religious movements and secular ideological movements replace the traditional religious thematic influence. However, it is important to remind ourselves that the secularization thesis has not been empirically validated, and perhaps we should not write off religious networks yet. Thus, in the context of a pluralistic moral basis for entrepreneurship, both mainstream and religious sects continue to motivate, and provide strong links for legitimacy and other resources for social entrepreneurs.

Notes

1. Based on paper presented at 3rd International Social Entrepreneurship Research Conference (ISERC), 18–19 June 2007 Copenhagen Business School Frederiksberg, Denmark.
2. The EMES criteria comprise economic and social dimensions defining social enterprise:

   Four factors to define the economic and entrepreneurial nature of the initiatives:

   1) a continuous activity producing goods and/or selling services;
   2) a high degree of autonomy (vs. dependency);
   3) a significant level of economic risk;
   4) a minimum amount of paid work.

   Five factors have been selected for the social dimensions of the initiatives:

   1) an initiative launched by a group of citizens;
   2) a decision-making power not based on capital ownership;
   3) a participatory nature, which involves the persons affected by the activity;
   4) limited profit distribution;
   5) an explicit aim to benefit the community.

3. Portes's definition of social capital: the ability to command scarce means by virtue of membership in social structures.
4. A quarter of regular churchgoers (among both Anglicans and other Christians separately) are involved in voluntary community service outside the church. Churchgoers overall contribute 23.2 million hours' voluntary service each month in their local communities outside the church.
5. Initially the plan was for a tram and roadway, but with the appointment of railway pioneer George Stephenson this changed to a locomotive and railway.
6. Note that one of the great founders of the CU movement, Friedrich Wilhelm Raiffeisen, also had strong religious links – his father was a minister and mayor of the village, but he died an alcoholic when Raiffeisen was 11 years old. In addition, his mother was a devout Christian (Lutheran), and she developed a strong sense of piety in her son. Raiffeisen built his model of co-operatives (CUs) on brotherly love and Christianity.
7. This was a 'co-operative association', since credit union legislation was not available in that state.

References

Aldrich, H. and Zimmer, C. 1985. Entrepreneurship through Social Networks. In Smilor, R. and Sexton, D. (eds), *The Art and Science of Entrepreneurship*: 3–23. Cambridge, MA: Ballinger.

Archbishop of Canterbury's Commission on Urban Priority Areas. "Faith in the city", 1985. Church House Publishing, Church House, Dean's Yard, London.

Archbishop of Canterbury's Commission on Rural Areas. "Faith in the countryside", 1990. Worthing, Churchman.

Borgaza, C. and Defourny, J. 2001. The Emergence of *Social Enterprise in Europe*. London: Routledge.

Dart, R. 2004. The Legitimacy of Social Enterprise. *NonProfit Management and Leadership*, **14**(4): 411–24.

Foster, D. 2006. Social Entrepreneurship: Exploring a Cultural Mode amidst others in the Church of England. In Nicholls, *Social Entrepreneurship*:181–202.

Granovetter, M. 1995. Economic Sociology of Firms and Entrepreneurs. In Portes, *Economics of Sociology of Immigration* 128–65.

Grenier, P. 2006. Social Entrepreneurship: Agency in a Changing World. In Nicholls, *Social Entrepreneurship*:119–43.

Hockerts, K. N. 2006. Bootstrapping Social Change, Towards an Evolutionary Theory of Social Entrepreneurship. *Academy of Management Conference*. Atlanta.

Kirby, M. 1993. Quakerism, Entrepreneurship, and the Family Firm. In Brown, J. and Rose, M. B. (eds), *Entrepreneurship, Networks, and Modern Business*:105–26. Manchester: Manchester University Press.

Laidlaw, A. F. and Coady, M. M. 1971. *The Man from Margaree*. Toronto: McClelland and Stewart Ltd.

Leadbetter, C. 1997. *The Rise of the Social Entrepreneur*. London: Demos.

MacPherson, I. 2005. Founders and the Formative Years of Caisses Populaires and Credit Unions in North America. In Tsuzuki, C., Hijikata, N. and Kurimoto, A. (eds), *The Emergence of Global Citizenship: Utopian Ideas, Co-operative Movements, and the Third Sector*:169–86. Robert Owen Association of Japan, Tokyo: JCCU.

Martin, D. 1991. The Economic Fruits of the Spirit. In Berger, B. (ed.), *The Culture of Entrepreneurship*:73–84. New Delhi: Tata McGraw Hill.

McCarthy, O. 1998. *The Role of Women Entrepreneurs in the Irish Credit Uunion Movement*. Paris: ICA Research Committee Conference: Women, Entrepreneurship and Co-ops.

Nicholls, A. (ed.) 2006. *Social Entrepreneurship*. Oxford: Oxford University Press.

Nyssens, M. 2006. *Social Enterprise at the Crossroads of Market, Public Policy and Civil Society*. London/New York: Routledge.

Polanyi, K. 1944. *The Great Transformation*. Boston: Beacon Press.

Portes, A. 1995. Economic Sociology and the Sociology of Immigration: a Conceptual Overview. In Portes, *Economics of Sociology of Immigration*:1–41.

Portes, A. (ed.) 1995. *The Economics of Sociology of Immigration*. New York: Russell Sage Foundation.

Steyaert C. and Hjorth, D. 2006. *Entrepreneurship as Social Change*. Cheltenham: Edward Elgar.

Swedberg, R. 2006. Social Entrepreneurship: the View of the Young Schumpeter. In Steyaert and Hjorth, *Entrepreneurship as Social Change*:21–34.

Weber, M. 1922. *The Theory of Social and Economic Organisation* (trans. A. M. Henderson and T. Parsons). New York: The Free Press.

4
Vision and Values: The Relationship between the Visions and Actions of Social Entrepreneurs

Paola Grenier

Introduction

> [Social entrepreneurs are] people with new ideas to address major problems who are relentless in their pursuit of their visions, people who simply will not take 'no' for an answer, who will not give up until they have spread their ideas as far as possible.
>
> (Bornstein, 2004: 1)

> ... what defines a leading social entrepreneur? First, there is no entrepreneur without a powerful, new, system changing idea. The entrepreneur exists to make his or her vision society's new pattern. He or she is married to that vision, in sickness or in health, until it has swept the field.
>
> (Drayton, 2002: 123)

Social entrepreneurs are consistently described as 'visionary'. The quotations above suggest that the defining characteristic of social entrepreneurs is that they have a vision which they pursue relentlessly, until that vision has been enacted and fulfilled. Vision is commonly associated with entrepreneurial behaviour, particularly in terms of leadership skills. The field of social entrepreneurship research and theory is in the early stages of development, and the role of vision and the relationship between vision and action has not been a focus for research. Yet it is suggested here that without more serious attempts to understand what is 'visionary' about social entrepreneurs the field of social entrepreneurship risks becoming overly focused on managerial issues, such as organizational growth strategies and metrics, and losing touch with what is exciting and distinct about social entrepreneurship. This is an exploratory study into how social entrepreneurs express their visions, and how their visions guide and shape their actions.

Vision is described by Burnside (1991: 178) as 'a living picture of a future, desirable end state'. He stresses the importance of the picture or image, and the fact that it is not about the how or the means but the ends results or outcomes. Similarly, Bennis and Nanus (1985: 82) state that:

> A vision articulates a view of a realistic, credible, attractive future for the organization, a condition that is better in some important ways than what now exists. A vision is a target that beckons.

Anecdotally, and in much of the popular leadership literature, vision is assumed to be an essential aspect of leadership. The centrality of vision to a successful entrepreneurial venture is highlighted by Shirley (1989), a successful entrepreneur herself. She comments that a good entrepreneurial vision is based in reality, which often encompasses accurate market research and trend analysis; the conversion of that analysis into action; and a willingness to put your money on the line. Vision, in other words, is said to be critical to entrepreneurial leadership, and is characterized as specific, realistic and achievable.

Theoretically, the centrality and role of vision in the entrepreneurial process have not been so well developed. Westley and Mintzberg (1989) propose a model of visionary leadership, suggesting that visionary leaders are entrepreneurial and that they are involved in setting up new organizations or changing existing organizations. They use a theatrical metaphor in setting out their theory. There is an initial period of 'rehearsal' or preparation, where the leader (or potential leader) becomes familiar with his or her field and develops the preliminary 'idea' or vision. This is followed by the communication of the vision – the 'performance'. The final element is the 'audience', which is conceived of as an active participant in the ongoing creation of the vision. The vision then undergoes change and development through interaction between the 'audience' and the leader. Vision is therefore dynamic in that it is constantly being redefined and rearticulated, and it is co-created through the interaction between leaders and 'audience' or followers. Westley and Mintzberg (1989) go onto stress the importance of leadership integrity and consistency, as well as the influence of context on the visioning process.

Goal-setting theory offers an alternative perspective on the nature of vision and the creation of a vision. Research supports the importance of goal-setting to the entrepreneurial process. Naffziger et al. (1994) propose a model of entrepreneurial motivation based on goal-setting theory, stating simply that entrepreneurs 'are motivated to accomplish goals they set for themselves'. Similarly, Gollwitzer (1996) found that goal-setting creates a perceptual readiness and guides a person's attention towards relevant opportunities. Kotter (1990) also stresses the primary importance of leadership in establishing the vision and goals that establish the direction for an organization.

Drawing on goal-setting theory, Bird (1988, 1992) has developed intentionality theory, which seeks to account for entrepreneurial behaviour. Intentionality is defined as 'a state of mind directing the person's attention (and therefore experience and action) toward a specific object (goal) or a path in order to achieve something (means)' (Bird, 1988: 442). The theoretical framework was developed in an inductive process from interviews with twenty entrepreneurs. Bird found that intentions guide an entrepreneur's behaviour in relation to goal-setting, communication, commitment and organization.

Intentionality does not offer a theory of vision, but it does help us to understand the actions of entrepreneurs. The intentional process involves three stages:

(i) Temporal tension: Bird proposes that entrepreneurial experience of time is 'different'. Entrepreneurs are 'here and now' and future orientated and do not spend time thinking about the past. They also have a wide range of task time horizons.

(ii) Strategic focus: the model proposes that entrepreneurs focus on end states and not means, and on organizational goals not personal goals.

(iii) Posture: there are two aspects to posture, first, the alignment of 'inner voices', particularly values, beliefs and wants so that there is no conflict between home life, work life and life style aspirations. The second aspect is attunement to the environment, which it is suggested is particularly important for ethically motivated entrepreneurs. Attunement is defined as the ability to send and receive information, and is demonstrated by open-mindedness and the ability to learn from mistakes.

Bird has applied the model to account for venture start-up (1992) and to develop a model of entrepreneurial competency (1995), demonstrating that the theory has a wide range of applications. Boyd and Vozikis (1994) have proposed an amendment to the model, with self-efficacy as a mediating variable, though they do not challenge the fundamentals of the theory.

Theory and research support the idea that vision, as 'desirable end state' 'a target that beckons', is an essential element in the entrepreneurial process. Westley and Mintzberg's (1989) approach to visionary leadership offers a dynamic approach to the creation of the vision, but not to how it is then followed through with actions. Intentionality provides a way of understanding the link between intentions and actions, though it does not incorporate the concept of vision.

The research question posed here is: how does vision guide the actions of social entrepreneurs? In order to focus the research, some specific areas for investigation were posed, which were informed by the theories of intentionality, goal-setting and visionary leadership outlined above.

1. *Vision:* Theory suggests that entrepreneurs work towards a vision, a 'desirable end state' (Burnside, 1991) where that vision is a clear 'picture' of a future state (Naffziger et al., 1994). Westley and Mintzberg (1989) propose that the vision develops over time and is 'co-created' by the leader and the 'audience'.

The present research examines whether social entrepreneurs have a vision that is a 'desirable end state', a vision that they consciously construct and can articulate to create an image of a possible future reality. The research seeks to identify whether there is anything distinctive about the content of entrepreneurial visions, whether that vision has changed and developed over time, and what factors have influenced those developments.

2. *Goal-setting Strategies:* Bird's (1988) theory of entrepreneurial intentionality and goal-setting theory both suggest that people who set clearly defined goals are more likely to be motivated and to achieve them. The present research examines whether social entrepreneurs make use of formal planning strategies, and to what extent they set and orient themselves to clearly defined goals.

3. *Actions:* Bird (1988) clearly states that intentions guide action, similarly Westley and Mintzberg (1989) talk about the communication of the vision as being in actions as well as in words, and stress the importance of consistency between what is said and what is done.

The present research examines whether the vision of individual entrepreneurs and non-entrepreneurs guides their actions, and seeks to identify what specific strategies are adopted by entrepreneurs in bringing their visions to life. This study also looks at the extent to which there is consistency between the vision statements and the actions pursued amongst both entrepreneurs and non-entrepreneurs, and seeks to identify distinguishing features between the two groups.

Research design and methods

The exploratory nature of this research meant that a qualitative research methodology was employed, involving both qualitative data collection and analysis. A comparative research design was adopted in order to identify what is distinctive about social entrepreneurs. A sample group of six social entrepreneurs were contrasted with a comparison group of six 'non-entrepreneurs' in similar organization and positions. Interviewees were guaranteed anonymity, hence none of the organizations are named and information that may indicate their identity has been anonymized.

For the purposes of this study, social entrepreneurs were defined as leaders of voluntary organizations[1] recognized for their impact and innovation. The six social entrepreneurs were identified through publications on the subject: two were identified from *The Rise of the Social Entrepreneur* (Leadbeater, 1997); two from *Staying the Course* (Thake, 1995); and two from *Practical People, Noble Causes* (Thake and Zadek, 1997). All six were therefore independently recognized as social entrepreneurs. This is referred to as the sample group in the text, and the individuals are labelled S1 to S6.

A matched sample of managers/directors of voluntary organizations were identified to make up the comparison group, and are labelled C1 to C6. They were matched on the basis of working in the same field as the social entrepreneurs, and as heading up organizations that were recognized as being effective but not highly innovative. Five were identified through talking with people in different specialist co-ordinating or umbrella bodies, who were both familiar with the field and also with individual organizations and projects. One project was identified from my own experience of working in that particular sector.

A number of factors became apparent that made it difficult to match the samples precisely.

- First, some fields are characterized by innovation, since organizations or projects simply would not survive otherwise. This applied to services for people who misuse drugs.
- Secondly, it was difficult to identify matched projects where the innovative project operated across field and sectors, providing a unique combination of services. This applied to multi-purpose community centres.
- Thirdly, the organizations were at different stages of development.

In spite of these factors, the matching was considered close enough for a meaningful comparison.

Data collection was through semi-structured interviews. The underlying assumption in collecting information in this way is that there is a relationship between the content of what someone says and their beliefs, attitudes and what they do, though this may not always be transparent (Smith et al., 1995). It is recognized that this study is dependent on the interviewees reporting what they have done reasonably accurately. As a check, the annual reports and other publicity materials of both the sample and the comparison groups were reviewed prior to

Table 4.1 Details of sample group (S) and comparison group (C)

Reference	Social entrepreneurs – SX Non-entrepreneurs – CX	Gender	Founder of organization	Length of time as director, years
S1	Drug project	F	No	0–5
C1	Alcohol service	M	No	0–5
S2	Membership network	M	No	6–10
C2	Membership network	M	No	0–5
S3	Church-based, multi-purpose centre	M	Yes	11+
C3	Church-based day centre	M	No	11+
S4	Housing co-operative	M	Yes	11+
C4	Housing co-operative	M	No	0–5
S5	Self-help homelessness project	M	Yes	0–5
C5	Mental health housing project	M	No	6–10
S6	Multi-purpose community centre	M	Yes	11+
C6	Day centre for homeless people	F	No	0–5

interview, so the interviewer had an idea of the particular organization and what it was doing, and could ask questions and probe on issues specific to the organization.

The interviews lasted between 20 and 45 minutes. An interview schedule was used, with four open questions representing the areas for investigation, and a number of probes. These covered questions on:

- the original vision;
- how that vision changed;
- what specific goals and plans were developed;
- what actions were undertaken.

In all cases the interviewees were encouraged to talk openly and to use their own words. Interviewees were also encouraged to give specific examples of what they had done and what had actually happened, as well as talking about their ideas and goals.

The researcher conducted each interview and the interviews were recorded and transcribed verbatim. Analysis was carried out concurrent to the interviews, and allowed for emergent themes to be followed up in later interviews. This was consistent with the exploratory nature of the research. Probes were added on attitudes towards funding and fundraising, and where they got their ideas from. This meant that the form and direction of each interview was slightly different.

The transcripts were analysed using cognitive mapping, a methodology set out by Jones (1985). The main themes and concepts discussed and the relationships between them were identified for each interview. It was important to identify where ideas or approaches were followed through with specific actions and examples, and where there were inconsistencies between their stated visions or ideas and their actions. These were then checked against the original transcript to hone in on the ideas more precisely. After analysing each interview in turn, the cognitive maps were compared and developed in an iterative way both within and between the sample and the comparison group. In this way the distinctive features and patterns characterizing the sample group were drawn out.

Findings

This section sets out the findings, and is organized around the three areas of investigation identified above–vision, goal-setting strategies and actions. The emphasis is on the social entrepreneurs, as the non-entrepreneurs are not of direct interest themselves, but rather as a point of comparison in determining what is distinctive about the social entrepreneurs.

There were clear differences between the two groups studied. Before even starting to analyse the data, this was clear in their reactions to being approached for interview and in the ways in which they related to me as a researcher.

- The social entrepreneurs responded quickly to phone calls and letters, and it was straightforward to set up an appointment. This was not always the case with the non-entrepreneurs, where I needed more persistence in contacting them and in setting up a meeting.
- All the social entrepreneurs provided written materials about their organizations, even if only an annual report, whereas most of those in the comparison group did not have anything available.
- All the social entrepreneurs asked for a copy of the research findings, although this was not offered. None of the non-entrepreneurs made this request.
- The energy during the interviews with the social entrepreneurs was more 'lively' and 'positive', and I left the interviews with a sense of excitement and conviction in what I had been told.

Vision

The social entrepreneurs did not present their visions as a living picture of a future, desirable end state (Burnside, 1991). They did not have a tangible, concrete picture in their minds of the future they were aiming for in the way that the literature suggests. When asked if they knew what they were trying to create from the beginning, two of the social entrepreneurs immediately and simply responded with 'no'.

> S3: It was just twelve people, a derelict building and me. There wasn't any grand plan...the whole thing began to happen and one thing led to another.

The social entrepreneurs expressed their visions, what they were aiming to create and achieve, as principles and values.

> Q: Did you have an idea of what you were trying to create?

> S6: Yes, but it wasn't like that. I think, an idea of the potential....We had two basic beliefs. One that there were better ways of doing

things and we were committed to finding new solutions. Secondly, to involving the whole community in the process. It wasn't going to be about getting professionals in to do things at us or for us, but to evolve solutions together that involved everybody.

Over the years we have gone in a wide range of different directions. These two basic principles underpin everything we do.

A commonly held value was the need to involve and empower people, in particular people affected by poverty and other socio-economic problems and people on the receiving end of services.

S1: It is always client led, it is responding to their needs and asking them what they want.

In some cases it was not possible to distinguish the ends from the means and the vision as values was both the ends pursued and the practice adopted.

S5: I am interested in involvement, involving people, giving people power at a local level. So in the case of XX it was enabling homeless people to decide what hours they worked, and how the whole project worked … and enabling them to make decisions.

S6: It is undoubtedly the glue that holds the organization together, a shared approach … it's a network of people with a shared set of goals and principles. It's not much else.

This challenges the notion of vision as a 'desirable end state', constructing vision more as a way of being and a way of acting based on a set of values and principles.

But differences between visions, expressed in terms of values and principles, did not clearly distinguish the social entrepreneurs from the comparison group. The non-entrepreneurs were also able to express clearly their values and how these were the starting point for their work and the work of their organizations. What distinguished the two groups was the way in which the vision was enacted, how such abstract and general values and principles were translated into specific goals, plans and actions.

A further distinction was the learning that took place. During the interviews, questions were asked about whether their visions had changed and developed over time. Developments, and more significantly learning, took place as a result of action and experiences. It was not the central and underpinning values that changed, though they may have became refined or more precisely articulated over time. Rather, what changed was how they were enacted and how they came to be translated into plans, programmes and projects that met social needs in novel ways.

> S6: Those basic principles have not changed. We would now look at those early education projects and think that they were naive in some respects, and you would learn from that and pick out what works and discount what doesn't work.

Several of the social entrepreneurs talked about spending several years getting to know the area, the issues, the people before their ideas for change developed.

> S3: You can't possible know from outside this community what's relevant. I spent two, three years loitering around getting to know people, sussing things out.

> S4: At that stage I was really just listening.

Goal-setting strategies

There was a clear distinction apparent between the goal-setting strategies of the social entrepreneurs and the comparison group. All the social entrepreneurs had up-to-date plans and clearly defined goals which formed the basis for the work of their organizations; none of the comparison group did.

> S6: Within any individual project we have very specific targets. We have just begun this system which we call Critical 100. This is 100 things we hope to achieve in the course of a year, some of which might be figures, outputs... we reckon that if we can achieve that we are maintaining the pace, constantly developing which is what we need to be doing.

They were able to translate their visions into practical proposals that established the work of the organization.

S5: I started with idealistic ideas about how you help people and ended up with practical proposals.

S2: We decided that all our work was urban, it was all a multi-purpose model of work, and it was in areas of deprivation... We turned that into a strategic plan... We broke the whole of the work down into three streams... urban policy, network development, and administration and grant-making... Not only did we create a strategic plan, we also broke the staff team down... the whole filing system, the computer system... The whole system is structured around the three strands of the strategic plan.

At the same time, all the social entrepreneurs were very different from one another in how they planned, how their plans were set out, and the exact role of the plans within the organization. In one case those plans were not even written but in the head of the social entrepreneur and communicated verbally.

S1: I am a very verbal person, and it's all in my head, but if you asked any of the managers they would all know.

In another case, plans were highly formalized and based on the structure of the organization. In another, plans were 'always' draft and constantly evolving.

S3: We have a business plan which we worked out with KPMG. But its draft, its always draft... Because it's growing and developing.

The social entrepreneurs presented ideas and plans at almost all stages of development, including referring to past ideas that were unrealistic or where conditions had changed which rendered them irrelevant. There was no sense of failure or loss if plans did not work out or were abandoned. This was partly because the social entrepreneurs had so many other plans and ideas ready to make an appearance that they seemed to move on easily to the next thing.

S1: I do get downcast but you have to have a buoyant nature and bounce back, because if you got depressed at every rejection you got you wouldn't carry on. I am always amazed that one of the ideas comes off.

S5: It's not an ideal way of working in some ways...but it's a reasonable way of spending my time.

In general, the comparison group did not have strategic plans nor had they developed specific goals in the way that the social entrepreneurs had done. Only one of the comparison group had a tangible goal, but it was a single goal with no further ideas or plans.

C1: Once the day centre is up and running that would be my ambitions complete... Once all that is up and running I'll have to see what else is around.

Two did have written plans, but in neither case did the plans relate closely to the actual work and activities of the organization. Plans were put together because they were expected from outsiders, rather than being internally motivated.

C3: In fundraising terms we have something we call a business plan.

C6: Last year we were going to completely rewrite it because so much had changed.

The other three of the comparison group who had no plans attributed this to the lack of organizational certainty and their lack of secure funding.

C2: It would be useful. But what's the point in writing it, you know, we've got no security at the moment.

C3: Most funding is for three years maximum. You can speculate... its all a bit hit and miss.

C5: It is difficult for a project manager or director to develop a project if there is no settled management committee, that was the main problem.

C6: I always felt dictated to...it always felt quite threatening to be completely honest with funders.

This contrasts with social entrepreneurs, who had all found ways of planning within an insecure and unpredictable future.

S2: We had two years [of secure funding]. The board and staff worked quite closely to try and get a strategy together.

S5: Yes and no – it keeps changing. . . . [but] I have a planned route. . . . Its quite hard to put together a business plan in terms of how am I going to become sustainable. All I can do is really throw out ideas.

The social entrepreneurs felt confident in planning because they had a sense of control over their environment and over their futures, and they set their own goals. Also notable was the fact that they approached funders and donors from a belief in their own value and independence, and not as subservient to or controlled by those who provided the money.

S2: I have negotiated with government what I want to do and they have either said yes you can or no you can't.

S4: You can do what you want and other people can do what they want. This is what our vision is for our little patch.

S4: If we don't get Housing Corporation grant it makes it difficult to build housing. But they can't stop us surviving, we've set up the organization in a way so that we're just not susceptible to that pressure.

S5: I talk to them [funders], I can be completely honest with them about how things are going.

S6: We are independent. Our power comes from the fact that we have no power. People come to us and talk to us about the problems they are having with their children, maybe abusing their children. We don't have the power to take them away. It's the same with principles. We don't have any other function in life, besides being a council department – statutory bodies. What we are here to do is fulfil certain objectives that we have established for ourselves.

Another clear difference between the social entrepreneurs and the comparison group was the number of ideas they had and the source of their ideas. The comparison group were very focused on their core day-to-day activities, and in some cases on the struggles and difficulties they were

Table 4.2 Sources of ideas

Ideas came from	S1	S2	S3	S4	S5	S6	C1	C2	C3	C4	C5	C6
Internal sources												
Personal experience	Y	Y	Y	Y	Y	Y	Y		Y	Y	Y	Y
Board members				Y				Y				
Clients/members	Y	Y	Y	Y	Y	Y			Y		Y	Y
Analysis	Y	Y	Y	Y	Y	Y			Y			
External sources												
From same field		Y			Y							
From different field	Y				Y							
Other				Y		Y						

experiencing, whereas the social entrepreneurs presented examples of their work to illustrate almost every comment they made.

The table above shows that the sample group gathered ideas from a wider range of sources, and in particular that they were more likely to get ideas from external sources. They also showed a closer engagement with their client group.

> S6: [Ideas come in] through the door. Either people want to do things and have ideas they want to develop with us or they identify needs...the vast majority of the time we respond to issues that present themselves.

> C6: it was depressing. As a worker you'd go away thinking more services to provide, more money to find.

Actions

Central to this research was analysis of how the visions were followed through with actions. All the social entrepreneurs had carried out specific actions in pursuit of their visions, ideas or stated objectives. The social entrepreneurs operationalized their values in a variety of ways, and were actively pursuing a wide range of new activities. They were very specific and gave concrete information about activities that they were planning or were already taking place.

S2: *Vision:* To try to link with each other so you can build an interdependency thing [between the members].

Action: We piloted a thing called the Skills Exchange, so again we were the brokers. A group out there said we are going to start a project about this, can you link us with someone who is already doing it. And now the Baring Foundation are funding to develop the initial year…and people are going on these skills exchange visits, to stop reinventing the wheel.

S5: *Vision:* Giving people power at a local level

Action: I work locally with projects that are in different parts of the country.

S6: *Vision:* To work on new things and where it works well to move it ever and ever closer to independent management.

Action: It might mean complete independence from us, or it might mean, [AB is] still based here but very much determining its own programs. …So t means different things for different projects. It all about people taking as much control as is reasonable and appropriate for that individual project and running it themselves.

This was markedly different from the comparison group, who were unable to identify specific activities that directly reflected their visions and gaols.

C2: *Vision:* There were ideas that we may be able to provide information and training services.

Action: But again that all fell apart.

C5: *Vision:* We wanted to set up different sorts of schemes such as a floating support scheme.

Action: We haven't actually followed through on them yet.

There was a consistent difference in that the social entrepreneurs were involved in a much wider range of activities than the comparison group, in the same way as they had more ideas and plans that they wanted to pursue.

Discussion and conclusions

In the quotation at the beginning of this report social entrepreneurs were described as 'relentless in their pursuit of their vision' (Bornstein, 2004). This study found that social entrepreneurs behave in ways that are consistent and distinct from non-entrepreneurs, confirming that social entrepreneurs are active and persistent in pursuing their vision.

The most surprising finding was that the social entrepreneurs interviewed did not have an image or picture of a 'desirable end state'. Rather, they tended to have a set of values or principles that guided what they did and how they did it. In many cases the ends and the means were the same. This belies a number of theoretical approaches which suggest that entrepreneurs focus on end states rather than the means or the 'how' (for example Bird, 1988; Burnside, 1991; Naffziger et al., 1994). Westley and Mintzberg's (1989) comment that vision may be 'products, services, markets, or organisations, or even ideals'. It is the 'even ideals' that social entrepreneurs seem to demonstrate.

Even though the content of the vision was not as expected, the scope and centrality of it were clearly expressed, both directly and indirectly in what the entrepreneurs were doing. There was, however, little evidence to support Westley and Mintzberg's proposition that the vision is co-created. Yet it was clearly the case that what was done or how the vision was implemented was strongly influenced by the people enacting it.

Interestingly, it was not their vision that differentiated social entrepreneurs from the non-entrepreneurs. Members of both groups were able to articulate their vision in terms of a set of values and principles. There were, nevertheless, several factors that did distinguish the social entrepreneurs.

The development of a wide range of activities consistent with the vision characterized the social entrepreneurs compared with the non-entrepreneurs. This has been intimated by Thake (1995) who credited social entrepreneurs with having a wish-list of ideas for potential funders. The close match between actions and vision amongst successful entrepreneurs is suggested by Westley and Mintzberg (1989), who comment on the importance of consistency and integrity.

However, neither Westley and Mintzberg nor Bird's model of intentionality account for the sheer quantity of ideas and activities that social entrepreneurs pursue. Bird does point to attunement to the environment as important, and this is certainly apparent among the social entrepreneurs. The findings are consistent with much anecdotal information that entrepreneurs are 'doers', have lots of 'energy', and are 'practical' in their approach.

Plans and the process of planning also played a key role in the work of the social entrepreneurs compared with that of the non-entrepreneurs. The development of specific targets was evident and supports the relevance of goal-setting theory to social entrepreneurship, as well as Bird's model of intentionality, which suggests that entrepreneurs with clear and specific goals are more successful. However, it is equally important not to lose sight of the idiosyncratic ways in which the social entrepreneurs approached goal-setting and planning. They all had very different ideas of what a 'plan' was, from something in their head, to a constantly revised draft, to a formally approved strategy document around which the whole organization was structured.

The sense of independence expressed by the social entrepreneurs was one of the strongest themes to emerge, and one that clearly differentiated the entrepreneurs from non-entrepreneurs. It was expressed as the belief that they could impact on the environment, and in particular on funders, and also that they were in a position to do what they wanted. In contrast, the non-entrepreneurs believed that they could not negotiate with funders and that their situation was too insecure for there to be any point in setting their own goals. The social entrepreneurs were confident in setting goals and in developing plans, and were not put off by the changing environment, funding uncertainties or the fact that some plans remained unfulfilled. Theoretically these imply an internal locus of control and high self-efficacy, as well as the over-optimism that is associated with social entrepreneurs (Busenitz and Barney, 1997).

The exploratory nature of this research means that the findings offer a starting point for researching social entrepreneurship and developing theory, and cannot provide clear-cut answers. The findings point to a number of areas for future research. More needs to be understood about what makes up a vision, how it is articulated, and the relationship between vision, goal-setting, the development of new ideas and action. The role of learning and attitudes to learning are clearly important, as are the way in which taking action is a creative process in itself and how learning takes place as a result.

This research was focused on identifying the distinctions between social entrepreneurs and non-entrepreneurs. There was much evidence to support the distinctiveness of social entrepreneurs in terms of their goal-setting strategies, their activities and their approach. At the same time, the differences between the social entrepreneurs, their styles and attitudes, was at least as striking as the differences between the two research groups. In presenting research that is looking for commonalities among social entrepreneurs it is easy to downplay these differences. There may be more to learn from studying the differences between social entrepreneurs than in attempting to demonstrate that social entrepreneurs are a clearly identifiable type of person.

Note

1. This study took place in the UK, and the terms voluntary organization and voluntary sector are widely used in that context. It is comparable to referring to non-profit organizations, which is the term more commonly used in the US, but it is broader than the legal concept of charity as used in the UK. The organizations studied here were charities, either formally registered with the Charity Commission or registered with the Inland Revenue.

References

Bennis, W. and Nanus, B. 1985. *Leaders: The Strategies for Taking Charge*. New York: Harper and Row.
Bird, B. 1988. Implementing Entrepreneurial Idea: The Case for Intention. *Academy of Management Review*, **13**(3): 442–53.
Bird, B. 1992. The Operation of Intentions in Time: The Emergence of the New Venture. *Entrepreneurship Theory and Practice*, **17**(1): 11–20.
Bird, B. 1995. Toward a Theory of Entrepreneurial Competency. In Katz, J. A. and Brockhaus, R. H. (eds.), *Advances in Entrepreneurship, Firm Emergence, and Growth*, **2**: 51–72. Greenwich, CT: JAI Press.
Bornstein, D. 2004. *How to Change the World. Social Entrepreneurs and the Power of New Ideas*. New York: Oxford University Press.
Boyd, N. G. and Vozikis, G. S. 1994. The Influence of Self-Efficacy on the Development of Entrepreneurial Intentions and Actions. *Entrepreneurship Theory and Practice*, **18**(4): 63–77.
Burnside, R. M. 1991. Visioning: Building Picture of the Future. In Henry, J. and Walker, D. (eds), *Managing Innovation*: 177–90. London: Sage Publications.
Busenitz, L. W. and Barney, J. B. 1997. Differences between Entrepreneurs and Managers in Large Organizations: Biases and Heuristics in Strategic Decision-Making. *Journal of Business Venturing*, **12**(1): 9–30.
Drayton, W. 2002. The Citizen Sector: Becoming as Entrepreneurial and Competitive as Business. *California Management Review*, **44**(3): 120–32.
Gollwitzer, P. M. 1996. *The Psychology of Action: Linking Cognition and Motivation to Behaviour*. New York: Guildford Press.
Jones, S. 1985. The Analysis of Depth Interviews. In Walker, R (ed.), *Applied Qualitative Research*: 56–70. Aldershot: Gower Publishing.
Kotter, J. P. 1990. What Leaders Really Do. *Harvard Business Review*, May–June, **68**(3): 103–11.
Leadbeater, C. 1997. *The Rise of the Social Entrepreneur*. London: Demos.

Naffziger, D. W., Hornsby, J. S. and Kuratko, D. F. 1994. A Proposed Research Model of Entrepreneurial Motivation. *Entrepreneurship Theory and Practice*, **18**(3): 29–42.

Shirley, S. 1989. Corporate Strategy and Entrepreneurial Vision. *Long Range Planning*, **22**(6): 107–10.

Smith, J. A., Harre, R. and Van Langenhore, L. (eds.) 1995. *Rethinking Methods in Psychology*. London: Sage.

Thake, S. 1995. *Staying the Course: The Role and Structure of Community Regeneration Organizations*. York: Joseph Rowntree Foundation.

Thake, S. and Zadek, S. 1997. *Practical People Noble Causes*. London: New Economics Foundation.

Westley, F. and Mintzberg, H. 1989. Visionary Leadership and Strategic Management. *Strategic Management Journal*, Special Issue, Summer, **10**: 17–32.

5
Divergent Orientations of Social Entrepreneurship Organizations

Heather Douglas

Introduction

Social entrepreneurship is now well established in the academic literature (Sullivan Mort and Weerawardena, 2007). A precise definition of the concept is, however, not yet agreed. Mair et al. (2006: 4–6) outline nine definitions used by different authors. Each definition establishes a connection with social goals and business processes, but varies in the emphasis placed on the individual social entrepreneur, organizational form and sector of operation, financial objectives and resource mobilization, and importance of the social mission and social impact. For example, Robinson (2006: 95) defines social entrepreneurship as a process: 'the identification of a specific social problem and a specific solution...to address it; the evaluation of social impact, the business model and sustainability of the venture...'. Cho (2006: 36) takes an organizational perspective: 'a set of institutional practices combining the pursuit of financial objectives with the pursuit and promotion of substantive and terminal values'. Mair and Noboa (2006: 122) include innovation: 'the innovative use of resource combinations to pursue opportunities aiming at the creation of organizations and/or practices that yield and sustain social benefits'. Hockerts (2006: 145) focuses on the sector of operation: 'hybrid enterprises straddling the boundary between the for-profit business world and social mission-driven public and nonprofit organizations. Thus they do not fit complete in either sphere'. Many other definitions of social entrepreneurship exist.

The common thread in definitions of social entrepreneurship is a business process that aims to generate beneficial social change to benefit a target group (see for instance Alter, 2007; Barraket, 2008: 127; Nicholls, 2006: 2; Townsend and Hart, 2008; Zietow, 2001). Additional elements included in some social entrepreneurship definitions are: an altruistic objective (Dorado, 2006); problem-solving (Johnson, 2000); civic engagement and mobilizing the community (Fowler, 2000; Henton et al., 1997); a catalyst for complex social change (Mair and Martí, 2006; Waddock and Post, 1991), especially for deprived populations (Mair and Schoen, 2007) in an uncertain environment (Haugh, 2005; Thompson and Doherty, 2006); conflicting objectives of multiple stakeholders (Dees, 1998); hybrid organizations (Hockerts, 2006); and a realignment of civic space (Shaw and Carter, 2007; Spear, 2006). Social entrepreneurship is applied in needy areas of developing countries and also in the first world (Fowler, 2000; Seelos and Mair, 2005). While it generally has a non-profit application, some suggest it may appear in public or even business domains (Chell, 2007; Eikenberry and Kluver, 2004; Light, 2005; Thompson et al., 2000). Thus social entrepreneurship is an economic process of civic innovation undertaken by hybrid organizational forms aiming to address complex social issues and achieve outcomes that benefit target groups rather than the founders.

Not only are different definitions apparent, considerable diversity in practice also is evident, particularly in the prominence of social goals and the extent of the application of entrepreneurial elements (Peredo and McLean, 2006). The conceptual approach to social entrepreneurship in the US reflects a distinctive institutional environment along with an expectation of private/business convergence, whereas in Western Europe there is more focus on government/social service and an expectation of complex social environments (Kerlin, 2006). In the US, social entrepreneurship includes the revenue-generating business activities of non-profit organizations, along with philanthropic contributions or corporate social responsibility programmes in any organization. There is more focus in the US on examining the practices of founding social entrepreneurs based on an expectation that they operate in similar ways to business entrepreneurs (Townsend and Hart, 2008). While there is variation among Western European countries, overall social entrepreneurship is situated more strongly in civil society than in the business sphere (Nyssens, 2006; Spear, 2006). While acknowledging for-profit activities, in general social entrepreneurship in Western Europe is anticipated to be situated in the non-profit sector, supported by national governments and the European Union (Haugh and Rubery, 2005). Change and the social impact of social entrepreneurship are central in Western Europe. There is more expectation than in the US that the affected community will be involved to some extent in the design or delivery of beneficial activities (Haugh, 2007). Social entrepreneurship

Social objectives ←_____ increasing attention to achieving _____→ Business objectives

Figure 5.1   Spectrum of social entrepreneurship

in the US is anticipated to address social issues in relation to market failure, but in Western Europe its focus is on 'market oriented economic activities serving a social goal', which is seen to be lacking in existing programmes (Dees, 2001; Nyssens, 2006: 4).

The extent of these variations in definitions and practices clearly indicates that social entrepreneurship organizations are not the same (Thompson and Doherty, 2006). Rather, social entrepreneurship can be viewed as a continuum between altruistic, voluntary organizations on the one hand, and commercial businesses (Figure 5.1). At one extreme of the spectrum, philanthropic commercial firms operate with a strong orientation to maximize profit while at the same time having some commitment to achieving a social objective. At the other end of the continuum are organizations aiming to achieve a social goal while operating with a small degree of business-like activity. These organizations have a 'volunteering service' orientation (Douglas, 2007). They are non-profit organizations with a strong altruistic vision and commitment to participatory practice in the provision of services for disadvantaged clients. In the middle of the social entrepreneurship continuum are entrepreneurial organizations with a mix of social goals and business activities. These organizations operate with a mix of social intentions, business functions and organizational forms. Some organizations have a greater concentration on achieving social goals; others are more strongly focused on their business activities. Present definitions of social entrepreneurship include all these organizational types, and undoubtedly the organizations across the spectrum are quite different.

Theoretical background

Robinson (2006) suggests that the theoretical traditions of business entrepreneurship are applicable to social entrepreneurship. He anticipates that disequilibria in the economic, social and institutional environments will lead to entrepreneurial opportunities for social as well as commercial entrepreneurs, with opportunities being converted in a similar way in social and commercial contexts. Others, however, suggest social entrepreneurship organizations have a greater need to adapt to expectations in their institutional environment than commercial firms, and this imperative of moral legitimacy differentiates the social and commercial domains (Dart, 2004). Organizations oriented towards communitarian, altruistic perspectives differ in significant ways from those with more rational, individualistic businesslike orientations (Johnstone and Lionais, 2004; Ridley-Duff, 2007). Dorado (2006) maintains that social entrepreneurship bridges a need to generate profit with a focus on service to disadvantaged groups, and so entrepreneurial concepts from the business domain are not relevant always to social entrepreneurship.

Given the evident extent of variation in social entrepreneurship organizations, it is reasonable to consider the similarities and differences of social entrepreneurship organizations at either end of the spectrum. Researchers and policy-makers would benefit from an improved appreciation of the plurality of social entrepreneurship orientations (Parkinson and Howorth, 2008). Authors from social and business traditions are aware of divergent orientations and practices, yet there has been little systematic consideration of how these differences affect operations of social entrepreneurship organizations (Austin et al., 2006). Differences in the underpinning principles influence operational decisions, but although this has been examined in commercial contexts, little is known about how organizational orientation affects social entrepreneurship organizations. The smallness of certain organizations is known to influence their survival, including those with a social mission, but how smallness affects how organizations operate is not understood (Chambre and Fatt, 2002; Hager et al., 1996).

This chapter aims to create a clearer understanding of how variations in orientations affect the functioning of different kinds of social entrepreneurship organizations. Drawing from interviews with founders of two nascent organizations, some of the differences in intentions and operational processes are described. Each organization displayed innovative, proactive and risk-taking behaviours, and thus met the social entrepreneurship definition outlined by Weerawardena and Sullivan Mort (2006). Both were constrained by concurrent needs to optimize the social mission, become viable organizations and respond to the environment. The two organizations were selected as exemplary organizations that highlight the spectrum of social entrepreneurship orientations; one operated with an altruistic volunteer orientation, the other had a higher focus on commercial activities to achieve the desired social goal.

Divergent types of social entrepreneurship organizations

The two organizations had many features in common (Table 5.1). Each was based in the same Australian capital city and operated as an

Table 5.1 Summary of two social entrepreneurship organizations

| Organization | Started | Legal form | Founders | | | Staff employed | | In 2007 | |
			number	M:F	education			# staff	status
Banksia	August 2002	incorporated association	4	3:1	university degrees	during 1st year		0.5	vulnerable
Hakea	May 2004	company	3	1:2	university degrees	At start up		4	almost viable

independent entity without a sponsoring or parent organization. Each had a social goal to improve the situation for a client group. Each had a clear understanding of its mission and aimed to address social issues by providing capacity-building services. Each undertook some business activities to generate revenue to achieve its organizational goals. Each was established at approximately the same time, with a small number of male and female founders.

One organization aimed to achieve local social change; the other initially operated with a local focus, but later expanded to a state service. Substantial financial and resource issues had occurred in both organizations, but the approach to overcoming the difficulties was very different. Although established about the same time, the two organizations differed significantly in their life stage, development history, decision-making patterns, management systems, staffing, volunteer and financial arrangements, strategic orientation, commercialization trajectory, and relationships with clients, members, donors and external advisors.

Organizational history

Banksia's target group was young people in part of a large Australian city where there were few facilities or services for young people other than schools, shops and churches. Banksia aimed to improve local youth facilities in the area and assist young people to organize functions and events. The events offered a means of connecting to young people, listening to their issues, and then responding either by advocating appropriate facilities or new service initiatives. Banksia's founders, three men and one woman, were aged 21 and 23 when the organization started. They had just completed university degrees in business management, in political science, urban planning and social work. The four founders all worked full time in professional jobs in business, government or non-profit organizations. Two of the founders had worked previously in their family's small businesses. The organization was immediately registered as an incorporated association on start-up. For the first year Banksia operated without a home base. Then the local government provided free office space, photocopying, telephone, Internet access and access to a meeting room. Banksia also aimed to build skills within the local population of young people and assist them to engage in change activities. This is a capacity-building approach which involves engaging with the targeted disadvantaged group, identifying volunteers who are interested, and then deliberately and systematically building up their knowledge and skills. The volunteers then have the capacity to engage in the change activities without the assistance of the facilitator. In Banksia's case, the volunteers, as their skills grew, started to organize appropriate activities to improve the local area. The Banksia activities included an interactive website, concerts three times a year with local rock bands, events for young people to discuss issues with local politicians and a small youth advocacy group based at a high school aiming to improve local recreation facilities and mental health services. Other activities had also been successful such as organized bike rides, a magazine and an attempt to form a representative youth council. All founders thought Banksia provided valuable services for local young people and expressed a sense of pride and achievement. Banksia 1 (B1) (formerly from Africa) said:

> We've really achieved a lot in three years. We started from nothing, and look what we've been able to do. The things we've done are really valuable for young people in this area. There's zilch out here...nothing would have changed, but we did it! And not only that, the things we do at Banksia is really good. [Volunteer experience] really helps them get jobs. B1.

Although the founders explicitly identified their mission and values, they did not prepare a business plan or conduct strategic planning until the third year. Since volunteers were core to the organization's goals and activities, locating and training committed volunteers was a high priority. Most volunteers were younger than the founders. At the end of the third year, all founders were bothered by what they considered still needed to be done to achieve Banksia's mission. They would have preferred the organization to be more productive. They all expressed personal difficulties managing the need to attend to their Banksia responsibilities while concurrently working full time in paid employment. Each of the four had considered leaving the organization at some time. As at 2007, none of the founders considered Banksia was fully viable.

> We're still a bit shaky...we're all really committed – but we're so busy with work and stuff. It's hard to keep going sometimes. It would be easy to give up. But I know what we're doing really helps young people. We've done some really good things that've helped – like our [music] days are really good and the kids out here really like it, they've been pretty well attended...but sometimes it's all so hard. I wonder

if I shouldn't just give up. We could just meet and be friends, not do all this stuff. It would be so much easier... B1.

Hakea had a single specific mission: to provide at-home reading support and coaching for a particular group of disadvantaged children to improve their life opportunities. The founders, one man and two women, had university degrees and had worked for some years. Before starting, the founders sought legal and financial advice. They registered the organization as a company with the three founders as Directors. Hakea invited a group of influential people to join an advisory group to offer important skills identified as lacking among the founders, for instance, law, accountancy, strategic planning, media relations and marketing. Volunteers delivered the programme and assisted in organizational management tasks. This period was difficult financially. Over several months the programme profile grew. The number of volunteers to provide the services grew slowly. Then Hakea received a small government grant. Hakea Founder1 (H1) took a calculated risk and moved the organization to commercial premises. This was intended to improve visibility and increase legitimacy for potential sponsors. In the second year a AUD 50,000 government grant enabled the organization to become better established financially. A full-time CEO was employed along with two part-time staff. The next year a major corporation selected Hakea as their Charity of Choice and donated AUD 100,000. The award was presented at a large social event, which generated considerable media coverage and improved Hakea's profile. The following year Hakea was awarded a government grant of AUD 100,000 per annum for three years. At the end of three years, both the CEO and H11 considered Hakea was almost viable:

> it does give us at least a three-year term, I guess, with a part-time Director and two part time staff, and our rent paid for. So we can at least continue to do what we're doing for three years, during which time hopefully we would generate more long term self sustainable revenue strategies... that will keep our organization alive for the next three years. H1

Relationships

Banksia founders met at least weekly for around two hours to make decisions and organize activities to achieve the organizational mission. Although not known to each other before becoming involved, the four Banksia founders became close friends who got together as much to enjoy each other's company as to do Banksia work. B4 said: 'We have fun...we don't want to have boring meetings'. Within the group, harmonious social interactions were valued and respectful interactions were agreed as a practice. Decisions were made by consensus within the group, although the four founders took more responsibility for strategic decisions. After five years, an internal review concluded that fully incorporating volunteers into the decision-making process had created difficulties for the organization's operations. In particular, it had been difficult to maintain focus on core decisions and activities rather than engaging in discussion on more peripheral issues. Subsequently, control and decision-making was centralized to the four founders in consultation with the other volunteers. Leadership was shared among the four founders. All contributed to the organization and its activities through their roles as President, Secretary and Treasurer. The fourth founder was responsible for developmental activities with the volunteers aimed to achieve the desired social change. Banksia identified its clients and primary stakeholders as young people aged 15–23 living in the area. Other stakeholders were parents, and local and state governments, but no attempt was made to include parents in activities or advisory groups. It was difficult for Banksia founders to engage extensively in networking activities because of their work commitments, so they requested employed staff to liaise with relevant youth organizations. The founders accepted advice from interested people they encountered in their external dealings, negotiations and meetings. At least once a year Banksia met local and state government politicians to keep them informed of the organization's goals and activities. Politicians were sometimes invited to events. Banksia founders built strong relationships with state and local government resource officers. In particular, two government officials offered extensive guidance to the founders over three years. Banksia valued these connections.

> At first we relied on [Resource Officer]. But [Banksia] was always ours. We could do whatever we wanted. [Resource Officer] would help...I think it was extremely important that [Resource Officer] was involved.... We've had no experience or learning on organizational management or organising events. So it really was a stab in the dark of what to do. We had the energy and motivation to do Banksia but needed specific steering and guidance in what to do. And what to do next.... I don't think any of us would've had the initiative or known to do it if it wasn't suggested to us. But I think the key thought is we knew what we wanted we had the energy to get there but needed

guidance to the steps to take to get there... we give him a really good understanding of the issues for young people. He uses our events to listen to them and find out about things... we've given lots of suggestions about [youth] concerns [in the area]... yep, we've influenced lots of things that wouldn't have happened otherwise. Like they did the consultation about the [a new] library and specifically did one for young people. B1.

Relationships among the three Hakea founders were cordial. The informal founders' meetings initially focused on both strategic and operational matters, but by year 3 there was more emphasis on discussing strategic issues. The three Directors maintained overall control of strategic decisions, with a clear division of roles. Hakea Founder2 took responsibility for the financial arrangements, while Founder3 was responsible for fundraising matters. The advisory group offered suggestions, but could not make or veto decisions. Operational responsibilities were divided between H1 and the CEO (H2). The CEO took responsibility for operational matters and outcomes including managing the business end of the organization. H1's prime responsibility was to manage relationships with stakeholders. From the beginning Hakea operated with the premise that stakeholder relationships were core to their success, so building networks of influence was a high priority. H1 identified her 'skill probably, is to draw a group together... [and] to identify the right people that have those [required] skills'. She took responsibility for creating good relationships with internal stakeholders, especially the volunteers who were vital as the workforce delivering the service. For future strategic use, H1 maintained a register of each volunteer's interests, skills and connections. She documented the needs of the client group and profiled these to build credibility and reputation. The organization's aims and achievements were shared via the website and regular promotional newsletters. H1 also took responsibility for establishing relationships with key individuals external to the organization, politicians, senior government officials, and major corporations identified as offering strategic advantage. The eventual aim was to establish strategic partnerships and corporate sponsorships and donations. Building strong institutional relationships became a priority:

I would say, with the exception of some of the key corporates, which we targeted as potential major um, corporate sponsors, we don't have trouble getting in the door with people. And you, you know, I think... that's a range of things, I think it's partly, as I said earlier, the simplicity of the programme makes it easy for people to understand what the program is. What the conversation would be about. Well, I think we certainly have the relationship development skills to open doors. Um, I think we have enough of a media profile for people to be wanting to talk to us and see the potential for them as an organization. So I'd say that they're only a couple of cases where that hasn't worked and who knows what reasons they are... We do very well in terms of relationship development. So we certainly have aligned ourselves with the [Children's] Minister and the Department of [Children], and they... are very helpful in terms of assisting us to do other things, like, put together our strategic framework in a way that's, you know, functional as well as works on paper. So they've been very helpful... helping us get our risk management strategy and our exit strategy together, that sort of thing. When we decided we wanted to look at expanding, the Minister provided us with the top 20 businesses [in her electorate]... she was very keen to have us up there. And has been really proactive about talking to people in industry about us. H2.

Business functioning

Banksia started with a clear idea of its mission, but with no assets, income, home base or staff. Within three months of starting, the founders identified three business projects to generate income for the new organization: a website with advertising and sponsorship, a youth magazine with advertising, and youth music events featuring local rock bands. The concerts also would assist the organization to establish connections and gain profile among local young people. These three business projects aligned well with the organization's mission and were achievable with the skills available in the founding group, but no systematic business planning occurred. Three months after starting, Banksia was awarded $1000 government grant and organized the first local youth activity. A further grant of $16,000 enabled a part-time project officer to be employed for six months to develop a youth council. The project officer set up preliminary organizational procedures and systems, wrote more grant applications, then left when the grant ran out. The founders continued capacity-building activities and recruited ten young volunteers. Two more small grants the following year were used to buy organizational and personal development training for the founders and volunteers. Another part-time project officer was employed to organize projects, recruit and train more volunteers. The new volunteers created four local programmes with assistance and guidance from the founders. The programmes were well attended, thus enhancing Banksia's profile and reputation, but they did not generate substantial income, or many new members or volunteers. In the second year the organization remained fluid without set structures and systems, even after a professional facilitator had conducted two strategic planning sessions. The website was launched three years after Banksia started; the magazine was started the following year. Even though both were launched without detailed business planning, market or competitor analysis, the activities succeeded in attracting a growing involvement by local young people in concerts, interactive discussions with local politicians and other events. Banksia achieved a profile among young people in the area, and recognition among government youth policy officers. Nearly five years after starting, Banksia had total assets of $14,000. No long-term sponsor had been identified. No financially viable business had been established. The website generated some income, but the magazine was not functioning well and had attracted limited advertising. Despite good patronage from local youth, the rock concerts did not produce much income. Banksia founders had not sought to build strong contacts with a business to establish business mentors, but they had identified a need for business training to improve the financial operations of the organization. There was insufficient revenue for Banksia to employ any ongoing staff. Despite the obvious financial limitations, B1 identified insufficient human resources as the main limiting factor to the future development of the organization rather than inadequate operational income:

> Our assets? Young people [the volunteers]. They're our achievement... we've four projects going now, and they run them all. With our help. We've a lot more we can do [to benefit the local area].... Our highest priority is for more people to organize projects. We need that more than anything. B1.

Two of Hakea's founders had extensive experience in business. Originally Founder1 (H1) had been a nurse, then for five years she had been the CEO of a successful small business. Founder2 ran his own construction business. Founder3 was an experienced fundraiser for non-profit organizations. Hakea founders all were members of service organizations such as Rotary; they used these contacts to forge productive links to influential people. Initially Hakea operated from H1's house with the organization funded from her personal savings. From the beginning, H1 worked in the organization full time: 'essentially...I volunteered to the organization I suppose for the first two years, 18 months'. Part time staff were added as funds became available. The government grant in the second year allowed a full-time CEO (H2) to be employed. Her background was in marketing and management as a senior strategist in government, but she found working in a small non-profit agency was different. Hakea identified clear and specific objectives at start-up. A business plan was developed and monitored closely. Overheads, costs, profit, opportunities and threats were monitored closely. Hakea designed a business strategy but maintained some flexibility: 'we certainly act first and then develop strategy after' (H2). A systematic approach to generate income through social functions was implemented. Corporate sponsorship was a key platform of the financial strategy, but not everything went according to plan. The CEO said: 'we've had less positive response to our sponsorship model that we would have expected'. Despite this, by 2007 the organization was almost viable. Not only had they achieved significant funding from the charity and a series of government grants, the enterprising business strategy had generated significant income. The additional income allowed Hakea to extend the service around the state. H1 was satisfied the organization was achieving its objectives, and confident it would continue to grow. H1 and the CEO considered they knew what it took to manage a successful social enterprise:

> any business rule is that you need...at least three different streams of income. You don't want your income coming solely from one customer. So we're looking at government, corporate and individual sponsorship...[then the organization needs] a group of people together who have the same vision and who can contribute to the four key areas of running a business...planning, financial, and a high profile media person who has um, a good network...I s'pose we have always started with the vision, you know, of something really quite large....I just know what it takes....I would suggest it is just would be best practice to have those sorts of people [accountants and lawyers] working for you from the beginning....I think, the key element is all, in a not-for-profit is always funding...that's just something that you just work towards. H1...and I think you also need something in the world of follow up. Because generally those kinds of skills are very high level and you know, much about, you know, identifying opportunities, but I think you do need to have a group of people or a person that can action the small parts of that. (H2)

Discussion

Banksia and Hakea had many features in common. The organizations were established around the same time, and both exhibited social entrepreneurial characteristics. The organizations were comparable in the number and educational backgrounds of the founders. The founders of each organization were proactive, innovative and committed to achieving the intended mission. Each organization had built strong internal and external relationships based on trust, cooperation and mutual benefit. Decision-making and organizational leadership was effective, and although the style of management varied, each was appropriate for the client group. Each organization considered it had been successful in achieving some of the intended goals. Banksia aimed to improve the life of young people in the local area, not simply to provide services for them. It wished to develop the skills and capabilities of young volunteers who wished to contribute to the organization and its change mission. Banksia valued harmony, inclusion, friendships and participatory decision-making. It achieved steady progression towards its objectives, became well known in government and influenced local youth policy to some extent. Hakea aimed to achieve financial stability as quickly as possible to allow further expansion of the service. It valued rapid entrepreneurial achievement based on competition, business monitoring and establishing a high public profile. Undoubtedly it was very successful in achieving its financial goals. It swiftly recruited many volunteers and quickly established its service profile. It rapidly became well established and visible in the service community, and was well on the way to becoming a significant organization in the state. So both organizations were successful in realizing their desired goals.

Clearly, these two organizations are not the same. They differed in the legal form (company or association), and commitment to generating income. They varied in the design of internal business management systems, the focus on financial arrangements, and the level of staffing after the first year. In essence, the two organizations had different orientations. Banksia displayed a volunteering service orientation, while Hakea displayed strongly entrepreneurial characteristics. This fundamental difference in orientation influenced the establishment process and how the organization went about its business. It affected the organizational form, prioritizing of activities, and functional procedures implemented to achieve the desired social goals. Orientation influenced how each organization positioned itself within the environment. It influenced what kinds of openings were sought, and how quickly arrangements were implemented to capitalize on opportunities. The organizations were managed with different arrangements for internal decision-making and monitoring systems, and the level of risk-taking. The organizational orientation affected the priority given to methodically implementing management systems and to attracting financial and human resources to achieve the desired mission. It affected the logic behind generating income and networking. It influenced how and with whom relationships with the external environment were developed. The variation in orientation resulted in the founders prioritizing different stakeholders, and affected the arrangements for engaging with stakeholders. Ultimately, the organizations had different outcomes: one rapidly became visible and financially viable, while the other was vulnerable after a longer period of development, and was still operating as a small, local organization. Hence, the divergence in orientation resulted in different kinds of social entrepreneurship organizations. Banksia had a stronger focus on achieving the social mission than on its business operation; Hakea had more focus on its business operation in order to achieve the desired social objective.

These two cases illustrate organizations with different orientations within the social entrepreneurship spectrum. Some set about achieving their social goal in a rational, businesslike and entrepreneurial way. They operate very much as a business to achieve the social goal. Other social entrepreneurship organizations utilize some business strategies, but overall have a stronger focus on achieving the intended social goal than on becoming a profitable enterprise. Both types of organizations have social goals; both engage in business activities, hence both are social entrepreneurship. However, social entrepreneurship organizations differ in the extent and commitment to achieving social goals compared with the commitment to achieving financially objectives. An entrepreneurial organization prioritizes acquiring strategic human and financial resources in order to achieve its objectives as quickly as possible. On the other hand, a more altruistic volunteer service organization operates from a self-sufficiency model to gain necessary knowledge, develop its capabilities and achieve its goals, but it has less commitment to business objectives. Gaining resources is a lower priority for the volunteer service organization than being self-determining, autonomous and independent. Volunteer service organizations have a non-profit social orientation. They prioritize engaging with their members and encouraging clients to participate in the organization. Non-profit social organizations may not attract as much attention as others that rapidly gain visibility, reputation and influence, but the volunteer service principles are as worthy and can also be successful in achieving the desired social goals. While orientation has consequences for how organizations develop and what actions are prioritized, it does not necessarily affect the success of the establishment process. Organizations operating from non-profit social orientations are tortoises compared with entrepreneurial hares that achieve rapid commercial success. Both types can be successful, but the orientation influences what founders perceived as a successful and worthwhile outcome, and what processes they implement to achieve their goals.

The orientation clearly affected the development trajectory of these two organizations, but other elements also may have been significant. Gender is an important element in many contexts, including entrepreneurship (Carter et al., 2003), social entrepreneurship (Dorado, 2006), and voluntary service organizations (Meinhard and Foster, 2003). However, as males and females were involved in both organizations the orientation does not appear to be related to a gender difference. Hakea founders had more experience in business that Banksia founders. This is likely to have affected the operation in the start-up of a social entrepreneurship organization (Thomas, 2004). The age, backgrounds and personal resources of the founders differed. Hakea's founders were older and had previous small business experience. These aspects of founder background are known to affect the outcome of commercial firms (Westhead et al., 2001). Previous successful experience is known to improve the survival of new businesses (Schindehutte and Morris, 2001) by influencing the founders to be more entrepreneurial (Begley, 1995). This is likely to apply also in social entrepreneurship. With business knowledge and capability, founders have a good understanding of start-up processes and can transfer these skills to social entrepreneurship start-ups (Sharir and Lerner, 2006).

The contexts in which these organizations operated may account for some differences. Each organization aimed to develop capacity with the non-profit sector, but while Banksia had a local focus, Hakea operated as a state-wide organization. A local venture may require fewer resources, whereas an organization with a larger purpose may need more capital. This may be a possible explanation for the orientations since size, scale, and access to start-up capital are considered to influence the survival and success of new non-profit (Twombly, 2003) and social entrepreneurship organizations (Sharir and Lerner, 2006). The choice of organizational form is likely to have been influenced by the institutional environment in which the organizations operated. In uncertain or ambiguous institutional environments, social entrepreneurship organizations vary in their choice of organizational forms (Townsend and Hart, 2008). Since both organizations operated in the same locality, however, the environmental context is unlikely to be sufficient to explain the obvious differences between these two organizations.

Each of these organizations could have developed successfully with the alternative orientation. Hakea could have engaged progressively with the social sector, grown the service base as resources became available, and slowly developed its profile and impact. In Australia this is a common approach to developing new service organizations, and it can be very successful. Banksia could have borrowed money and immediately commended the three business projects, used the profit to organize capacity-building projects, and quickly grown its influence and reputation. Banksia's founders had opportunities to engage with business, for instance their families managed small businesses, and there were ample opportunities to establish strategic alliances with local businesses. Additionally, Banksia could have sought business mentoring, joined local business networks or leveraged their workplaces to develop business partnerships. Many similar organizations develop strong associations with the corporate sector through collaborative ventures, cause-related marketing, social alliances or similar practices. Banksia did not engage in any of these possibilities, but decided to develop as an independent, participatory, volunteer oriented service organization. It chose to initiate a proactive social change process with a self-reliant approach, rather than to operate from a strongly entrepreneurial framework. Similarly, Hakea made a rational choice to develop the organization via a rapid and dynamic pathway despite the high risks associated with this strategy. These founders decided on logical and specific, detailed and closely monitored business planning. There was clearly a good fit between the founders' values and actions and the goals in each of these organizations. The organizational orientation emerged from internalized presumptions of the founders that then influenced the organizational culture and its operation. The orientation was a fundamental set of unspoken principles which influenced future goals as well as development actions.

Organizational orientation, therefore, is chosen by the founders. It emerges from their values, principles and ideals as much as from wisdom gained through social networks and previous business experience. Values are internal and invisible, but are embedded in organizational practices and affect all decisions. Orientation is agreed among the group of key individuals who create the organization. It does not reside in a single individual social entrepreneur even if leadership appears to be strongly centralized. Once chosen, the orientation has a significant influence on the future direction of the organization and the strategies it employs. Orientation influences how much and quickly organizational growth is desired, which activities are thought appropriate to engage in, who to build alliances with and what resources are considered to be necessary. Values, integrity and reputation are central to all organizations with social or non-profit goals, hence social entrepreneurship organizations develop according to the founders' ideals (Hemingway, 2005; Voss et al., 2006). Since social entrepreneurship commits to achieving a public good, the organization's values are important for all involved: staff, volunteers, board members, clients and partner organizations. Hence it is helpful for the founders of social entrepreneurship organizations to identify and articulate their values to ensure those associated with the organization appreciate the intended approach.

Different kinds of social entrepreneurship

Social entrepreneurship is a way of creating social change through a set of processes initiated by committed activists. It involves some degree of organizational self-reliance and business activity. Both the goal for public change and self-sufficiency are important. Social entrepreneurship has two core principles: recognition of a need to initiate social change to benefit a target area or group, and the application of business like approaches; but it is operationalized as a continuum. Some organizations are more oriented towards the social end of the spectrum while others are positioned closer to the entrepreneurship endpoint. Outcomes vary (Haugh, 2006). The extent of strategic orientation varies: organizations may be more or less enterprising, deliberately planned, and rationally structured (Douglas et al., 2007; Hockerts, 2006). Social entrepreneurship is not one single form, but rather multiple variations in the application of core principles of achieving social change. The wide variation in orientation explains the variations in social entrepreneurship definitions evident in the literature. Present definitions of social entrepreneurship do not reflect the diversity of organizations. Since organizations undoubtedly differ markedly across the spectrum, a review of the definition of social entrepreneurship is warranted. The definition needs to indicate more precisely the variations in organizations.

A social entrepreneurship typology is proposed that accounts for differences in orientation. The typology has two elements: commitment to achieving social change and business orientation (Figure 5.2). These

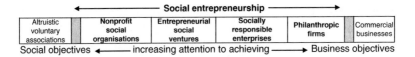

Figure 5.2 Spectrum of social entrepreneurship organizations

two elements result in different organizations with orientations, organizational forms and practices of social entrepreneurship. The proposed typology offers a systematic terminology for distinguishing among the different kinds of organizations. At either end of the spectrum are altruistic voluntary associations and commercial businesses. Neither of these are social entrepreneurship. Altruistic voluntary associations are concerned to provide services without an intention of generating income via business processes; commercial business firms are concerned with profit and have no commitment to achieving social change goals. Organizations identified as social entrepreneurship sit between these two extremes. There are four steps in this typology, according to the extent of business orientation and commitment to social change.

The legal form (organization, venture, enterprise or firm) indicates the extent of prioritizing of business activities over social goals. Organizations closest to altruistic voluntary associations are 'non-profit social organizations'. These operate in a manner similar to Banksia, with some intention to generate operating income, but a higher commitment to achieving the social goals. There is a close connection to the client group, and participatory processes are valued and promoted. Next are 'entrepreneurial social ventures'. These have been described by Dorodo (2006) and termed 'community enterprises' by Haugh (2005) and others (e.g. Tracey et al., 2005). These ventures are hybrids. Some are registered as companies, others are non-profit organizations. Entrepreneurial social ventures bridge profit and service. They are dedicated to achieving a desired social change, but at the same time are committed to generate substantial income from business processes to keep the organization operational. Hence, entrepreneurial social ventures have a delicate balance between achieving the desired social goal and an imperative to maintain a sustainable venture. When difficult compromise decisions are made, the social goal is given a higher priority than achieving higher profits. The third step in social entrepreneurship is 'socially responsible enterprises'. These operate as a business enterprise. Profit is a priority, but at the same time, there is a firm commitment to address a social change agenda. Hence there is a constant juggle to achieve both profit and social goals. Socially responsible enterprises may sacrifice some profitability in order to achieve the desired social agenda, but being more business oriented than entrepreneurial social ventures, maintaining a reasonable profit is given a higher priority than the social goal if a compromise is required. Philanthropic firms sit at the fourth step in social entrepreneurship. These are businesses that make donations of money or goods to address an identified social disadvantaged group or place. The actions usually have public relations motives. While there is an intention to achieve some social good, the social agenda is only important to a philanthropic firm because ultimately it provides benefits for the firm. Hence the social agenda is evaluated as a cost or benefit for the firm. Philanthropic firms and their actions are well described in the corporate social responsibility literature (Garriga and Melé, 2004; Jamali and Keshishian, 2008).

Implications

This typology is important for setting the boundaries of social entrepreneurship. It will start the process of defining social entrepreneurship more clearly. It helps define variations among different kinds of social entrepreneurship organizations that are not yet acknowledged in research or practice. A less unambiguous concept of social entrepreneurship will enable practitioners and researchers to more clearly define the kind of organization they are attending to. This will assist to distinguish important elements in each of the four kinds of organizations in their social orientation and business practices. The typology will assist in understanding how and why some organizations prioritize business when others do not. It will help distinguish why some social entrepreneurship organizations engage in planning, and prioritize accessing human and financial resources, when others do not. It will help an appreciation of how and why different kinds of social entrepreneurship organizations relate to their environment in particular ways. It will assist practitioners in describing their organization in terms that are easily understood by researchers and policy-makers. Ultimately, these understandings may assist social entrepreneurship organizations to be more successful in achieving their goals.

There are both practice and theory implications of diversity in social entrepreneurship. For practice, an understanding of orientation may facilitate successful development of organizations across the social entrepreneurship spectrum. Social entrepreneurship organizations do not all seek the same things. Orientation has a significant influence on how founders recognize and exploit opportunities and what social entrepreneurship organizations strive to achieve. Not all aspire to be large and well recognized, or wish to expand and maximize potential resources in the environment. Orientation drives what they decide to do and how they organize to achieve their goals. It affects the strategies organizations use to attract human and financial resources, and whether the organization strives for rapid growth and achievements. Orientation influences how relationships are developed and with whom, whether recognition and networking are prized and prioritized. It affects whether clients or recipients of the service are perceived as integral to the organization or as customers in a market-like perspective. Orientation affects a social entrepreneurship organization's functioning, but not its capacity to deliver the social mission. All kinds of organizations can realize the desired social mission. While some organizations may be more strategic, others may still achieve their goals. Although a visible, energetic, high-profile and dynamic approach may be more spectacular, an incremental, participatory and collaborative orientation may achieve excellent long-term outcomes. One process may be faster and more impressive, but it is not the only way to achieve quality results. Indeed, since social entrepreneurship is a change process, then arguably skill transfer to the clients may be more likely to achieve sustainable, long-term change. Non-profit social organizations, entrepreneurial social ventures and highly entrepreneurial socially responsible enterprises can be equally successful in achieving a desired social change. When seeking to assist the development of new social entrepreneurship organizations we should not expect a single approach or process, but rather be mindful of possible different orientations and different kinds of organizations.

Conclusion

Successful social entrepreneurship organizations may be entrepreneurial, well organized and accountable, but not all have this competitive market driven posture, nor may this approach be necessary. Even though they operate less visibly and on a smaller scale, organizations with a non-profit social orientation may be as successful in achieving their objectives as those with a market-driven entrepreneurial framework. If the organization benefits from a dynamic and progressive outlook, then an entrepreneurial orientation is very appropriate. If, however, compassion and sensitivity are required, then a participatory, collaborative non-profit social approach may be more fitting. Social entrepreneurship founders and advisors may need to choose appropriate processes to match the organizational orientation, rather than follow a single model. Present definitions of social entrepreneurship do not distinguish clearly among organizations with different orientations. Reviewing the definition of social entrepreneurship may assist in the clarification of different types of organizations that operate with different kinds of orientations. This chapter has outlined distinct orientations in social entrepreneurship organizations. It proposes a typology to distinguish among four different kinds of social entrepreneurship. Different organizational forms can be distinguished along a spectrum of social entrepreneurship, and each type has distinct characteristics. Each type varies in orientation towards prioritizing social or business objectives. Some have a mutual, participatory volunteer service stance, while others use a more businesslike and entrepreneurial approach. Entrepreneurial organizations tend towards competitive, market-driven approaches, while non-profit social organizations are more oriented to traditional social collaboration frameworks. These different orientations are linked to the intent of the founders. They are demonstrated by variations in relationship-building, strategic intent to seek and capitalize opportunities to attract resources as well as the prioritizing of networking, positioning, reputation and status. Each of the four types of social entrepreneurship has its place. Each offers benefits to improve society. Being clearer in our understanding of the type of organization we are discussing will improve our understanding of social entrepreneurship.

References

Alter, K. 2007. Definitions of Social Enterprise. Retrieved 1 April, 2008, from http:// www. virtueventures. com/ setypology/ index. php?id= DEFINITION&lm=1.

Austin, J., Stevenson, H. and Wei-Skillern, J. 2006. Social and Commercial Entrepreneurship: Same, Different, or Both? *Entrepreneurship Theory and Practice*, 30(1): 1–22.

Barraket, J. (ed.) 2008. *Strategic Issues for the Not-For-Profit Sector*. Sydney: University of New South Wales Press.

Begley, T. M. 1995. Using Founder Status, Age of Firm, and Company Growth-Rate as the Basis for Distinguishing Entrepreneurs from Managers of Smaller Businesses. *Journal of Business Venturing*, 10(3): 249–63.

Carter, N. M., Gartner, W. B., Shaver, K. G. and Gatewood, E. J. 2003. The Career Reasons of Nascent Entrepreneurs. *Journal of Business Venturing*, 18(1): 13–39.

Chambre, S. M. and Fatt, N. 2002. Beyond the Liability of Newness: Nonprofit Organizations in an Emerging Policy Domain. *Nonprofit and Voluntary Sector Quarterly*, 31(4): 502–24.

Chell, E. 2007. Social Enterprise and Entrepreneurship: Towards a Convergent Theory of the Entrepreneurial Process. *International Small Business Journal*, **25**(1): 5–26.

Cho, A. H. 2006. Politics, Values and Social Entrepreneurship: A Critical Appraisal. In Mair, J., Robinson, J. and Hockerts, K. (eds), *Social Entrepreneurship*, 34–56. Basingstoke: Palgrave Macmillan.

Dart, R. 2004. The Legitimacy of Social Enterprise. *Nonprofit Management and Leadership*, **14**(4): 411–24.

Dees, J. G. 1998. Enterprising Nonprofits. *Harvard Business Review*, **76**(1): 54–67.

Dees, J. G. 2001. The Meaning of 'social entrepreneurship'. Fuqua School of Business, Duke University, Center for the Advancement of Social Entrepreneurship (CASE), Durham, NC.

Dorado, S. 2006. Social Entrepreneurial Ventures: Different Values, so Different Process of Creation, no? *Journal of Developmental Entrepreneurship*, **11**(4): 319–43.

Douglas, H. 2007, 18–19 June. *Comparing Orientations in Social Entrepreneurship Organizations*. Paper presented at the 3rd International Social Entrepreneurship Research Conference (ISERC), Copenhagen.

Douglas, H., Sullivan Mort, G. and Cuskelly, G. 2007, 6–9 February. *Analyzing Elements Affecting the Survival of New Nonprofit Organizations in the Context of Social Entrepreneurship Ventures*. Paper presented at the 4th International Entrepreneurship Research Exchange, Australian Graduate School of Entrepreneurship Brisbane.

Eikenberry, A. M. and Kluver, J. D. 2004. The Marketization of the Nonprofit Sector: Civil Society at Risk? *Public Administration Review*, **64**(2): 132–40.

Fowler, A. 2000. NGDOs as a Moment in History: Beyond Aid to Social Entrepreneurship or Civic Innovation? *Third World Quarterly*, **21**(4): 637–54.

Garriga, E. and Melé, D. 2004. Corporate Social Responsibility Theories: Mapping the Territory. *Journal of Business Ethics*, **53**(1/2): 51–71.

Hager, M., Galaskiewicz, J., Bielefeld, W. and Pins, J. 1996. Tales from the Grave: Organizations' Accounts of their Own Demise. *The American Behavioral Scientist*, **39**(8), 975–95.

Haugh, H. 2005. The Role of Social Enterprise in Regional Development. *International Journal of Entrepreneurship and Small Business*, **2**(4): 346–57.

Haugh, H. 2006. Social Enterprise: Beyond Economic Outcomes and Individual Returns. In Mair, J., Robinson, J. and Hockerts, K. (eds), *Social Entrepreneurship*, 180–206. Basingstoke: Palgrave Macmillan.

Haugh, H. 2007. Community-led Social Venture Creation. *Entrepreneurship Theory and Practice*, **31**(2): 161–82.

Haugh, H. and Rubery, E. 2005. Educating Managers to Lead Community Enterprises. *International Journal of Public Administration*, **28**(9/10): 887–902.

Hemingway, C. A. 2005. Personal Values as a Catalyst for Corporate Social Entrepreneurship. *Journal of Business Ethics*, **60**(3): 233–49.

Henton, D., Melville, J. and Walesh, K. 1997. The Age of the Civic Entrepreneur: Restoring Civil Society and Building Economic Community. *National Civic Review*, **86**(2): 149–56.

Hockerts, K. 2006. Entrepreneurial Opportunity in Social Purpose Business Ventures. In Mair, J., Robinson, J. and Hockerts, K. (eds), *Social Entrepreneurship*, 142–54. Basingstoke: Palgrave Macmillan.

Jamali, D. and Keshishian, T. 2009. Uneasy Alliances: Lessons Learned from Partnerships between Businesses and NGOs in the Context of CSR. *Journal of Business Ethics*, 84(2): 277–95.

Johnson, S. 2000. *Literature Review on Social Entrepreneurship*. Alberta, Canada: Canadian Centre for Social Entrepreneurship, University of Alberta.

Johnstone, H., and Lionais, D. 2004. Depleted Communities and Community Business Entrepreneurship: Revaluing Space through Place. *Entrepreneurship & Regional Development*, 16(3): 217–33.

Kerlin, J. A. 2006. Social Enterprise in the United States and Europe: Understanding and Learning from the Differences. *Voluntas*, 17(3): 247–63.

Light, P. C. 2005, 17–18 November. *Searching for Social Entrepreneurs: Who they Might be, Where they Might be Found, What they do*. Paper presented at the Association for Research on Nonprofit and Voluntary Associations.

Mair, J. and Martí, I. 2006. Social Entrepreneurship Research: A Source of Explanation, Prediction, and Delight. *Journal of World Business*, 41(1): 36–44.

Mair, J. and Noboa, E. Social Entrepreneurship: How Intentions to Create a Social Venture are Formed. In Mair, J., Robinson, J. and Hockerts, K. (eds), *Social Entrepreneurship*, 121–36. Basingstoke: Palgrave Macmillan.

Mair, J., Robinson, J., and Hockerts, K. 2006. *Social Entrepreneurship*. Basingstoke: Palgrave Macmillan.

Mair, J. and Schoen, O. 2007. Successful Social Entrepreneurial Business Models in the Context of Developing Economies. *International Journal of Emerging Markets*, 2(1): 54–68.

Meinhard, A. G. and Foster, M. K. 2003. Differences in the Response of Women's Voluntary Organizations to Shifts in Canadian Public Policy. *Nonprofit and Voluntary Sector Quarterly*, 32(3): 366–96.

Nicholls, A. 2006. Introduction. In A. Nicholls (ed.), *Social Entrepreneurship: New Models of Sustainable Social Change*, 1–35. Oxford: Oxford University Press.

Nyssens, M. (ed.) 2006. *Social Enterprise at the Crossroads of Market, Public Policies and Civil Society*. Abingdon, Oxon, UK: Routledge.

Parkinson, C. and Howorth, C. 2008. The Language of Social Entrepreneurs. *Entrepreneurship & Regional Development*, 20(3): 285–309.

Peredo, A. M. and McLean, M. 2006. Social Entrepreneurship: A Critical Review of the Concept. *Journal of World Business*, 41(1): 56–65.

Ridley-Duff, R. 2007. Communitarian Perspectives on Social Enterprise. *Corporate Governance-an International Review*, 15(2): 382–92.

Robinson, J. 2006. Navigating Social and Institutional Barriers to Markets: How Social Entrepreneurship Identify and Evaluate Opportunities. In Mair, J., Robinson, J. and Hockerts, K. (eds), *Social Entrepreneurship*. 95–120. Basingstoke: Palgrave Macmillan.

Schindehutte, M. and Morris, M. H. 2001. Understanding Strategic Adaptation in Small Firms. *International Journal of Entrepreneurial Behaviour & Research*, 7(3): 84–107.

Seelos, C. and Mair, J. 2005. Social Entrepreneurship: Creating New Business Models to Serve the Poor. *Business Horizons*, 48(3): 241–46.

Sharir, M. and Lerner, M. 2006. Gauging the Success of Social Ventures Initiated by Individual Social Entrepreneurs. *Journal of World Business*, 41(1): 1–15.

Shaw, E. and Carter, S. 2007. Social Entrepreneurship: Theoretical Antecedents and Empirical Analysis of Entrepreneurial Processes and Outcomes. *Journal of Small Business and Enterprise Development*, **14**(3): 418–34.

Spear, R. 2006. Social Entrepreneurship: A Different Model? *International Journal of Social Economics*, **33**(5/6): 399–410.

Sullivan Mort, G. and Weerawardena, J. 2007. Social Entrepreneurship: Advancing Research and Maintaining Relevance. In A. Sargeant, Wymer, W. Jr. (ed.), *A Companion of Nonprofit Marketing*, ch. 12: 209–24. London and New York: Routledge.

Thomas, C. 2004. *The Role of Social Entrepreneurship in Community Development*. Unpublished Master of Business Administration, University of Witwatersrand, Johannesburg.

Thompson, J. and Doherty, B. 2006. The Diverse World of Social Enterprise: A Collection of Social Enterprise Stories. *International Journal of Social Economics*, **33**(5/6): 361–75.

Thompson, J., Alvy, G. and Lees, A. 2000. Social Entrepreneurship – a New Look at the People and the Potential. *Management Decision*, **38**(5/6): 328–39.

Townsend, D. M. and Hart, T. A. 2008. Perceived Institutional Ambiguity and the Choice of Organizational form in Social Entrepreneurial Ventures. *Entrepreneurship Theory and Practice*, **32**(4): 685–700.

Tracey, P., Phillips, N. and Haugh, H. 2005. Beyond Philanthropy: Community Enterprise as a Basis for Corporate Citizenship. *Journal of Business Ethics*, **58**(4): 327–44.

Twombly, E. C. 2003. What Factors Affect the Entry and Exit of Nonprofit Human Service Organizations in Metropolitan Areas? *Nonprofit and Voluntary Sector Quarterly*, **32**(2): 211–35.

Voss, Z. G., Cable, D. M. and Voss, G. B. 2006. Organizational Identity and Firm Performance: What happens When Leaders Disagree About 'Who We Are?'. *Organization Science*, **17**(6): 741–55.

Waddock, S. A. and Post, J. E. 1991. Social Entrepreneurs and Catalytic Change. *Public Administration Review*, **51**(5): 393–401.

Weerawardena, J. and Sullivan Mort, G. 2006. Investigating Social Entrepreneurship: A Multidimensional Model. *Journal of World Business*, **41**(1): 21–35.

Westhead, P., Wright, M. and Ucbasaran, D. 2001. The Internationalization of New and Small Firms: A Resource-Based View. *Journal of Business Venturing*, **16**(4): 333–58.

Zietow, J. T. 2001. Social Entrepreneurship: Managerial, Finance and Marketing Aspects. *Journal of Nonprofit & Public Sector Marketing*, **9**(1/2): 19–43.

Part II

Discovery and Exploitation of Social Opportunities

6
Social Entrepreneurship: A Study on the Source and Discovery of Social Opportunities

Javier Monllor

Introduction

Social entrepreneurship practice has progressed immensely in the last 30 years. Close to 80 million adults (Drucker, 1989) work for nearly 2 million citizen sector organizations of which 70% were established in the last 30 years (Davis, 2002). There has been a 40% increase in their number in the last decade (Johnson, 2000), 5% more than new business formation (Austin et al., 2006). Sensing the need to educate this new wave of social entrepreneurs, programs catering to the education of social entrepreneurs have begun to emerge in major and elite universities such as Columbia, Harvard, Yale, Duke and others.

The growth and evolution of social entrepreneurship has created a new wave of hybrid organizations, termed social purpose business ventures (Hockerts, 2006), that combine aspects of both non-profit and for-profit ventures. These hybrid organizations have a mission to create both economic and social value and are therefore no longer at opposite ends of a continuum. This in turn has made it difficult for researchers to catalogue social entrepreneurship and to find the defining characteristics that differentiate it from business entrepreneurship. To try to differentiate the two, some researchers have singled out entrepreneurial motives while others use the priority that is given to the created value (social or economic).

Opportunity recognition is widely recognized as a central and defining aspect of entrepreneurship (Shane and Venkataraman, 2000; Zahra and Dess, 2001), and although it has also been acknowledged as an important part of the social entrepreneurship process (Dees et al., 2002; Seelos and Mair, 2005; Thompson, 2002; Thompson et al., 2000) researchers in this area have largely ignored the opportunity recognition process of social entrepreneurs.

Embracing opportunity recognition opens the door for cross-fertilization between social and business entrepreneurship and provides researchers with a discernible roadmap to follow. Some questions that researchers should be asking are: how are social opportunities created? How do social entrepreneurs recognize opportunities? Why do they recognize different opportunities from business entrepreneurs? How are these opportunities evaluated and exploited? And what type of value is created from different opportunities?

In the following sections, this chapter will analyze where social opportunities come from and how the concept and study of the discovery, evaluation and exploitation of social entrepreneurial opportunities can have a positive impact on the social entrepreneurship field. It is our hope that it will open the discussion of social opportunity recognition, initiate future research opportunities for the field and attempt to establish social opportunity recognition as a differentiating characteristic between the two types of entrepreneurship.

Literature review

Development of social entrepreneurship research

Social entrepreneurship is not a new phenomenon, and examples of early social entrepreneurship exist in the literature, including Florence Nightingale (pioneer of modern nursing), abolitionist William Lloyd Garrison (Drayton, 2002) and the creation of Victorian private hospitals (Thompson et al., 2000). Still, there is no denying that compared with business entrepreneurship, it is still in its infancy. However, compelling evidence points to the fact that this development gap that separates the two types of entrepreneurship is closing. Just as in business, the social arena is now headed by 'independent, competitive citizen created and citizen-run organizations' (Drayton, 2002).

Peter Drucker was one of the first to notice this transition from early bureaucratic and monopolistic to 'entrepreneurial, competitive and innovative social organizations' (Drayton, 2002). In an article published in the *California Management Review* Drucker (1989) states that the best management practices and most innovative methods are not coming out of Fortune 500 corporations, but from non-profit social organizations such as the Salvation Army and the Girl Scouts. Not only are social venture's management practices rivaling those of for-profits, their growth is also extraordinary.

Table 6.1 Sample of social entrepreneurship programs (Brock, 2006)

Institution	Program
Berea College	Entrepreneurship for the Public Good
Columbia University	Research Initiative on Social Entrepreneurship (RISE)
Duke University	Center for the Advancement of Social Entrepreneurship (CASE)
Harvard Business School	Initiative on Social Enterprise
University of Navarra	IESE Business School
New York University	Stewart Satter Program in Social Entrepreneurship
Oxford University	Skoll Centre for Social Entrepreneurship
Roberts Wesleyan College	Institute for Social Entrepreneurship
Seattle University	The Center for Non-profit and Social Enterprise Management
Stanford University	Center for Social Innovation
Sterling University	McVay Social Entrepreneurship Center
Yale School of Management-Goldman Sachs Foundation	Partnership for Non-profit Ventures

Academic institutions have also noticed the shift in the development of social entrepreneurship and the increasing interest by practitioners in social enterprises, and have started to establish programs and centers dedicated to catering to the needs of individuals and organizations interested in for-profit and non-profit social ventures (Table 6.1 provides a sample list of programs that exist in various academic institutions).

For all the growth in the social entrepreneurship sector and the creation of academic programs that cater to this new breed of entrepreneur, until recently, academic research has shown little interest (Prabhu, 1999) and lags behind that of business entrepreneurship (Johnson, 2000).

Opportunity recognition in social entrepreneurship research

Entrepreneurship has been defined as 'the process of first, discovering and second, acting on a disequilibrium *opportunity*' (Kaish and Gilad, 1991: 46) and as 'the attempt to create value through the *recognition of business opportunity...*' (Hulbert et al., 1997: 68). It is clear from these definitions that opportunity recognition is an integral part of the field of entrepreneurship and represents one of its most important early aspects (Hills et al., 1999). In fact, the most successful entrepreneurs are opportunity-focused (Craig and Lindsay, 2002) and most of them believe they have a special sensitivity or alertness towards opportunities (Craig and Lindsay, 2002).

Social entrepreneurship research has consistently acknowledged opportunity recognition as a vital feature of social entrepreneurs. Seelos and Mair (2005) state that social entrepreneurs recognize and act upon opportunities to improve systems, create solutions and invent new approaches (to social problems). Thompson et al. (2000: 328) defined social entrepreneurs as people who 'realize where there is an *opportunity* to satisfy some unmet need that the state welfare system will not or cannot meet...'. The author (Thompson, 2002: 416) later adapted Sykes's three-stage entrepreneurial process to develop a four-step process of social entrepreneurship composed of the following:

- envisioning – *perceiving an opportunity*;
- engaging – engaging the opportunity with a mind to do something about it;
- enabling – ensuring something happens by acquiring the necessary resources;
- enacting – championing and leading the project.

As can be seen from the process model, opportunity perception is the first step in the process. Thompson studied two cases, both examples of outstanding contributions from a database of 82 schemes, to illustrate these four key themes in his social entrepreneurship framework. In both cases, the author found that *opportunity* was at the heart of the ventures.

Dees (1998; Dees et al., 2002) defines social entrepreneurs by stating that they play the role of change by:

- adopting a mission to create and sustain social value;
- *recognizing and relentlessly pursuing new opportunities to serve that mission;*
- engaging in a process of continuous innovation, adaptation and learning;
- acting boldly without being limited by resources currently in hand;
- exhibiting heightened accountability to the constituents served and for the outcomes created.

He makes the case that social entrepreneurs *see opportunity* where others see problems. Following that same line of thought, Drayton (2002) affirms that both types of entrepreneurs (business and social) *recognize* when a part of society is stuck and provide new ways to get it unstuck.

Finally, Peredo and McLean (2006) conducted a critical review of the social entrepreneurship concept and concluded that social entrepreneurship is exercised in part when a person or group shows 'a capacity to *recognize* and take advantage of opportunities to create that value' (64).

Surprisingly, even though social entrepreneurship scholars acknowledge opportunity recognition as a central and important aspect in the process of social entrepreneurship, and it is considered a primary definition for business entrepreneurship, little, if any, effort has been made to understand it. In a comprehensive review of the social entrepreneurship literature, Johnson (2000) provides a list of gaps that are present in the social entrepreneurship literature, and while valuable, the lack of a mention of opportunity recognition as a research gap is unanticipated.

In their seminal piece, Shane and Venkataraman (2000: 218) define the scholarly domain of entrepreneurship as the

> examination of how, by whom, and with what effects opportunities to create future goods and services are discovered, evaluated, and exploited. Consequently, the field involves the study of sources of opportunities; the processes of discovery, evaluation, and exploitation of opportunities; and the set of individuals who discover, evaluate, and exploit them.

In subsequent writings, they also acknowledged that outcomes on the level of industry and society should be considered as well (Davidsson, 2005; Zahra and Dess, 2001). Notice how their delineation of the field does not limit entrepreneurship research to business entrepreneurship where economic value alone is created, since outcomes on the societal level should also be considered.

If we dissect the previously developed definition, we can discern four distinguishable parts (see Figure 6.1): first we have the source of opportunities, second we have the discovery of those opportunities, third we have the evaluation of such opportunities and, finally, we have the exploitation of opportunities through social entrepreneurship. In the following sections, I explain each of these steps in detail and identify variables that affect each of these steps with the idea of generating a research agenda that can guide future research on the topic of social entrepreneurship opportunity recognition.

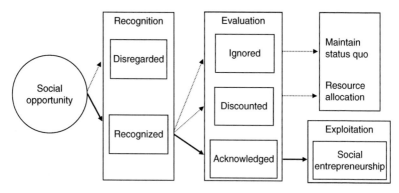

Figure 6.1 Social opportunity identification process (adapted from Gaglio (2004))

Sources of social opportunities

In one of the few studies to examine the source of opportunities for social purpose business ventures, Hockerts (2006) created a conceptual framework for social entrepreneurial opportunities and came up with three sources: activisms, self-help and philanthropy. The author defined social purpose business ventures as 'hybrid enterprises straddling the boundary between the for-profit business world and social mission-driven public and nonprofit organizations' (Hockerts, 2006: 145). This chapter wishes to expand Hockerts's conceptual framework and examine the source of opportunities for all social entrepreneurial ventures, including not for-profits and social purpose business ventures, and the process of recognizing them.

Shane and Venkataraman (2000) have posited that the study of sources of opportunities is one of the fundamental aspects of entrepreneurship research. In this section I build on the research by Dean and McMullen (2002, 2005) and Cohen and Winn (2005) on market failure and entrepreneurial opportunity and on the research on government failure to describe how social opportunities are created. But, before continuing, we must first define what is a social opportunity. Hockerts (2006) explains that in order to keep their balance, social purpose business venture (those that are on the boundary of for-profit and social mission-driven) need to discover opportunities to create both social and economic value. Weerawardena and Mort (2006) conclude that social entrepreneurs seek market opportunities that will enable them to create better social value. Given the scope of this study, social opportunities are defined as those that, when exploited, will allow the entrepreneurs to create enhanced social value. With this definition in hand, we can carry on with the study of sources of social opportunities.

Economists call an ideal state where no clear social welfare improvement is possible a Pareto optimal condition. When Pareto optimal conditions are achieved, the only way for one person to make himself better off is if he makes someone else worse off. To reach a Pareto optimal state, Pareto optimal improvements need to take place. Pareto optimal improvements are transactions where one individual is made better off by a given exchange while at the same time compensating the losers. For economists, a system that is not in a Pareto optimal condition is one where market inefficiencies and failures exists, but for entrepreneurship researchers it is the perfect system to find market opportunities. As Dean and McMullen (2002) explain, in a Pareto efficient economy, the system conditions are stable, there are no potential gains to trade and therefore no entrepreneurial opportunities. But, in a system that has yet to reach a Pareto optimal condition, entrepreneurs see opportunities everywhere to gain through trade. The conditions where markets fail to achieve the Pareto efficient ideal have often been categorized by the general term of market failure.

The five primary classes of market failure that are mentioned in the welfare economics literature are: *imperfect information, monopoly power, public goods, externalities and market pricing.* Below I delineate how each one of these types of market failures create social opportunities in specific ways and provide examples of current entrepreneurs who have perceived and acted upon these opportunities.

Imperfect information: Neoclassical economics suggests that everyone has perfect information. This implies that sellers and buyers have all possible information available (Cohen and Winn, 2005). However, in reality, knowledge is never perfect and this situation is one of the primary causes of market failure and, therefore, the creation of entrepreneurial opportunities. As Kirzner (1973) explains, entrepreneurs have an alertness towards opportunities, their possession of knowledge of time and place allows them to perceive and exploit opportunities that others do not recognize. Recognizing that consumers do not have all the information all the time, Kailash Satyarthi created Rugmark. This program labels rugs created in India by factories that agree to be regularly inspected as 'child-labor-free'. By labeling these products, Kailash is informing consumers in developed countries of how their expensive Indian rugs are made and of the existence of rugs that utilize child labor in their factories. With this new information, he dissuades consumers from purchasing rugs that are made in factories that use child labor and therefore is reducing this social problem.

Monopoly Power: The condition of monopoly is one in which there is only one seller (Dean and McMullen, 2005). In perfect competition models, the assumptions state that the sellers are numerous and therefore each seller's decision has no effect on market price. When a monopoly exists, the firm will aim for profit maximization through the under-provision and over-charging for goods, and it is for this reason that it is considered a market failure. As Dean and McMullen (2002) explain in their paper on market failure and entrepreneurial opportunities, to make use of these opportunities, entrepreneurs must discover 'production technologies that operate efficiently at a small scale'. Fabio Rosa, from Brazil, is a textbook example of a social entrepreneur who was able to perceive the opportunities that arose as a result of monopoly power. In the late 1990s Brazil's electric industry was privatized and the new owners, being a monopoly power, refused to provide service to the countryside, claiming that the profit margins were too low. Rosa then decided to use solar technology and established IDEAAS. The company now rents solar equipment to farmers, which provides them with electricity and a better life. By utilizing solar power technology, Rosa was able to operate at a small scale and in a way that is affordable for poor farmers.

Public Goods: The most important characteristic of public goods is that they are non-excludable. If one person is able to consume the public good, then others cannot be excluded from consuming it (Dean and McMullen, 2005). This characteristic has two important implications: it stimulates over-use when one person's use diminishes the amount or quality of the good available to others and it provides incentives for 'free riders' (Ackerman, 1996) since there is little economic motivation for entrepreneurial production because non-payers cannot be excluded from consumption. These situations are commonly referred to as the 'tragedy of the commons'. Rivers are a good example of a public good. No one is excluded from consuming the water or from using it for other purposes such as washing clothes, bathing, and so forth. As stated above, the use of the river diminishes the quality of the water available for others. As can be seen around the world, people who live downstream of rivers have to bathe in and drink water that has been utilized by people for the same purposes further upstream. This causes a large amount of people to become sick and die from drinking water that is infected with bacteria. LifeStraw is a small device created by Torben Vestergaard that allows people in these situations to filter their drinking water. The technology lasts for about a year and it costs close to US$2 only, allowing people in developing countries that are very poor to afford it, potentially saving thousands of lives. With this invention, the social entrepreneur attempts to solve a problem, in this case unsafe drinking water, which was created by a public good market failure.

Externalities: Another assumption of economics is that of exclusivity (Cohen and Winn, 2005). This assumption states that one firm's actions has no effect on the well-being of bystanders. Externalities are a deviation from this assumption and can be viewed as side effects of one individual's actions on the utility of another individual (Dean and McMullen, 2005). Externalities can be positive or negative: a positive externality is one that has a beneficial effect on another individual while a negative externality has damaging effects on other individuals. Externalities may be one of the largest and most pervasive deviations from classical economics. In response, an entire discipline has emerged, environmental economics, to study how and when firms do or do not bear their share of environmental costs in conjunction with the benefits of rents. Examples of negative environmental externalities are ground water pollution, textile runoffs, toxification of land from cotton farming, global warming, global dimming, ozone depletion, and such like. Dean and McMullen (2005) explain that to make use of opportunities that are created by externalities, entrepreneurs must find ways to reduce the transaction costs that are associated with them. In their paper, they make reference to entrepreneur Richard Sandor, creator of the Chicago Climate Exchange (CCX). The CCX serves as a marketplace where members can trade carbon emission allowances. Companies that produce small amounts of carbon emissions or that have implemented new technologies to reduce them can sell their credits to other firms. The systems has reduced transaction costs of carbon trading, reduced the aggregate emissions and therefore reduced environmental degradation.

Flawed pricing mechanisms: When markets are perfectly competitive, items are traded at market clearing or equilibrium price. To reach equilibrium price, the prices of all products must be determined by equating the demand for the product with the supply (Cohen and Winn, 2005). But, up to now, firms have largely ignored the demand for their products in developing countries. As firms seek to extract the highest possible profit from every item sold, they ignore the opportunities that are available from the demand from people who cannot pay those high prices. By meeting the demand for their products in developing countries, firms counter the decrease in profits from lower prices by increasing sales volume. Aravind Eye Hospital and Aurolab are examples of entrepreneurial ventures that have noticed the discrepancies between supply and demand for medical technology that result in exorbitant prices. Dr Govindappa Venkataswamy and David Green have created the company with the sole purpose of making medical technology and health care services accessible and affordable. By meeting the demand for medical products in the developing world, they have been able to reduce the price of, for example, replacement lenses from $150.00 a pair to just $10.00 a pair and improved the life of thousands by restoring their eyesight.

One accelerating factor to market failure is state or political failure. When the state fails in its goal as a service provider of law and order, stable property rights and/or welfare redistribution, it contributes to economic under-performance and poverty. State or government failure is analogous to market failure in the public sector. Government failure occurs when governments do not efficiently allocate goods and/or resources to government consumers. Just as in market failure, government failure is not failure to bring a particular solution into existence but rather a systemic problem that prevents efficient government solutions to a problem. Another similarity with market failure is that there are also many types of government failures, although, compared with market failures, they have only just begun to be studied and it has never even been looked at in the area of entrepreneurship. The government failures that will be addressed in this chapter are: *pursuit of self-interests, short-term solutions and imperfect information.*

- *Self-interests* – when politicians and civil servants are operating in pursuit of self-interests rather than operating on behalf of citizens, misallocation of resources occur.
- *Short-term solutions* – since many government leaders are only in office for a short term, there might be a tendency to fixate on short-term fixes and ignore large, complex problems. Myopic decision-making will only provide short-term relief to particular problems but does little to address structural problems.
- *Imperfect information* – similar to market failure gathering sufficient information in regulatory agencies is no easier for the regulatory agency than for individual actors. Because there are monetary and time costs associated with gathering information, and the benefits of doing so are limited, legislators frequently do not research the matters on which they vote.

All these forms of government failure are sources of opportunity for social entrepreneurs in themselves or through their correlation with market failure. When government failures occur, resources are not efficiently allocated and citizens, as consumers of the services that governments provide, end up suffering the consequences. By legislating for their self-interest, acting for the short term by using imperfect information, governments can inadvertently cause or increase market failures. As an example, a politician who passes legislation in benefit of a particular firm might cause other firms to disappear, resulting in a case of monopoly power. Through imperfect information, a politician might also regulate air pollution, unaware that this may increase water pollution, increasing the effects of externalities.

As mentioned in the literature, market failures are a source of entrepreneurial social opportunities. In a system that has yet to reach a Pareto optimal condition, where market failures are prevalent, entrepreneurs see opportunities everywhere to gain through trade (Dean and McMullen, 2002). I therefore propose that:

P1: Social opportunities are the result of market and government failure.

In the preceding paragraphs, it has been argued that social opportunities are the result of market and government failures. It is implicitly assumed in this argument that social opportunities are exogenous phenomena independent of the entrepreneur. It is up to social entrepreneurs to discover these opportunities and exploit them to create a desired social value. In the next section, I elucidate how these opportunities can be discovered.

The recognition of social opportunities

Once an opportunity is created by any of the types of failures explained above, an individual can disregard such opportunity or recognize it in order to evaluate and exploit it (depicted in Figure 6.1). Market and government failure create a need or set of needs for society that entrepreneurs have to address, but the existence of that need does not guarantee that an entrepreneur will exploit it. Shane (2000) posits that there are three major dimensions of prior knowledge that are important to the process of entrepreneurial discovery:

• prior knowledge of markets;
• prior knowledge of ways to serve markets;
• prior knowledge of customer problems.

As we can see from Shane's dimensions, not only is the knowledge that there exists a need necessary, but the means to satisfy that need have to exist and this is not always the case. For example, there are numerous diseases that affect people all over the world but a cure is not available to treat those diseases. Therefore, there is a social need to save the lives of people suffering from those diseases but since the means to satisfy that need is unavailable, it does not represent an opportunity for a social entrepreneur. While entrepreneurs might not possess the knowledge to cure that disease, this fact does not stop them from creating value in other ways. They might possess knowledge on how to increase the lifespan for those people through better care, so they might create an organization to do just that. They might also possess knowledge on how to gather funds, so they might create an organization to reach out and finance research scientists working to find a cure for the said disease. Possessing the knowledge of, not only the need, but of the means to satisfy that need are therefore necessary conditions for social opportunity recognition. Examples of the effects of knowledge can be seen in any available case of social entrepreneurship. Muhammad Yunus has a PhD in economics, which gave him the knowledge necessary to start Grameen Bank. Fabio Rosa was an electrical engineer, which, again, gave him the necessary training to create his innovative use of solar technology to bring electricity to the poor.

> P2: Social entrepreneurs' prior knowledge will influence their discovery of social opportunities.

It is important to mention in this section the concept of embeddedness put forth by Mair and Martí (2006) which argues that it is impossible for social entrepreneurs to be detached from the environment (community, society, etc.) in which they are operating. Weerawardena and Mort (2006) proposed that social entrepreneurs are not only responsive but also constrained by environmental dynamics. This implies that not only will social entrepreneurs recognize opportunities in environments in which they are immersed in but these environments will also limit the ideas they recognize to a particular environment. Shane (2000) posited that entrepreneurial action creates 'knowledge corridors' that open up new opportunities for the entrepreneur to discover in his field of action. Thompson's (2002) case study found that social entrepreneurs had trouble focusing because more and more *opportunities* became apparent during the development of the venture and none of them had originally envisioned what he had created. Therefore, individuals who are immersed in an environment have greater knowledge and are better prepared to perceive existing needs, but these perceptions will also be limited to those he can grasp from the environment he is embedded in.

While prior knowledge of needs and means to satisfy those needs are required, they are not sufficient for the recognition of social opportunities. Both have to be cognitively linked together for the opportunity to be realized (Shrader, 2006). Kirzner was the first to realize that entrepreneurs possess a distinct quality that allows them to see opportunities, which he called alertness. He defined it as an 'attitude to available (but hitherto overlooked) opportunities' (Kirzner, 1973). Alertness has been recently conceptualized as a chronic cognitive schema, and entrepreneurs who discover opportunities are able to break their existing means–ends framework and create alternative ones through counterfactual thinking and/or mental simulations (Gaglio, 2004).

Opportunity recognition, then, has a series of necessary requirements. The entrepreneur must first identify a need that was created through market or government failure. As explained previously, this condition is not enough since the entrepreneurs must also identify a means to satisfy that need, which creates social value. Finally, he must cognitively unite those two pieces of knowledge into one coherent object that can now be called a social opportunity. The earlier examples of Muhammad Yunus and Fabio Rosa again demonstrate that their knowledge was not a sufficient condition for them to discover their respective social opportunities. Both entrepreneurs had to tie in a particular social need (extreme poverty and lack of electricity) to their knowledge of a way to satisfy those needs (micro lending and solar technology).

P3: Social opportunities are recognized when the entrepreneur cognitively links his knowledge of a social need and a means to satisfy that need.

One final variable that can have a significant impact on the recognition of social opportunities are social networks. Past research on entrepreneurial opportunity recognition has looked at the effect and has found that other people in the entrepreneur's network, such as customers, employees, acquaintances and so forth, are important sources of opportunities (Shrader and Hills, 2003). Ardichvili et al. (2003) also propose that alertness is heightened by social networks. Entrepreneurs might not be able to recognize a social opportunity, but these opportunities might 'fall in their lap' through people in their networks. In social entrepreneurship research, various authors have emphasized the importance of social networks since they not only serve as a source of social opportunities but also provide access to information, resources and support (Mair and Martí, 2006).

> P4: Social networks will greatly increase social entrepreneurs' alertness to social opportunities.

Once an opportunity has been recognized, entrepreneurs must evaluate it in order to decide if they should exploit it. In the case of social entrepreneurs, the ability to extract social value out of the opportunity is of the highest priority. Therefore, as will be argued in the next section, social value will have an important position in the evaluation of social opportunities that have been discovered.

The evaluation of social opportunities

The preceding section explained that social entrepreneurs recognized opportunities when they cognitively linked existing social needs with the means to satisfy those needs. There are three possibilities that arise once a social opportunity is recognized. Of these, only one leads to the exploitation of the opportunity and the development of a social entrepreneurial enterprise. This outcome is achieved when an individual perceives the opportunity and acknowledges it. The entrepreneur now evaluates the opportunity and decides that exploiting it can create the necessary social values to diminish or possibly eradicate that social need. The question that remains now is what factors do social entrepreneurs use to evaluate that opportunity and decide that it is a meaningful one, well worth their investment.

The literature on social entrepreneurship has made clear that social entrepreneurs' main concern is the creation of social value. For social entrepreneurs, their social mission is explicit and central, and this affects how they perceive and assess opportunities (Dees, 1998). The literature emphasizes social entrepreneurs' motivation to 'make a difference', their need to be committed to 'helping others' (Thompson et al., 2000) and their concern with caring and helping rather than making a profit (Thompson, 2002). For some researchers, social entrepreneurship promises an altruistic form of capitalism, is aimed at benefiting society rather than maximizing individual profits, and develops a continuum of social entrepreneurs dependent on their degrees of altruism (Tan et al., 2005), while others hint that altruism is a possible motivation for social entrepreneurs (Prabhu, 1999). Prabhu (1999) asserts that the need to be *true to one's values and beliefs*, the need to *match with one's self concept* and be socially responsible are further motivations of social entrepreneurs. Social entrepreneurs will seek opportunities to create enhanced social value to both existing and potential clients (Weerawardena and Mort, 2006).

P5: Social entrepreneurs will evaluate social opportunities based on the social value that can be created through the exploitation of that opportunity.

The resources that are available to entrepreneurs at the moment of opportunity evaluation will also play an important role in their decision to exploit the opportunity. Entrepreneurs must have the resources necessary (Shane, 2003; Shrader, 2006), such as financial capital or access to government funding, in order to be able to get their social enterprise on its feet. If the entrepreneur does not have the resources necessary, then the possibility of acquiring those resources through personal networks is of especial importance.

P6: Social entrepreneurs will evaluate social opportunities based on their access to resources that will allow them to exploit said social opportunity.

If the social value that can be created is not considered productive or if the resources available to the entrepreneur are not deemed sufficient, the entrepreneur might then follow any of the other two steps possible during opportunity evaluation (see Figure 6.1). The first option is to ignore the opportunity. The individual recognizes the opportunity but decides that the state of affairs is inevitable. This perpetuates the situation and does not provoke any change at all. The second possibility is that the individual discounts the situation. In this case, the individual understands that the situation should and needs to change, but decides that exploiting the opportunity through the creation of a social enterprise is not a worthwhile endeavor. This type of evaluation may lead to other types of actions to try to satisfy the existing need. For example, the individual may decide to donate funds to a philanthropic organization or volunteer his or her time to a worthy goal. While commendable, these actions do not represent social entrepreneurship. Individuals might also talk about their ideas to others, who might take on the idea and develop it, just as I have discussed previously.

The evaluation of the opportunity is an essential step in the process. Once social entrepreneurs deem an opportunity to be worthy of exploitation, they proceed to act upon it and create social value. Without exploitation, social entrepreneurship would not exist. In the following section, I discuss the process of social opportunity exploitation and propose which variables are essential during this step.

The exploitation of social opportunities

As explained in the sections above, how a social opportunity is exploited depends on how the individual evaluates the social opportunity. Evaluation leads to three possible effects, one of which will lead to the actual exploitation of the opportunity and eventual social value creation. In the case that the individual ignores the opportunity, no action is taken and the status quo remains. If, on the other hand, the individual discounts the opportunity, exploitation does not take place, but the individual might still act through other methods to attempt to diminish the social need. Some of the actions that the individual might take are philanthropy, volunteering, donations, activism, and so forth. The final possibility is that the individual decides that the opportunity is one worthy of exploitation and pursues it through the creation of a social entrepreneurial venture. During exploitation, social entrepreneurs enact the different strategies that will make their social enterprises successful. There are various strategies available to social entrepreneurs that they can rely on to exploit social opportunities. Which strategies will be utilized depends on the various factors I examine below.

Access to resources not only affects the evaluation of the social opportunity but will also facilitate or constrain the implementation of specific strategies (Shrader, 2006). Dees (1998, 2002) defined social entrepreneurs by stating that they play the role of change by 'Acting boldly without being limited by resources currently in hand'. As an example, Mair and Martí (2009) have explored the concept of bricolage as a process of exploiting opportunities that originate from institutional voids. In their paper, the define bricolage as 'to make do with "whatever is at hand"'. This strategy is especially salient in developing countries, which possess environments characterized by scarcity of resources and institutions. This strategy has also been explored in the entrepreneurship literature under the name effectuation (Sarasvathy, 2001). Effectuation entails looking at the available set of means and selecting between the many possible effects that can be created with that set of means. There is no predetermined path, not one single strategy to follow. Effectuation leads to a process of experimentation and iteration to discover new effects with the available set of means. Both bricolage and effectuation entail for the entrepreneur to act, utilizing the means he has available at his disposal.

P7: The availability of resources to the social entrepreneur will have a significant effect on the strategy that will be implemented during the exploitation phase.

In the evaluation stage, the value that can be created through exploitation is one of the main aspects used to decide whether to pursue a social opportunity. A social opportunity can not only create social value but, depending on the strategy utilized, can also create economic value through the creation of a social purpose business venture. As explained by Hockerts (2006), these ventures are hybrids that walk the line between for-profit and non-profit ventures. If, during the evaluation stage, an individual perceives that the social opportunity can only create social value, he will then have no option but to create a non-profit organization. If, on the other hand ,during evaluation the individual perceives that he can not only create social value but also profit from the opportunity, he might decide to exploit the opportunity through the formation of a social purpose business venture that can create both types of value (social and economic). The value that the individual perceives can be created during the evaluation stage will therefore affect the strategy that is implemented in the exploitation stage.

P8: The perceived value that can be created through exploitation will have a significant effect on the strategy that will be implemented during the exploitation phase.

As in the recognition stage, social networks will also have a significant impact on the exploitation stage of opportunity recognition, specifically on the strategy utilized to develop the social venture. Social ventures are characterized by existing in environments with scarcity of resources and institutions. These ventures must then rely on institutional or resource bricolage to get their social programs started and on their way to sustainability (Mair and Martí, 2009). Bricolage allows them to mobilize the actors' skills and resources and learn from the process of moving ahead. As Sarasvathy (2001) explains, entrepreneurs who follow a process of bricolage, or effectuation, will rely on strategic alliances and pre-commitments from stakeholders as a tool to reduce uncertainty. These social networks are sources of information, capital and support for the social entrepreneurs (Mair and Martí, 2006). We can therefore expect that social entrepreneurs, who have a large social network, will tend to use this network to form strategic alliances, access resources, gain capital and form competitive barriers. The quality of these networks, the trust and respect that they have, can also have an effect as they may

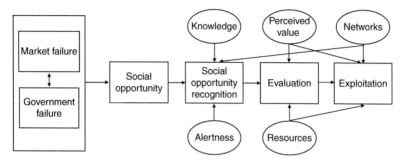

Figure 6.2 Conceptual framework of social opportunity recognition and exploitation

lead to utilization of different strategies such as the use of cooperative activity.

P9: Access to networks will have a significant effect on the strategy that will be implemented during the exploitation phase.

In sum, the process of social opportunity recognition and the variables that are believed to have a significant effect in the process have been depicted in Figure 6.2.

Conclusion

Business entrepreneurship and social entrepreneurship research have progressed in parallel, but almost in isolation from each other, with the gap between them widened by the ideological differences between the two sets of researchers (Prabhu, 1999). For this reason, research on social entrepreneurship lags behind that of business entrepreneurship (Thompson et al., 2000). But the gap that separates business entrepreneurship practitioners from social entrepreneurship practitioners is closing. It is time for researcher of business entrepreneurship and social entrepreneurship to do the same and close the gap.

Except for a few researchers (e.g. Hockerts, 2006), social opportunity recognition has been largely overlooked by social entrepreneurship scholars. This author believes that the omission is one of the main reasons why social entrepreneurship research still lags behind that of business entrepreneurship. One of the fundamental aspects that has been signaled as essential to the study of entrepreneurship is 'the set of individuals who discover, evaluate, and exploit them (opportunities)'.

In the case of social entrepreneurship, unraveling the variables that allow entrepreneurs to recognize social opportunities vs. business opportunities is of vital concern if the field is to gain legitimacy.

In this chapter, I have provided a process and conceptual model in order to initiate the dialogue on social opportunity recognition. I believe this is an important contribution and provides many areas for scholars to concentrate on, in order to better understand how social entrepreneurs recognize opportunities and attempt to grasp any differences between the process by social and business entrepreneurs. It is the author's belief that identifying differences is of the utmost importance. Research studying social entrepreneurs has focused on personality traits, entrepreneurial motives and value created to try to distinguish them from business entrepreneurs; but it is our belief that the social opportunity recognition process is a worthy area of inquiry to try to delineate further differences (Monllor and Attaran, 2008). As seen in the conceptual model, it is proposed that value creation has a significant impact on the evaluation and exploitation of social opportunities. This factor in itself might provide social entrepreneurship and business entrepreneurship scholars with valuable insights that are worth our attention. It is plausible that value created in itself is not the only differentiating characteristic. How value affects the opportunity recognition process could also be considered a factor that is distinct in social entrepreneurs and could lead them to recognize different opportunities altogether.

Opportunity recognition is the first step in the entrepreneurial process and draws a clear, comprehensible and easily recognizable dividing line that separates the two types of entrepreneurship. Business entrepreneurs recognize gaps in the economic system (business opportunities) and evaluate and exploit these opportunities to create economic value. Social entrepreneurs, on the other hand, recognize gaps in the social system (social opportunities created by market and government failure) and evaluate and exploit these opportunities according to their perceived potential to create social value. They focus their entrepreneurial talent on *recognizing* and solving social problems (Drayton, 2002). Contrary to business entrepreneurs who consider an attractive opportunity as one that will provide positive economic profit, for social entrepreneurs an attractive opportunity is 'one that has sufficient potential for positive social impact to justify the investment of time, energy and money required' (Guclu et al., 2002). Social entrepreneurs pursue opportunities to catalyze social change or address social needs (Mair and Martí, 2006). Not only is perceived social value of great importance to the evaluation of the idea, but, as has been argued, the strategy that is utilized to exploit it (non-profit vs. social purpose business ventures) might also be contingent on the perceived social value that can be created. If we were to adapt Shane and Venkataraman's (2000: 218) domain definition of entrepreneurship to social entrepreneurship it would read as the 'examination of how, by whom, and with what effects opportunities to create future *social* goods and services are discovered, evaluated, and exploited. Consequently, the field involves the study of sources of *social* opportunities; the processes of discovery, evaluation, and exploitation of *social* opportunities; and the set of individuals who discover, evaluate, and exploit them'.

As a research starting point, social entrepreneurship scholars should look into the existing literature and methodologies as a guide in their research. Research in opportunity recognition has advanced and researchers are using highly sophisticated methodologies in an attempt to understand the process. Although duplication should not be an aim, these research studies should be thought of as a guide. Shane (2000) conducted an important study of prior knowledge on the effect of opportunity recognition that could provide a useful stepping stone. Gaglio (2004) has concentrated on cognitive research and counterfactuals in an attempt to understand the black box that is opportunity recognition which could provide useful ideas to social entrepreneurial cognition. Shrader and Hills (2003) have developed a highly detailed questionnaire on opportunity recognition which is currently being adapted for the study of social entrepreneurs.

Social entrepreneurship provides a unique opportunity for the field of entrepreneurship to challenge, question and rethink important concepts and assumptions in its effort towards a unifying paradigm (Mair and Martí, 2006). The study of social entrepreneurial organizations can give mainstream entrepreneurship researchers useful insights into the process of evoking values and ideology among members during the organization creation process (Prabhu, 1999) and as proposed here, during the opportunity recognition process.

References

Ackerman, S. R. 1996. Altruism, Nonprofits, and Economic Theory. *Journal of Economic Literature*, 34(2): 701–28.
Ardichvili, A., Cardozo R. and Ray, S. 2003. A Theory of Entrepreneurial Opportunity Identification and Development. *Journal of Business Venturing*, 18(1): 105–23.

Austin, J., Stevenson H. and Wei-Skillern, J. 2006. Social and Commercial Entrepreneurship: Same, Different, or Both? *Entrepreneurship Theory & Practice,* **30**(1): 1–115.

Brock, D. D. 2006. *Social Entrepreneurship Teaching Resources Handbook.* Kentucky: Entrepreneurship of the Public Good Program, Berea College.

Cohen, B. and Winn, M. I. 2005. Market Imperfections, Opportunity and Sustainable Entrepreneurship. *Journal of Business Venturing,* **22**(1): 29–49.

Craig, J. and Lindsay, N. 2002. *Quantifying "Gut Feeling" in the Opportunity Recognition Process.* Frontiers of Entrepreneurship Research, December. Babson College.

Davidsson, P. 2005. *Researching Entrepreneurship.* Springer Science+Business Media, Inc.

Davis, S. 2002. Social Entrepreneurship: Toward and Entrepreneurial Culture for Social and Economic Development. In *Youth Employment Summit,* Alexandria, Egypt. September 7–11.

Dean, T. J. and McMullen, J. S. 2005. Toward a Theory of Sustainable Entrepreneurship: Reducing the Environmental Degradation through Entrepreneurial Action. *Journal of Business Venturing,* **22**(1): 50–76.

Dean, T. J. and McMullen, J. S. 2002. *Market Failure and Entrepreneurial Opportunity.* Academy of Management Proceedings, Academy of Management Meeting, Denver, CO.

Dees, J. G. 1998. The Meaning of Social Entrepreneurship. Fuqua School of Business, Duke University, Center for the Advancement of Social Entrepreneurship (CASE), Durham, NC.

Dees, J. G., Emerson, J. and Economy P. 2002. *Strategic Tools for Social Entrepreneurs.* New York: John Wiley & Sons.

Drayton, W. 2002. The Citizen Sector: Becoming as Entrepreneurial and Competitive as Business. *California Management Review,* **44**(3): 120–32.

Drucker, P. F. 1989. What Business can Learn from Nonprofits. *Harvard Business Review* (July–August 1989), 88–93.

Gaglio, C. M. 2004. The Role of Mental Simulations and Counterfactual Thinking in the Opportunity Identification Process. *Entrepreneurship: Theory & Practice,* **28**(6): 533–52.

Guclu, A., Dees, J. G. and Anderson, B. B. 2002. *The Process of Social Entrepreneurship: Creating Opportunities Worthy of Serious Pursuit.* Fuqua School of Business, Duke University, Center for the Advancement of Social Entrepreneurship (CASE), Durham, NC.

Hills, G. E., Shrader, R. C. and Lumpkin, G. T. 1999. *Opportunity Recognition as a Creative Process.* In Reynolds (ed), Frontiers of Entrepreneurship Research, 216–27, Boston, MA: Wellesley.

Hockerts, K. 2006. Entrepreneurial Opportunity in Social Purpose Business Ventures. In Mair, J, Robinson, J. and Hockerts, K. (eds.), *Social Entrepreneurship,* 143–54. Basingstoke: Palgrave Macmillan.

Hulbert, B., Brown, R. B. and Adams, S. 1997. Towards an Understanding of 'Opportunity'. *Marketing Education Review,* **7**(3): 67–73.

Johnson, S. 2000. *Literature Review on Social Entrepreneurship.* Canadian Centre for Social Entrepreneurship, Canada: University of Alberta School of Business.

Kaish, S. and Gilad, B. 1991. Characteristics of Opportunities Search of Entrepreneurs Versus Executives: Sources, Interests, General Alertness. *Journal of Business Venturing*, 6(1): 45–61.

Kirzner, I. M. 1973. *Competition and Entrepreneurship.* Chicago: University of Chicago Press.

Mair, J. and Martí, I. 2006. Social Entrepreneurship Research: A Source of Explanation, Prediction and Delight. *Journal of World Business*, 41(1): 36–44.

Mair, J. and Martí, I. 2009. Entrepreneurship in and around Institutional Voids: A Case Study from Bangladesh. *Journal of Business Venturing*, 24(5): 419–35.

Monllor, J. and Attaran, S. 2008. Opportunity Recognition of Social Entrepreneurs: An Application of the Creativity Model. *International Journal of Entrepreneurship and Small Business*, 6 (1): 54–67.

Peredo, A. M. and McLean, M. 2006. Social Entrepreneurship: A Critical Review of the Concept. *Journal of World Business*, 41(1): 56–65.

Prabhu, G. N. 1999. Social Entrepreneurship Leadership. *Career Development International*, 4(3): 140–5.

Sarasvathy, S. D. 2001. Causation and Effectuation: Toward a Theoretical Shift from Economic Inevitability to Entrepreneurial Contingency. *Journal of Management Review*, 26(2): 243–63.

Seelos, C. and Mair, J. 2005. Social Entrepreneurship: Creating New Business Models to Serve the Poor. *Business Horizons*, 48(3): 241–46.

Shane, S. 2003. *A General Theory of Entrepreneurship: The Individual-Opportunity Nexus.* Cheltenham: Edward Elgar.

Shane, S. 2000. Prior Knowledge and the Discovery of Entrepreneurial Opportunities. *Organization Science*, 11(4): 448–69.

Shane, S. and Venkataraman, S. 2000. The Promise of Entrepreneurship as a Field of Research. *Academy of Management Review*, 25(1): 217–26.

Shrader, R. C. 2006. Perception and Pursuit of Opportunity: Toward a General Theory of Entrepreneurship. In Hills, G. E. and Monllor, J. (eds.), *UIC Research Symposium on Marketing and Entrepreneurship.* Chicago: IL, University of Illinois.

Shrader, R. C. and Hills, G. E. 2003. Opportunity Recognition: Perceptions of Highly Succesful Entrepreneurs. *Journal of Small Business Strategy*, 14(2): 92–108.

Tan, W., Williams J. and Tan, T. 2005. Defining the 'Social' in 'Social Entrepreneurship': Altruism and Entrepreneurship. *International Entrepreneurship and Management Journal*, 1(3): 353–65.

Thompson, J. L. 2002. The World of the Social Entrepreneur. *International Journal of Public Sector Management*, 15(5): 412–31.

Thompson, J. L., Alvy G. and Lees, A. 2000. Social Entrepreneurship – A New Look at the People and the Potential, *Management Decision*, 38(5): 328–38.

Weerawardena, J. and Mort, G. S. 2006. Investigating Social Entrepreneurship: A Multidimensional Model. *Journal of World Business*, 41(1): 21–35.

Zahra, S. and Dess, G. 2001. Entrepreneurship as a Field of Research: Encouraging Dialogue and Debate. *Academy of Management Review*, 26(1): 8–10.

7
Entrepreneurial Opportunity Evaluation: A Discrete Choice Analysis of Financial and Social Entrepreneurial Opportunity Attributes

Brett R. Smith, Jill R. Kickul and Fiona Wilson

Introduction

How does a potential entrepreneur evaluate an opportunity? One of the most compelling questions in the field of entrepreneurship concerns the evaluation of an entrepreneurial opportunity. The evaluation of an opportunity is critical because it is in this decision-making process that an individual either initiates or forgoes action that may lead to the fruits of social wealth generated by entrepreneurial activity. Therefore, in order to achieve the *raison d'être* promised by entrepreneurship (Venkataraman, 1997), a prospective entrepreneur must engage in the evaluation of an opportunity during the entrepreneurial process.

The domain of entrepreneurship research has been defined as the three processes of discovery, evaluation and exploitation of opportunities (Shane and Venkataraman, 2000). With growing interest in a cognitive perspective (Mitchell et al., 2002), the processes of opportunity discovery and exploitation have continued to receive a considerable amount of theoretical and empirical attention. By comparison, relatively less attention has focused on the critical processes of how individuals evaluate an opportunity. Given that the three processes of discovery, evaluation and exploitation are non-linear and interrelated, increased attention on opportunity evaluation is needed to gain a more holistic understanding of the entire entrepreneurial process.

While comparatively under-represented, the existing work on opportunity evaluation tends to focus on the assessment of whether or not any given idea is in fact an opportunity (e.g. Keh et al., 2002). The implicit assumption in much of this work in the mainstream entrepreneurship literature is the notion that the evaluation of an opportunity is focused primarily on the economic viability of an opportunity. For example, Ardichvili and colleagues (2003: 111) suggest the evaluation of an opportunity is to 'assess whether the value that a particular combination of resources can deliver will translate into economic success'.

While financial attributes are likely to be an important consideration for many potential entrepreneurs, other opportunity attributes are also likely to be important in the evaluation of an opportunity. For example, an individual may be drawn to the environmental aspects of an entrepreneurial opportunity for creating clean technologies that will benefit the health of the planet. Recognizing that entrepreneurial opportunities are multi-dimensional, we extend the work on opportunity evaluation by focusing on the assessment of opportunities that contain both financial and social-value creation attributes to understand how the various types of opportunity attributes affect the evaluation of an entrepreneurial opportunity. Specifically, we examine two related research questions:

1) *What are the relative utilities of different financial and social value creation opportunity attributes?*
2) *Which opportunity attribute, or what combination of opportunity attributes, is/ are likely to motivate an individual from inaction to action?*

To examine these research questions, we introduce discrete choice analysis (McFadden, 2001) to the field of entrepreneurship as an important methodology to examine the multi-attribute decision process of opportunity evaluation. Discrete choice analysis has been used to model choice processes of decision-makers in a variety of academic disciplines including marketing, operations management, urban planning, hospitality, and natural resource economics (e.g. Louvière and Timmermans, 1990; Verma et al., 1999; Verma and Plaschka, 2005). The use of discrete choice analysis allows us to address two important issues in the domain of entrepreneurship and social entrepreneurship research. First, we provide a means to address the issues associated with how to deal with variation in the opportunity itself (Shane et al., 2003). In this research, we use choice experiments that present individuals with different sets of entrepreneurial opportunities that vary in their opportunity attributes. This approach eliminates concerns about how variation in the opportunity itself may affect an individual's evaluation of the opportunity and allows us to focus on the evaluation of both the economic and other non-economic reasons for individual preferences. Second, through the example of discrete choice analysis, we introduce a sophisticated econometric modeling approach to the field of entrepreneurship that holds great promise for many aspects of entrepreneurial decision-making. In this research, the use of discrete choice analysis allows us to determine the relative weights that individuals attach to various characteristics of an entrepreneurial opportunity and to understand the combination of opportunity attributes or 'bundle' that is likely to motivate an individual from inaction to action. While discrete choice analysis has seen significant use among econometricians, it has been rarely employed in studying entrepreneurship. Given the ability of discrete choice analysis to predict, not just explain, it is particularly useful in understanding the genesis and evolution of venture preferences and evaluation.

Taken together, this chapter makes at least three important contributions to the entrepreneurship and social entrepreneurship literature. First, this research adds to the important work on opportunity evaluation by examining the choice process through which individuals assess the relative utilities of different attributes of an entrepreneurial opportunity. Second, the chapter provides insight into how and why individuals overcome their inertia to become entrepreneurs. Finally, it utilizes discrete choice analysis as a way to experimentally examine the decision-making process of opportunity evaluation.

This chapter will proceed as follows. First, we develop the theoretical framework of opportunity evaluation as a utility maximizing approach that motivates our research questions. Second, we provide an introduction to the methodology of discrete choice analysis. Finally, we present findings and discuss the implications of the results while providing direction for future research.

Background

Opportunity evaluation as utility maximization

The evaluation of an entrepreneurial opportunity can be thought of as a decision-making process where the prospective entrepreneur decides whether or not to pursue an entrepreneurial opportunity. In the field of entrepreneurship, utility models have been proposed as a means to examine entrepreneurial decision-making, including the career choice to become an entrepreneur (e.g. Douglas and Shepherd, 2000). 'Utility models of human decision-making postulate that individuals select the course of action which promises, in prospect, the greatest utility (or psychic satisfaction)' (Douglas and Shepherd, 2000: 234). In this research, we use a utility maximization approach to opportunity evaluation to understand how various attributes of the opportunity affect the evaluation of an entrepreneurial opportunity. As such, we argue that a potential entrepreneur will evaluate an entrepreneurial opportunity based upon the prospective assessment of satisfaction that will be gained from pursuing the opportunity.

Opportunity as a multi-dimensional construct

In the study of consumer behavior, researchers seek to identify the choices made by the consumer based upon the different attributes of various products or brands (e.g. McFadden, 1986). Adopting a similar approach, we seek to understand how potential entrepreneurs make choices about which opportunities they see as attractive. In so doing, we propose that an entrepreneurial opportunity is a multi-dimensional construct that is comprised of many different attributes (economic, social, environmental, etc.) and that all these different attributes potentially matter in the evaluation of an opportunity.

To date, much of the work on opportunity evaluation has been concerned with the evaluation of whether or not an opportunity is financially viable or economically attractive. This approach recognizes the economic roots of the field of entrepreneurship. Early entrepreneurship theory assumed economic motives as the sole, or primary, purpose of new organization creation (Baumol, 1993; Cole, 1965; Kirzner, 1985; Schumpeter, 1934). The 'traditional' entrepreneur is seen to be motivated by self-interest to pursue opportunities for creating economic profits and personal wealth (Amit et al., 2001; Kent, 1982; Zahra et al., 2006).

While not discounting economic considerations, the purpose of this research is to move beyond a primary focus on economic considerations to recognize the multi-dimensionality of opportunities and its effect on opportunity evaluation. In their seminal work, Shane and Venkataraman (2000) explicitly acknowledge that entrepreneurship occurs for reasons other than for profit, but then focus exclusively on economic considerations. This limitation is unfortunate because we know that 'entrepreneurs, like anyone else, have a host of personal motives' (Cyert and March, 1963). As such, we follow the lead of Amit and his colleagues (2001) who find that wealth attainment is only one of many decision dimensions important to entrepreneurs. In this research, however, we focus on attributes of the opportunity rather than the motive of the individual, which represents a subtle, but important difference.

Indeed, in the emerging field of social entrepreneurship, the non-economic considerations are beginning to receive increased attention. While definitional challenges still exist, nearly all definitions of social entrepreneurship involve, at least in part, the aspiration to achieve some socially desirable objective (Zahra et al., 2006). While financial considerations may be of significant importance, the emerging work in social entrepreneurship suggests that social considerations may also be compelling to a prospective entrepreneur because 'social goals can replace profit maximization as a powerful motivating influence' (Yunus, 1998: 62). Given the multi-dimensionality of opportunities and the utility maximizing approach, our first research question is:

What are the relative utilities of different financial and social opportunity attributes?

Overcoming inertia: moving from preference to action

The identification of a desirable opportunity does not guarantee that an individual will pursue the opportunity. While the evaluation of the opportunity is conditional upon its identification, evaluation is also integral to the pursuit of entrepreneurial action. In developing a theory of entrepreneurial action, McMullen and Shepherd (2006) differentiated between third-person and first-person opportunities. A third-person opportunity represented an opportunity for someone in the marketplace. By contrast, a first-person opportunity is an opportunity upon which a given entrepreneur believes they should act. In their framework of entrepreneurial action, this transition from a third- to a first-person opportunity occurs as a decision-making process whereby the individual considers whether the potential reward of pursuing the opportunity is worth the potential cost that will be incurred. However, this decision-making process is undermined by doubt and uncertainty. This uncertainty is what creates the inertia of inaction which, in turn, causes many identified third-person opportunities to remain unexploited. 'Therefore, the question... is similar to the classic 'risk / return' dilemma in which the prospective actor must ask him/herself whether he or she believes that the payoff of the third-person opportunity justifies bearing the uncertainty necessary to attain it' (McMullen and Shepherd, 2006: 141).

As previously noted, the evaluation of the 'payoff' of entrepreneurial action has often been limited to economic considerations. Returning to the multi-dimensionality of an opportunity and the utility maximizing framework, an individual must decide whether the potential 'payoff' of psychic satisfaction derived from the various opportunity attributes is worth incurring the risk of pursuing the opportunity. If the utility gained from the opportunity attribute(s) is (are) sufficient, then the prospective entrepreneur is able to overcome the inertia of uncertainty and engage in entrepreneurial action. This leads to our second research question:

What opportunity attribute or combination of opportunity attributes motivates an individual from inaction to action?

Research design: discrete choice analysis and multinomial logit models

As mentioned, McFadden's (2001) discrete choice analysis approach uses an elegant framework to associate discrete micro-level decisions with macro-level predictors. Given our proposed research questions, this approach allows us to include both the financial and social attributes of an entrepreneurial opportunity. Like conjoint analysis, discrete choice analysis assumes individuals act to maximize their self-interest. However, unlike conjoint analysis (wherein respondents rank or rate their preferences using experimental profiles), discrete choice analysis requires that respondents make explicit choices in simulated situations derived from realistic variations of expected scenarios.

More specifically, in conjoint analysis, several problems can arise when asking participants to rate or rank multiple profiles. For the procedure to work correctly, participants must rank or rate all the conjoint profiles. For example, while reviewing a series of 24 profiles representing different entrepreneurial opportunities, it is likely that study participants would be able to select which one they like best and the one they like the least. However, difficulty arises when they are asked to rank their fifth or sixth choices. Forcing participants to carefully rank or rate choices/alternatives that they would never choose can make the task imposed by conjoint somewhat different from real-world selection behavior. Unfortunately, accurate rankings or ratings of all the profiles are needed for conjoint analysis to provide meaningful results. With discrete choice analysis, we avoid impossible combination and forced choice problems, while preserving and even extending the estimating power of conjoint. Using discrete choice analysis, participants are exposed to different attributes of an entrepreneurial opportunity alongside different levels of each attribute in a series of scenarios. Participants are asked to examine each scenario, and respond to a single question: if these were all the choices available, which entrepreneurial opportunity would you choose to act on, if any? Given the simplicity coupled with its sophisticated methodology (to be discussed later), discrete choice analysis can be applied to the most complex evaluative choices, including why individuals start entrepreneurial ventures.

Aside from offering participants a more realistic and natural task, representations of opportunity choices within discrete choice analysis can be customized to match entrepreneurial /marketplace reality. Each choice can have its own attributes and attribute levels. Several opportunities with many of the same but some different attributes can appear side by side in the scenarios, allowing for direct measurement of the opportunity attribute effects. Finally, discrete choice analysis can handle certain experimental designs more easily than conjoint analysis. In discrete choice analysis, many opportunities can share one large experimental design, or each opportunity can have its own conjoint-style design. As such, even relatively large designs, those requiring 64 or 128 scenarios, can be fractionalized more easily (as opposed to complex gyrations required in splitting conjoint analysis designs).

Designing discrete choice analysis experiments

Discrete choice experiments involve careful design of profiles and choice sets (a bundle of opportunity attributes) in which two or more alternatives are offered to respondents. The design of the experiment is under the control of the researcher, and consequently, the decision-makers' choices (dependent variable) are a function of the attributes of each alternative, personal characteristics of the respondents, and unobserved effects captured by the random component (e.g. unobserved heterogeneity or omitted factors). (For a more detailed theoretical and statistical background of discrete choice analysis, see Ben-Akiva and Lerman [1991] and McFadden [1986].)

Discrete choice analysis applications based on choice experiments typically involve the following steps:

- identification of attributes;
- specification of attribute levels;
- experimental design;
- presentation of alternatives to respondents; and
- estimation of the choice model.

Although design of choice experiments and estimation of multinomial logit models requires sophisticated training and skills, implementing the estimated model(s) in spreadsheet-based decision support systems is fairly easy. Hence, discrete choice analysis is very useful for practicing managers and is used here to explore the respondents' preferences and evaluation of the attributes of a new venture opportunity.

Methodology

Participants were 137 students enrolled in an undergraduate entrepreneurship program located in the US Midwest. Of the 137 participants, the average age was 20.82 years and 67% were male (over 90% were Caucasian). All participants were told that we were conducting research to better understand their attitudes and beliefs regarding entrepreneurial ventures. In their questionnaire, we provided the respondents with scenarios of different entrepreneurial opportunities that are designed to assess the attractiveness of nine key attributes of an entrepreneurial opportunity; these scenarios provide the input for our discrete choice analysis.

Survey design

In our survey, respondents had to make a choice in 16 three-choice sets regarding which type of business venture they preferred to start. Each choice set offered two different entrepreneurial opportunity scenarios that they were asked to choose between, as well as the option to select 'neither'.

Prior to the creation of scenarios, the first stage of the design of our discrete choice analysis study involved the identification of relevant opportunity attributes. As suggested, the selection of opportunity attributes was balanced between the inclusion of all salient attributes and the restriction of an exponentially large experimental design (Verma et al., 1999). Based on previous research (Krueger et al., 2006), we included six attributes that are both highly salient to the assessment of an entrepreneurial opportunity, and are relatively non-overlapping. Each attribute has two levels. These were high growth versus slow/non-growth, competing on price versus competing on quality (e.g. low-cost leadership vs. differentiation), high-tech versus low/no-tech, prospector versus defender strategy (e.g. Miles and Snow's Typology), bootstrapped versus externally funded, and competitive environment (e.g. constantly changing vs. remaining stable). In addition to these six attributes, we also included three additional attributes of interest that comprise the commonly referred to triple bottom line, or issues related to environmental and social concerns As such, these variables included: economic sustainability (profitability), environmental sustainability, and social impact (emphasis on improving some social condition in society such as the reduction of poverty). Finally, we used a fractional factorial design that simultaneously created both the entrepreneurial opportunity scenarios, as well as the choice sets into which to place them (Verma et al., 1999; Please see Appendix 7A for a sample choice set).

Choice analyses

We used the LIMDEP program by econometric software (www.limdep. com) to estimate multinomial logit choice models for all respondents using a maximum likelihood estimation technique. The multinomial logit model is expressed as

$$(P_j | C_n) = \frac{e^{V_j \mu}}{\sum_{k=1}^{n} e^{v_k \mu}} \tag{7.1}$$

where V_j represents the systematic component of utility (U_j) of a choice alternative j (Ben-Akiva and Lerman, 1991). The model assumes that the utilities (U_j) are comprised of a systematic component (V_j), which can be estimated, and random error (ε), which is independent and identically distributed according to a Gumbel distribution with a scale parameter μ. $P_j | C_n$ represents the probability of selecting an alternative, and therefore the expected preference. Representing an opportunity as a bundle of its attributes, and by assuming an additive utility function, an alternative's systematic utility can be calculated as:

$$V_j = \sum_{a \in \Lambda} \beta_a X_{aj}$$

where β_a is the relative utility (part-worth utility) associated with attribute a.

Rather than going through the statistical details of the estimated choice models, in this chapter we describe the results in a more user-friendly format. At the same time we would like to assure readers that the estimated models are statistically significant, and meet all the established criteria established within the academic community. While the relationships are likely to be complex, our design and methodology will allow us to tease out critical linkages. This information can then be applied to design strategies and educational programs tailored to how individuals make choices, trade-offs, and weight their attitudes and intentions regarding new venture opportunities.

Results

The main analysis approach utilized by discrete choice analysis researchers is the estimation of the multinomial logit model based on a maximum likelihood estimation technique. Using LIMDEP, we found our overall model to be significant at the .05 level and the essential goodness-of-fit measures (including the log-likelihood ratio; McFadden's ρ^2) demonstrated excellent statistical properties (Louvière et al., 2000). Multinomial logit models are similar to ordinary least square regression in that they are derived by estimating β weights for the predictor variables within the proposed model.

In the examination of our first research question, '*What are the relative utilities of different financial and social opportunity attributes?*' we were able to use the estimated β weights (shown in Table 7.2) to derive the relative utility (importance) of all our variables. That is, the relative utility for each variable represents the value of the construct (rescaled between 0 and 1 from highest to lowest) and were derived from the β weights of the constituent attributes (e.g. the weights of all attributes included within each construct were added together to obtain the composite score for each construct). In examining the relative utilities, we found that respondents placed the highest relative importance on firm growth, and within this attribute they preferred ventures that are 'growing very fast' (relative utility of 1.00). Noticeably, the second most important attribute was social impact (e.g. emphasis on improving some social condition in society, such as the reduction of poverty; relative utility = .9286; see Table 7.1, which shows the relative importance of each of the attributes).

The economic sustainability of the venture was third in importance (relative utility = .8163), followed by the strategic preference for quality (relative utility of .8061). It is noteworthy that two of the three aspects of triple bottom-line model are among the top priorities for aspiring entrepreneurs. After these top four attributes, there was a decrease in the reported importance of other strategic attributes of entrepreneurial opportunities. For example, attributes such as the third component of the triple-bottom-line model, environmental sustainability (from the relative utility of .7347) was lower in importance.

Table 7.1 Relative utilities of each attribute

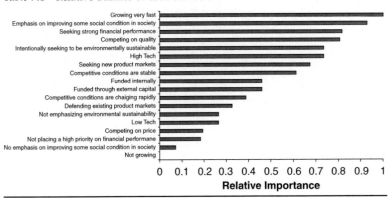

	Relative Utilities
Growing Very Fast	1.0000
Low Growth/Not Growing	0.0000
Competing on Quality	0.8061
Competing on Price	0.1939
High Tech	0.7347
Low Tech	0.2653
Seeking new product markets	0.6735
Defending existing product markets	0.3265
Funded through external capital	0.4592
Funded internally	0.4592
Seeking strong financial performance	0.8163
Not placing a high priority on financial performance	0.1837
Emphasis on improving some social condition in society	0.9286
No emphasis on improving some social condition in society	0.0714
Intentionally seeking to be environmentally sustainable	0.7347
Not emphasizing environmental sustainability	0.2653
Competitive conditions are changing rapidly	0.3878
Competitive conditions are stable	0.6122

In addition to analyzing the level of importance that each participant placed on their perceptions of a venture opportunity, we were also able to examine within each of the attributes, and investigate how the two levels differed. Table 7.1 displays the differences within each of the attributes. Table 7.2 provides detailed statistical analysis and β weights used to answer our first question. As shown in Table 7.2, significant differences were also seen within eight of the nine attributes (see Table 7.2).

For our second research question, we were interested in investigating '*What opportunity attribute or combination of opportunity attributes*

Table 7.2 Detailed statistical analysis of choice model and attributes

Variable	Beta Weight	Std Error	t-Statistic	P-value
Intercept	−0.44	0.05	−9.11	0.00
1) Growth versus non-growth (1 = growing very fast, −1 = not growing)	0.49	0.05	9.85	0.00
2) Competing on price versus competing on quality (1 = quality, −1 = price)	0.30	0.04	6.18	0.00
3) High-tech versus low/no-tech (1 = cutting-edge high tech industry, −1 = low/no-tech industry)	0.23	0.05	4.67	0.00
4) Prospector versus defender strategy (1 = seeking new product-markets, −1 = defending existing product-markets)	0.17	0.05	3.45	0.00
5) Bootstrapped versus externally funded (1 = funded through external capital, −1 = funded internally – bootstrapping)	−0.04	0.05	−0.85	0.40
6) Economic sustainability (1 = seeking strong financial performance, −1 = not placing a high priority on financial performance)	0.32	0.05	6.33	0.00
7) Social Impact (1 = Emphasis on improving some social condition in society, −1 = No Emphasis on improving some social condition in society)	0.42	0.05	8.64	0.00
8) Environmental sustainability (1 = intentionally seeking to be environmentally sustainable, −1 = not emphasizing environmental sustainability)	0.24	0.05	4.84	0.00
9) Competitive environment (1 = competitive conditions are changing rapidly, −1 = in an industry where competitive conditions are stable)	−0.11	0.05	−2.33	0.02

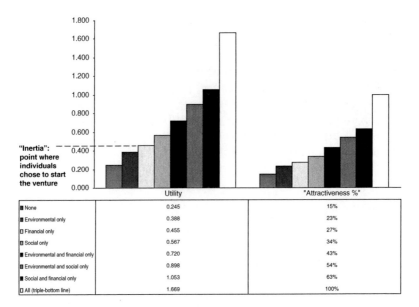

	Utility	"Attractiveness %"
■ None	0.245	15%
■ Environmental only	0.388	23%
□ Financial only	0.455	27%
◪ Social only	0.567	34%
■ Environmental and financial only	0.720	43%
◪ Environmental and social only	0.898	54%
■ Social and financial only	1.053	63%
□ All (triple-bottom line)	1.669	100%

Figure 7.1 Utility and attractiveness in percent (economic and non-economic attributes)

motivates an individual from inaction to action?' To fully examine this question, we calculated a number of scenarios where either the economic or social or some combination was present. For each individual and combination of attributes, we estimated the overall utility and the percentage of attractiveness (as determined by the utility function, see Figure 7.1).

As a baseline, the combination of financial, social, and environmental served as the maximum utility in which the percentage of attractiveness was calculated. When removing any of the attributes, we saw a decrease in overall attractiveness. Additionally, given that we incorporated the intercept (termed in discrete choice analysis as 'inertia') in our multinomial logit model analyses, we also determined which single or combination of attributes propeled a prospective entrepreneur from inaction to action. Given a negative intercept (i.e. more individuals had low intentions to start an actual business overall), we examined which attribute(s) would overcome this negative inertia and motivate individuals to launch the venture. While all combinations positively influenced individuals to consider starting a business, results revealed that either social or financial (although marginally) by itself was sufficient in overcoming the negative inertia. However, environmental was not sufficient to overcome the inertia of inaction.

In relation to investigating the utility and inertia, it was also interesting to examine the perceived attractiveness of each of the attribute(s). Consistent with our previous findings, social and financial performance had the second highest level of attractiveness (63%), followed by social and environmental (54%) and financial and environmental had the lowest of all combinations at 43% level of attractiveness. Social impact had the highest single level of attractiveness (34%) followed then by financial performance (27%). By not emphasizing any of the three attributes, overall attractiveness decreased to a minimal 15%.

Discussion and conclusion

In this study, we found that prospective entrepreneurs greatly valued both financial and social opportunity attributes. Specifically, we found that social value creation attributes of an opportunity were second only to growth considerations, and superseded even financial considerations in the evaluation of an opportunity. While many of the individuals were reluctant to become an entrepreneur, we also found that certain combinations of opportunity attributes may generate enough utility to motivate the individual from inaction to action. The main findings from this study suggest that opportunity evaluation and entrepreneurial action may benefit from a broader conceptualization of the multi-dimensionality of an entrepreneurial opportunity. In this research, we also introduced the methodology of discrete choice analysis to the field of entrepreneurship. This research has several implications for research related to entrepreneurial motivation, social entrepreneurship and quantitative methodologies.

One important implication of this work is the need to disentangle the desirability and the feasibility of an entrepreneurial action. Research on entrepreneurial intentions (e.g. Krueger et al., 2000) and entrepreneurial action (McMullen and Shepherd, 2006) suggest that both intent and behavior are a function of the desirability and feasibility of outcomes. While much of the existing work on opportunity evaluation has been focused on assessing the financial feasibility of the opportunity, we move beyond feasibility to include the desirability of pursuing an opportunity. In assessing the desirability of an opportunity, it is important to understand the motivation of the prospective entrepreneur. Despite the disappointing results of previous studies of entrepreneurial motivation (Busenitz and Barney, 1997), we concur with Shane and his colleagues

(2003) that there is much to be gained from understanding how human motivation may affect entrepreneurship.

A longstanding approach to psychology stems from a functional perspective (e.g. Katz, 1960). To gain a more fine-grained and perhaps useful understanding of how motivation affects the entrepreneurial process, we suggest the development of a functional approach to entrepreneurial motivation. A functional approach to motivation suggests it is important to examine not only in what action the entrepreneur is engaging but also what function the action is fulfilling for the individual. According to McMullen and Shepherd (2006), the desirability analysis of an opportunity is focused on whether the entrepreneurial action 'will fulfill the motive for which it is being sought' (McMullen and Shepherd, 2006: 141). Therefore, to gain further insight into the evaluation of an entrepreneurial opportunity, it is important to begin to map the underlying motivations of the entrepreneur to various opportunity attributes. This type of joint mapping process would respond to calls to focus research on the individual–opportunity nexus rather than simply on the individual or the opportunity (Busenitz et al., 2003). Such an approach would tie together this study with the work by Amit and his colleagues (2001) and may lead to the development of an individual–opportunity *fit perspective* (Kristof, 1996) where the motivation of the individual could be matched to the attribute of the opportunity.

Another important implication of this research is that it calls attention to the potential reciprocal benefits of research on social and commercial entrepreneurship. In this research, we found that social value creation attributes of entrepreneurial opportunities were particularly salient in the evaluation of any given opportunity. As the emerging work on social entrepreneurship begins to expand the knowledge frontiers of this domain, there are likely to be many benefits that can accrue to the study of commercial entrepreneurship. In comparing social and commercial entrepreneurship, Austin and his colleagues (2006) identified four key areas that differentiate commercial and social entrepreneurship: the social nature of the opportunity, motivation due to fundamentally distinct missions, human and resource mobilization, and performance measurement. Each of these areas represents an important potential contribution between the domains of commercial and social entrepreneurship. For example, in their theoretical work on social entrepreneurship, Zahra and his colleagues (2006) introduced the construct of social wealth as a means to measure the social value created after accounting for the associated financial and social costs incurred. While the creation of financial value is often the dependent variable of choice when measuring the contribution of entrepreneurship, the performance measurement of social wealth may complement these efforts and be more consistent with the *raison d'être* of entrepreneurship. As such, we believe our results suggest that the study of any form of entrepreneurship may be incomplete without the inclusion of social wealth.

In the same way, research in the area of social entrepreneurship can advance more quickly by utilizing the universe of knowledge gained in the study of commercial entrepreneurship. 'We should build our theory of social entrepreneurship on the strong tradition of entrepreneurship theory and research. Social entrepreneurs are one species of the genus entrepreneur' (Dees, 2001: 2). The logic of this approach is tied to the idea that both social and commercial entrepreneurship address similar conceptual questions about the processes of discovery, evaluation and exploitation of opportunities and the set of individuals who engage in these actions (Shane and Venkataraman, 2000). The increased recognition that social and commercial entrepreneurship exist on a continuum (rather than as a dichotomy) and the continued blurring of boundaries between social and economic value creation suggest there may be numerous examples of cross-fertilization of knowledge between commercial and social entrepreneurship.

With recent attention focused on the quantitative methodologies in the field of entrepreneurship (Dean et al., 2007), we noticed an absence of the use of discrete choice analysis in the field of entrepreneurship. In the current study, we have used discrete choice analysis not only to examine the evaluation of opportunity attributes but also to highlight its potential range of applications to a myriad of decision-making choices in entrepreneurship. A broader use of discrete choice analysis and its associated choice experiments may be beneficial for entrepreneurial research particularly for areas related to opportunities where it is difficult to control for variance in opportunities (Shane et al., 2003). The use of discrete choice analysis may also be helpful to gain further insight into many other decisions within the entrepreneurial process such as the selection of founding teams and the decisions by providers of capital (i.e. angel investors, venture capitalists, etc.). In order for the field of entrepreneurship to continue to gain legitimacy in the larger social sciences and to more accurately understand the underlying phenomenon, it is important to continue to increase the rigor of our research methodologies.

Although this research makes several important contributions, these contributions must be considered within the context of the limitations of this study. One limitation is the use of a student sample from a single university. Given this sample, the findings of this study may not generalize to the evaluation process of existing entrepreneurs. However, there are at least two issues that mitigate this problem. First, all the students in this sample had signed up for elective academic coursework in entrepreneurship, indicating some interest in becoming an entrepreneur. Second, nearly 30% of the sample indicated they already had some entrepreneurial experience. While these answers reflect self-response data, the answers also highlight the notion that many are already engaged in some level of entrepreneurial activity. Another limitation of this research is that the study is cross-sectional in nature. While our results permit us to make generalizations regarding respondents' evaluation of opportunities, future research is needed that tracks the same set of respondents as they further contemplate and continue developing ventures of their own, specifically as they leave the university setting and encounter many of the opportunities and barriers that exist in the opportunity development (Ardichvili et al., 2003) and new venture creation process. This research is a first step in understanding how individuals evaluate multidimensional opportunities. Third, we need to consider with additional data the use of a priori criteria for student segmentation. Future research could use latent class and other segmentation techniques to allow student segments to emerge from the data itself, thus accounting for heterogeneity that may exist between different student segments (Degeratu et al., 2000).

Despite these limitations, this research offers a promising approach to understanding how individuals evaluate entrepreneurial opportunities. By highlighting the multi-dimensionality of opportunities, this study offers an interesting look at the attributes that prospective entrepreneurs value. The inclusion of non-economic attributes illustrates some of the reciprocal benefits of commercial and social entrepreneurship research. Finally, this chapter introduces discrete choice analysis to the field of entrepreneurship as an important methodological approach to understand multi-attribute decision-making.

References

Amit, R., MacCrimmon, K., Zietsma, C. and Oesch, J. 2001. Does Money Matter? Wealth Attainment as the Motive for Initiating Growth-Orientated Technology Ventures. *Journal of Business Venturing*, **16**(2): 119–43.

Ardichvili, A., Cardozo, R. and Ray, S. 2003. A Theory of Entrepreneurial Opportunity Identification and Development. *Journal of Business Venturing*, **18**(1): 105–23.

Austin, J., Stevenson, H. and Wei-Skillern, J. 2006. Social and Commercial Entrepreneurship: Same, Different or Both? *Entrepreneurship Theory and Practice*, 30(1): 1–22.

Baumol, W. J. 1993. Formal Entrepreneurial Theory in Economics: Existence and Bounds. *Journal of Business Venturing*, 8(3): 197–210.

Ben-Akiva, M. and Lerman, S. 1991. *Discrete Choice Analysis*. Cambridge, MA: MIT Press.

Busenitz, L. and Barney, J. 1997. Differences between Entrepreneurs and Managers in Large Organizations: Biases and Heuristics in Strategic Decision-Making. *Journal of Business Venturing*, 12(1): 9–30.

Busenitz, L.W., West III, G.P., Shepherd, D., Nelson, T., Chandler, G.N. and Zacharakis, A. 2003. Entrepreneurship Research in Emergence: Past Trends and Future Directions. *Journal of Management*, 29(3): 285–308.

Cole, A. 1965. An Approach to the Study of Entrepreneurship: A Tribute to Edwin Gay. In Aitken, H. (ed.), *Explorations in Entrepreneurship*, 30–44. Cambridge, MA: Harvard University Press.

Cyert, R.A. and March, J.G. 1963. *A Behavioral Theory of the Firm*. Englewood Cliffs, NJ: Prentice-Hall.

Dean, M., Shook, C. and Payne, T. 2007. The Past, Present and Future of Entrepreneurship Research: Data Analytic Trends and Training. *Entrepreneurship Theory and Practice*, 31(4): 601–18.

Dees, J. G. 2001. The Meaning of Social Entrepreneurship. Fuqua School of Business, Duke University, Center for the Advancement of Social Entrepreneurship (CASE), Durham, NC. The article is available online at http://www.fuqua.duke.edu/centers/case/documents/dees_sedef.pdf.

Degeratu, A., Rangaswamy, A. and Wu, J. 2000. Consumer Choice Behavior in Online and Regular Stores: The Effects of Brand Name, Price, and Other Search Attributes. *International Journal of Research in Marketing*, 17(1): 55–78.

Douglas, E. and Shepherd, D. 2000. Entrepreneurship as a Utility Maximizing Response. *Journal of Business Venturing*, 15(3): 231–51.

Katz, D. 1960. The Functional Approach to the Study of Attitudes. *Public Opinion Quarterly*, 24(2): 163–204.

Keh, H., Foo, M. and Lim, B. 2002. Opportunity Evaluation under Risky Conditions: The Cognitive Processes of Entrepreneurs. *Entrepreneurship Theory and Practice*, 27(2): 125–48.

Kent, C. 1982. *Encyclopedia of Entrepreneurship*. Englewood Cliffs, NJ: Prentice Hall.

Kirzner, I. M. 1985. *Discovery and the Capitalist Process*. Chicago: University of Chicago Press.

Kristof, A. 1996. Person-Organization Fit: An Integrative Review of its Conceptualizations, Measurement and Implications. *Personnel Psychology*, 49(1): 1–49.

Krueger, N., Reilly, M. and Carsrud, A. 2000. Competing Models of Entrepreneurial Intentions. *Journal of Business Venturing*, 15(5/6): 411–32.

Krueger, N., Kickul, J., Gundry, L., Wilson, F. and Verma, R. 2006. Discrete Choices, Trade-offs, and Advantages: Modeling Social Venture Opportunities and Intentions. Paper presented at *2nd International Social Entrepreneurship Research Conference*, New York, NY.

Louvière, J., Hensher, D.A and Swait, J.D. 2000. *Stated Choice Methods: Analysis and Application.* Cambridge, U.K.: Cambridge University Press.

Louvière, J. and Timmermans, H. 1990. Stated Preference and Choice Models applied to Recreation Research: A Review. *Leisure Science,* **12**(1): 9–32.

McFadden, D. 1986. The Choice Theory Approach to Market Research. *Marketing Science,* **5**(4): 275–97.

McFadden, D. 2001. Economic Choices. *American Economic Review,* **91**(3): 351–78.

McMullen, J. and Shepherd, D. 2006. Entrepreneurial Action and the Role of Uncertainty in the Theory of the Entrepreneur. *Academy of Management Review,* **31**(1): 132–52.

Mitchell, R., Busenitz, L. Lant, T., McDougall, P., Morse, E. and Smith, J. 2002. Toward a Theory of Entrepreneurial Cognition: Rethinking the People Side of Entrepreneurship Research. *Entrepreneurship Theory and Practice,* **27**(2): 93–104.

Schumpeter, J. 1934. *The Theory of Economic Development.* Cambridge, MA: Harvard University Press.

Shane, S. 2003. *A General Theory of Entrepreneurship The Individual-Opportunity Nexus.* Cheltenham: Edward Elgar.

Shane, S. and Venkataraman, S. 2000. The Promise of Entrepreneurship as a Field of Research. *Academy of Management Review,* **25**(1): 217–26.

Shane, S., Locke, E. and Collins, C. 2003. Entrepreneurial Motivation. *Human Resource Management Review,* **13**(2): 257–79.

Venkataraman, S. 1997. The Distinctive Domain of Entrepreneurship Research: An Editor's Perspective. In Katz, J. and Brockhaus, R. (eds.), *Advances in Entrepreneurship, Firm Emergence and Growth,* **3**: 119–38. Greenwich, CT: JAI Press.

Verma, R. and Plaschka, G. 2005. Predicting Customer Choices, *MIT Sloan Management Review,* **47**(1): 7–10.

Verma, R., Thompson, G. and Louvière, J. 1999. Configuring Service Operations Based on Customer Needs and Preferences. *Journal of Service Research,* **1**(3): 262–74.

Yunus, M. 1998. Poverty Alleviation: Is Economics any help? Lessons from the Grameen Back Experience. *Journal of International Affairs,* **51**(1): 47–65.

Zahra, S., Gedajlovic, E., Neubaum, D. and Shulman, J. 2006. Social Entrepreneurship: Domain, Contributions and Ethical Dilemma. *University of Minnesota Conference on Ethics and Entrepreneurship.*

Appendix 7A New business venture preferences

This section contains 16 tables, each containing two hypothetical new venture opportunities that you may prefer. We would like you to evaluate each set and choose the venture (or neither) in which you would *prefer* to start or launch as a new business.

Please note that there are no right or wrong answers. We are only interested in knowing your venture preferences.

Venture Set No. 1	Option 1	Option 2	
Firm Growth	Growing very fast	Not growing	
Industry Competition	Competing on Price	Competing on Quality	
Technology Profile	Cutting-edge high tech industry	Low/no-tech industry	
Firm Strategy	Defending existing product-markets	Seeking new product-markets	
Funding Strategy	Funded internally— bootstrapping	Funded through external capital	
Economic Sustainability	Seeking strong financial performance	Not placing a high priority on financial performance	
Social Impact	Emphasis on improving some social condition in society (such as the reduction of poverty)	No emphasis on improving some social condition in society (such as the reduction of poverty)	
Environmental Sustainability	Not emphasizing environmental sustainability	Intentionally seeking to be environmentally sustainable	
Competitive Environment	Competitive conditions are changing rapidly	Competitive conditions are stable	Neither?
I would prefer to start this business (choose one)			

8
The Thread of Inchoate Demand in Social Entrepreneurship

Jeffrey G. York, Saras D. Sarasvathy and Andrea Larson

Introduction

> In a new *Time*/ABC/Stanford University poll, 85% of respondents agree that global warming is probably happening. Moreover, most respondents said they want some action taken (*Time*, April 3, 2006).

There is an emerging belief amongst non-profit, environmental and business leaders that social entrepreneurship may present an alternative solution to many of the issues we face. Whether the problem is homelessness (Hibbert et al., 2002), funding for non-profit art organizations (Hughes and Luksetich, 2004), or environmental degradation (Cohen and Winn, 2007), one can find active new ventures led by those labelling themselves as 'social entrepreneurs'. As with the broader field of entrepreneurship, there has been a struggle to define social entrepreneurship and its contribution as a field of study (Venkataraman, 1997). Some scholars have focused on outlining key differences with and similarities to 'traditional' entrepreneurship (Austin et al., 2006; Dees, 1998) and others have focused on the prioritization of a social mission in these organizations (Dees, 1998; Mair and Martí, 2006). Attempts to create a taxonomy delineating non-profit, for profit, and complementary profit models have been advanced (Fowler, 2000). While some have chosen to squarely place social entrepreneurship within the realm of non-profit organizations utilizing traditional business techniques (Zietlow, 2001), others describe social entrepreneurship as crossing non-profit, business and government boundaries (Austin et al., 2006). On the whole, it appears as though the focus of attention is on the 'social' in social entrepreneurship rather than the 'entrepreneurship' that goes into addressing social issues of interest.

From a non-academic perspective, there may be even less focus on the 'entrepreneurship' in social entrepreneurship. Instead, the phrase 'social entrepreneurship' seems to be rapidly becoming a catch-all for anything involving business and a social cause – implying also the troublesome separation thesis that business and social causes are non-overlapping domains to begin with (Freeman, 1994). For those of us who believe that there is something inherently interesting and useful in the application of entrepreneurship to problems outside the conventional realm of for-profit business, an exclusive focus on what social entrepreneurs *are* (profit, non-profit, MBAs, NGO leaders, values-driven, opportunity-driven) is not the best intellectual investment for our efforts. Rather, paying attention to what entrepreneurs actually *do* and how entrepreneurial (as opposed to political or legal) actions affect social issues seems more promising. In this chapter we proceed on the latter premise to examine one recent thread of theorizing that impacts on entrepreneurship research in a significant manner – namely, Geroski's notion of the role of inchoate demand in the creation and evolution of new markets (Geroski, 2003). It turns out that this thread is just as easily and meaningfully woven into phenomena of primary interest to social entrepreneurship researchers.

Organization of this chapter

We begin our analysis with a review of Geroski's theory of market evolution, detailing the journey from inchoate demand to market formation (Geroski, 2003). We then examine four case studies that exemplify this journey, from an industry level to that of a large corporation, a new venture, and an organization founded around the concept of social entrepreneurship. Next, a preliminary multiple-case analysis suggests interesting commonalities, each embodying the transformation of inchoate demand into a dominant design through an entrepreneurial new combination of technologies and resources at hand. We conclude with a discussion of our findings in terms of key theoretical constructs in current entrepreneurship research including Schumpeterian new combinations (Schumpeter, 1942), bricolage (Baker and Nelson, 2005), exaptation (Dew et al., 2004) and principles of an effectual logic (Sarasvathy, 2001).

Two preliminary matters before we proceed:

- Social entrepreneurs as defined in the literature can be understood to be fundamentally concerned with addressing an issue that is of public interest (Austin et al., 2006). Our exposition is in agreement with this baseline definition; however, we do not delineate social entrepreneurship to the realm of non-profit enterprise. Rather, we leverage Venkataraman's (1997: 120) definition of entrepreneurship as *'how opportunities to bring into existence "future" goods and services are discovered, created, and exploited, by whom and with what consequences'* to examine the creation of new markets, in particular, markets that address issues of public interest.

- We take the demand for environmental preservation as a quintessential example of inchoate demand. We proceed on the assumption that no one chooses to buy environmentally damaging products or services for the sake of the adverse ecological impacts they cause; markets simply fail to account for environmental goods (Cohen and Winn, 2007; Dean and McMullen, 2007). Yet, despite their vague belief that we should not engage in environmental degradation, consumers are unable to articulate a specific demand for goods and services that meet this criteria.

Theoretical development

The creation and evolution of new markets – inchoate demand to dominant design

The concept of inchoate demand is not new. The role of ill-formed demand for some societal need has been examined in the realms of law and corporate governance (Mitchell, 2005), national policy development (Fainstein and Fainstein, 1978), international development (Council, 1937), business strategy (Wiltbank et al., 2005), and entrepreneurship (Dew et al., 2004; Sarasvathy and Dew, 2005). The concept of inchoate demand must be differentiated from latent demand. While latent demand describes the unmet, but identifiable of consumers (Earl and Potts, 2000), which Kirznerian entrepreneurs satisfy through their alertness (Kirzner, 1997), inchoate demand is unformed, and thus, is not latent, non-existent in an articulated form. Thus, while latent demand could be brought into clarity through consumers' articulating desire, inchoate demand can be met only through entrepreneurial action to offer a new good or service. Geroski (2003), through an examination of the formative years, what he refers to as the the first 3 minutes of industries ranging from automobiles to telephones to the internet, makes a persuasive argument for the role of inchoate demand in the formation of new markets.

New products emerge from new technologies, and they can be driven by either articulated demand (consumers articulate a clear desire or inchoate vague demand for a solution to a problem) or a supply side push (new scientific knowledge coupled with business folks push a product or service to market). We commonly understand consumer demand to be articulated demand. Geroski (2003: 28), however, argues for the necessity to differentiate articulated from inchoate demand and clearly outlines the basis for such differentiation:

> On the one hand, consumers can have what one might call a 'inchoate' or general demand for things that *meet certain broadly defined types of needs* or perform certain functions; on the other hand they also can have 'articulated' or specific demand for a *particular product with particular characteristics*...An inchoate demand for something exists whenever consumers respond affirmatively to the question: *'wouldn't it be nice (or useful)* if this sort of thing were available?'; an articulated demand exists whenever consumers respond affirmatively to the question: 'would you like to buy this particular thing at that price?'...An inchoate demand for A exists whenever A is the kind of thing that a consumer feels might, in principle, be of some use in some circumstances...
>
> (28–9, emphasis added)

Beyond simply articulating what inchoate demand is, Geroski shows that it is this type of demand with which we must be concerned in exploring the entrepreneurial construction of new goods and services. As he simply states it, 'The demand for products that do not as yet exist cannot be anything other than an inchoate demand. This leaves us with a story that if demand stimulates the kind of innovative activity which leads to the creation of new markets, it is inchoate demand that does the work' (Geroski, 2003: 29).

The puzzle, then, is how demand goes from inchoate to articulate. In Geroski's model most innovation is supply-driven, because consumers do not know what they want most of the time to clearly articulate demand (Geroski, 2003: 57). Inchoate demand sets broad priorities and goals that can serve as guideposts for innovative activity; for example, the emergence of AIDS has created a demand for new drugs that has altered the research agenda of many pharmaceutical companies, although the demand was too general to express the exact drug required (Geroski, 2003: 53). As inchoate demand drives suppliers to innovation, a variety of new goods and services begin to be offered, and demand evolves through the selection process. Rather than viewing new ventures as identifying a gap in the market (Kirzner, 1997), Geroski views them as engaging in an intersubjective process of creating a new market (Davidson, 2001). Most innovation is actually 'pushed' to market from the supply side, creating an almost autonomous process through which consumers and entrepreneurs collectively create a new reality (Sarasvathy and Dew, 2005).

This means that the formation of new markets does not wait for demand to be articulated. A new market begins to be formed when a flood of firms offering a myriad of products comes into existence, all attempting to capitalize on the new innovation and gain 'first mover advantage' (Geroski, 2003: 97). Geroski (2003: 97) describes the early genesis of markets:

> the wave of entry that acts as a vehicle for the new product variants which flood very young markets tends to be the work of a small, highly, non-random sample of the full population of would-be entrepreneurs in the economy. Most of the entrants are from 'near' the new market, guided by individuals who are familiar with the new technology and feel sanguine about its opportunities. This *non-randomly selected* group of individuals seem to appear on the market in a highly *non-random* fashion. In part, the rush of entry that brings most of them to the market in a very short time is driven by the social dynamics associated with the transmission of information... The consequence is that *the race starts before the track has been fully laid out.*
>
> (97, emphasis added)

Two key points in this passage are that early entrants to a new market are non-random; they are driven by a set of beliefs about the nature of inchoate demand in their industry, and generally, are close to the industry. Second, the concept that the market-formation begins without guide rails or even a fully laid track helps us understand the nature of entrepreneurial innovation. There is no conscious choice to discover and exploit an opportunity in many cases; rather, the new firms are creating opportunity by shaping inchoate demand into tangible articulations.

This flood into the new market is self-perpetuating in that the entry by competitors provides a confirming signal to would-be entrepreneurs that there is a genuine opportunity. The key turning point is the emergence of the 'dominant design', a 'consensus good' that is a compromise of all users' needs in an effort to gain the mass market (Geroski, 2003: 111). The establishment of a dominant design invariably leads to a shakeout amongst the firms in the market and the variety of products offered. If a dominant design does not emerge, the new market is unlikely to form in any meaningful way (Geroski, 2003: 142).

An 'S-curve' of demand then forms, with demand sky-rocketing, huge profits made, and wide dissemination of the product. In Figure 8.1, we illustrate this process.

The cycle will begin anew when the leading firms become established and slow to innovate, setting the stage for 'creative destruction' (Geroski, 2003: 187). Thus, the process of new market formation and subsequent destruction continues to foster innovation and new technology.

Geroski's argument is an elegant and clear way to view the phenomenon of new market formation. In the next section we apply Geroski's model to three illustrative examples, starting with his own example of the market for television, proceeding through Toyota's introduction of the Prius Hybrid, and the founding of Method home cleaning products. These cases are not meant to illustrate social entrepreneurship, but to further develop the model of market formation and inchoate demand. We then apply explore the model's implications for social

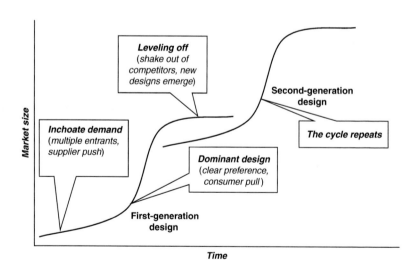

Figure 8.1 The journey from inchoate demand in market formation

entrepreneurship by examining the work of Ashoka, an organization founded 'to shape a citizen sector that is entrepreneurial, productive and globally integrated, and to develop the profession of social entrepreneurship around the world' (Ashoka, 2006). Finally, we discuss the implications of our theory for future research in social entrepreneurship.

Inchoate demand and entrepreneurial action

In this section we further develop and illustrate the concept of inchoate demand through several illustrative examples. The examples move from a purely commercial example (television), to more entrepreneurial ventures that directly address environmental issues (Method Products). We then apply the model to social entrepreneurship through a revelatory case model to social entrepreneurship through a revelatory case study of the work of Ashoka (Yin, 2002).

Television

We use the case of television to illustrate the role of inchoate demand in what now appears a 'traditional' and predominantly 'for-profit' industry.

In 1872, Joseph May, a worker for the Telegraph Construction and Maintenance company of the United Kingdom noticed that the ability of selenium to conduct electricity was impacted on by light (Geroski, 2003). It was quickly realized that his discovery could be used to translate pictures into an electrical current. Most of these subsequent and supplementary inventions were the pet projects of scientists fascinated by the idea of 'seeing by radio'.

There was, however, no public demand for 'seeing by radio' since it simply did not exist, except for the scientific community and the readers of scientific journals (generally not the marketer's target demographic). Early transmissions on the flickering, small screen included such riveting content as pictures of smoke rings, which failed to stoke the fires of public interest (Geroski, 2003).

How then can we explain the emergence of television as the predominant form of entertainment all over the world as articulated demand? As Geroski points out, most consumers at the time were grappling with the newly emerging concept of radio and movie house; conceiving of television was not really on anyone's agenda, other than those innovators like David Sarnoff who had a vision for profits, and scientists who were merely interested in tinkering with technological possibilities. The case for inchoate demand is rooted in one simple fact about human behavior and history: once night falls humans have always looked for ways to entertain themselves.

However, as laid out in Table 8.1, the critical point is that the television industry was not created from the spotting of a gap in consumers' lives, but by addressing an inchoate demand (the need for information and entertainment in the home) through a new combination (transmission of images through electrical current) that led to the emergence of a dominant design (the ubiquitous screen in a box with open standards of broadcasting). Table 8.1 shows similar transformations in the next three cases, each of which more directly and explicitly involved the development of solutions to environmental problems.

Table 8.1 Translating inchoate demand into dominant design

	Inchoate demand	Innovative new combination	Dominant design
Television Industry	• Information and entertainment available at home	• Transmission of pictures through electrical current	• Open broadcast standard • Glass screen • Multiple channels • Advertising
Toyota Prius	• Would be nice to be able to have the advantages of a car without contributing to global warming	• Integrate reduced emissions with new car design that advertises the owners commitment	• Hybrid engine drive train dominates market and is purchased by competitors
Method Home Products	• Don't want poisons in the home	• Toxin-free chemical compositions coupled with pleasing design aesthetic	• Household cleaning products easily available in major retailers without toxic components
New Youth Village Welfare Association	• Need to have water during droughts	• Combine cultural beliefs about water with effective irrigation systems independent from government	• Community based, self-sufficient resource management networks

Overlapping Considerations	• Demand could not be clearly articulated into a specific product or service
	• Entrepreneurs created a new combination that would enable a solution by taking action even in the absence of articulated demand.
	• Because the solutions overcame tradeoffs and provided synergies between seemingly conflicting values and preferences, consumers supported the solution that then grew into the dominant design
	• Elements of entrepreneurial action, such as new combinations, bricolage, exaptation and effectuation were present in the process of transforming inchoate demand into dominant design

Toyota Prius

In late 2005, Toyota Motor Company, Japan's largest company and the world's second largest auto manufacturer, announced that global sales of its hybrid vehicles had topped the 500,000 mark (Larson and O'Brien, forthcoming). Earlier, Toyota had estimated that it would sell only 47,000 of its Prius hybrid cars that year – but sales were booming as Prius spent less time in dealership lots (measured in hours, not days) than any other car in the US. To be sure, total hybrid global sales in 2005 could be dismissed as insignificant when compared with sales of the combined Toyota and Lexus brands (6.11 million units from January to September 2005). However, Toyota had clearly created a new market for hybrid vehicles, selling close to 200,000 hybrid vehicles in 2006 (Woodyard, 2006).

For Toyota in the 1990s, taking an environmental perspective on its strategic options revealed the following cases of inchoate demand: in addition to universal industry concern for product quality and cost, there was rising public anxiety about climate change, local air pollution, and concern about dependence on foreign sources of oil. In Table 8.1, we highlight how Toyota's engineering innovation translated the public's concerns about environmental issues into a predominant design within the industry.

When the hybrid first appeared at US auto shows it was received like any other 'concept car' – a sci-fi toy, something interesting we might move towards in the future; but as a technology to put head-to-head with the conventional automobile, the hybrid was largely dismissed as unpractical. Besides, Americans were buying SUVs and Hummers, gas was cheap, and fuel standards were for sissies.

But then came the war in the Persian Gulf, Hurricane Katrina and the rising specter of China's growing demand for oil. And as the price of petroleum lurched upwards, the hybrid car began to appeal to a wider segment of global buyers. In 2005, if you were an auto company that did not make a hybrid, you were at risk of losing serious market share.

It cannot be argued that Toyota catered to existing articulated demand when it first introduced the hybrid, for Toyota's own estimate of the demand was much smaller than what the market actually turned out to be. The most plausible conclusion, therefore, is that Toyota's hybrid engine was designed in response to inchoate demand; and by not sacrificing convenience or performance it has become the dominant design in whole new market for environmentally friendly automobiles.

The Prius story does not provide us with an example of social entrepreneurship as it is commonly understood, since it stemmed from the actions of an established, publicly held for-profit corporation; but it again illustrates that the journey from inchoate demand to dominant design can have a *social* as well as *economic* impact. The same journey is undertaken by smaller new ventures when they successfully introduce products that move an industry towards greater environmental awareness. Method Home Products is one such company.

Method home products

No one would consciously choose to clean their home with products that are linked with increased cancer rates, pollution of water supplies and toxic chemicals that can be deadly if consumed in more than miniscule amounts. Yet this would describe the choice that consumers make every day on the aisles of grocery stores around the world. Since the publication of Rachel Carson's book *Silent Spring,* there has been inchoate demand for environmental and health-friendly cleaning. However, because the available products were hard to get, they were distributed through odd, 'hippie' health food stores or simply did not work well – no dominant design had emerged (Carson et al., 2003). For example, while Ecover brand cleaning products was begun in 1980, the innovative Belgian company's products remain widely unavailable to most US consumers, available only through specialty retailers such as Whole Foods Markets.

Method Home Products Inc. (Method) was founded on the notion of using formulas that emphasized *both* the environmental and economic aspects of household cleaners (Clifford, 2006). Because there was inchoate, but not articulated, demand for these products, the founders of Method were able to exploit the inaction by larger, established firms to engage in the necessary research to formulate safe and effective cleaning products. Method founders Adam Lowry and Eric Ryan saw the size of the cleaning products industry as an advantage that would allow them to push a new design into the market.

'You have all your domestic experiences in that house or wherever you live,' Adam Lowry explains (York, 2007). 'And so from the furniture you buy to your kitchenware, you put a lot of thought and emotion into what you put in that space. Yet the commodity products that you use to maintain this very important space tend to be uninteresting, ugly, and toxic – and you hide them away. Why did that have to be?' (York, 2007; see StartupNation.com, 2005). Lowry and Ryan decided to take the opposite approach; if they could create products that were harmless to humans and the natural environment, attractively designed with interesting colors and aromas, they could disrupt an industry populated with dinosaurs (York, 2007). By differentiating themselves from the competition in a significant and meaningful way, Lowry and Ryan hoped to offer an attractive alternative that also had a positive environmental impact. 'It's green clean for the mainstream,' says Lowry, 'which wouldn't happen if it wasn't cool' (York, 2007).

To make green cool, Method took a two-pronged approach. First, they formulated new product mixtures that performed as well as leading brands while minimizing environmental and health impacts. With a degree in chemical engineering from Stanford, and experience researching 'green' plastics at a climate-change think-tank, Adam Lowry saw these issues as opportunities.

'I knew as a chemical engineer that there was no reason we couldn't design products that were non-toxic and used natural ingredients,' he said (York, 2007). 'It would be more expensive to do it that way. But that was okay as long as we created a brand that had a "premiumness" about it, where our margins would support our extra investments in product development and high quality ingredients' (York, 2007).

The second prong of Method's attack on the entrenched cleaning products industry was to utilize design and brand to appeal to consumers tired of the same old products. In an industry rife with destructive price competition, Method realized the new product would have to be different. He believed that the competition was so focused on price that 'They weren't able to invest in fragrance or interesting packaging or design,' Lowry explains, 'Our idea was to turn that reality on its head and come up with products that absolutely could connect with the emotion of the home. We wanted to make these products more like "home accessories." We believed there was an opportunity to really reinvent, and in the end, change the competitive landscape' (York, 2007). By focusing their marketing and packaging as the solution 'against dirty' they tapped into consumers' disquiet with the ingredients in their household cleaners, and the inchoate demand for an alternative.

In bringing together chemical engineers, cutting-edge designers and the nationwide distribution power of Target and Home Depot stores, the founding team brought disparate resources to bear to create a new market place (Larson et al., forthcoming). Consumers could now purchase readily available, attractive and effective environmentally sound cleaners. By 2007 the company had 45 employees and annual revenues of over USD 40 million (Clifford, 2006). The inchoate demand for environmentally friendly cleaners was transformed into a well-defined market through entrepreneurial action that *combined* economics and eco-sensitivity – and did not trade them off. This is reminiscent of Toyota's not trading off fuel efficiency against consumer considerations of cost and performance in automobiles. Through entrepreneurial actions, socially focused ventures not only generate new socially valuable options, but also provide new information to society regarding costs and benefits of solutions, thereby allowing products with more synergies to win over those with more tradeoffs of benefits that consumers value. In the case of Method, the small company's success has demonstrated that consumers will pay a premium for more ecologically sound cleaning products, *if* they are marketed and distributed effectively. This has created a new way for producers to define and interpret the category and for consumers to change their perceptions and preferences over the effectiveness of different types of products. As illustrated in Table 8.1, the new combination of improved technology and distribution with standard functionality and ease of use in the customer value chain has created a new market of environmental home cleaning products readily accessible to most consumers.

Both Toyota and Method exemplify entrepreneurial action, with a broader focus on environmental issues, in the for-profit realm. Next we turn to a demonstration of the same process in a non-profit setting. Our aim here is to simply trace common elements involved in the transformation of inchoate demand for environmental friendliness into articulated demand for a variety of new products and services.

The role of inchoate demand at Ashoka

Methods

To better understand the role of inchoate demand in social entrepreneurship, we developed a revelatory case study (Yin, 2002) on the activities of Ashoka, an organization founded 'to develop the profession of social entrepreneurship around the world' (Ashoka, 2006). The study employed an embedded design, in which analysis occurs at two levels.

We first analyzed an existing, publicly available case study of an Ashoka fellow's work; thus the first level of analysis is around the work of a social entrepreneur receiving support from Ashoka. Second, we looked at the activities of Ashoka in developing its relationship with financial institutions; thus, the second level of analysis occurs at the organizational level. We believe that this allows us to see the role of inchoate demand as a driver of social entrepreneurship when addressing tactical, local issues, as well as when addressing larger societal and institutional change. While not intended to be a comprehensive study, we believe it provides us with initial grounding for understanding social entrepreneurship as a process of transforming inchoate demand into a dominant design.

Our study is based on three data sources: (1) a series of interviews with Arthur Wood, Vice President of Social Financial Services at Ashoka, (2) a site visit to Ashoka's North American offices, (3) secondary sources such as videos, reports, and websites developed by Ashoka.

Background

Ashoka was founded in 1980 by Bill Drayton, who was recently named by US News as one of America's top 25 leaders. While working as a McKinsey fellow, following a stint as Assistant Administrator of the US Environmental Protection Agency, Drayton noticed that ordinary people had found local solutions to a variety of social problems such as poverty, illiteracy, and so on. But they could not scale up these ventures without adequate capital or at least a fighting chance to grow the venture without endangering the basic economic well-being of their families. Drayton formulated a solution in the form of Ashoka. The inchoate focus of his new venture was to 'give identity to the philosophy of entrepreneurship'. In concrete terms, Ashoka awards fellows a three-year living wage stipend to assist them in founding social ventures. To date, Ashoka has funded over 2000 Fellows in 63 countries. Of these, approximately 300 have value propositions that directly address environmental degradation.

Water warriors of Laporiya

In Rajasthan, a drought-prone state situated at the edge of the Thar Desert of western India, the effects of changes in the natural environment were being felt as early as the 1970s. Water shortages had led to a barren landscape without enough water for drinking and bathing needs, much less irrigation. Laxman Singh is a citizen of Laporiya, a village that was 'on the edge of starvation' (Ashoka Case Study, 2006). Singh decided there was a better way to manage the fortunes of his village than to rely on the government-run public water supply system, and left his university studies to pursue the idea. By appealing to the villagers' cultural beliefs in community and reverence for water, he educated and mobilized thousands in an effort to rebuild and augment the village's water supply system. Through rebuilding embankments, re-silting ponds and constructing new irrigation channels, Singh and his 'Water Warriors', youth volunteers recruited from a variety of villages, reversed the environmental degradation of the desert village and established a thriving agricultural economy. His organization, the New Youth Village Welfare Association, has grown from a local volunteer effort to over 40 employees and 8000 volunteers with an annual budget of USD 93,000. Their practices have spread across the region, providing a lush natural environment for local animals while improving the lives of thousands of families. The case study on which this example of an Ashoka fellow in action was based may be viewed at http://www.ashoka.org/casestudies.

In what ways was Laxman Singh acting as an entrepreneur? Current entrepreneurship theories do provide useful explanations. For example, we could argue that Singh was alert to an opportunity that others missed (Kirzner, 1979) and acted in an innovative way, fostering the creative destruction of the government water supply monopoly (Schumpeter, 1942). In leaving formal education, he took upon himself a variety of risks and even uncodifiable uncertainties, where others would not (Knight, 1921). It is easy to see that the relevant question here does not really seem to be whether Singh is an entrepreneur, but rather *why* and *how* Singh came to target his efforts against the social and environmental issues faced by his village. And why did he not turn to political campaigns and governmental action, which, in the Indian context, is a more 'normal' path to pursue in dealing with social issues? The fact remains that Singh seized upon an inchoate demand for reversing environmental degradation without sacrificing the water needs of the villagers and proceeded to solve the problem in an entrepreneurial fashion. Whether he was motivated by altruism or a desire for self-fulfilled satisfaction, his actions created both economic value and environmental solutions for his consumers, as did the Toyota Prius and Method Home Products.

We believe the process of moving from inchoate demand to dominant design can be seen in Singh's story as clearly as in the evolution of the market for hybrid cars or environmentally friendly cleaners. Singh's venture worked for reasons he could not have predicted, just as Toyota and Detroit could not very well predict the success of the Prius. In Singh's own words:

> When I started going out on my own with a spade and shovel to repair the only existing talaab (tank), which had been breached, people joined me because they felt beholden to help their Raja (King). When I started repairing the talaab, the villagers thought it was blasphemy that I should be doing this menial work, but I welcomed it. The numbers gradually swelled until the entire village was involved. Caste system lines have also blurred due to this culture of volunteerism and a common goal.
>
> (Ashoka Case Study, 2006: 3)

Singh's actions were *entrepreneurial* in the sense in which Sarasvathy (2001) describes *effectual* action. Singh's very first action was to get his friend and the village priest to take up shovels and assist him in repairing the embankment. He then began to recruit other members of the village into implementing his idea; he built an initial small stakeholder group based simply on his relationship to other villagers. Through their actions, working to rebuild the embankment surrounding the village's pond, they brought in more volunteers, doubling in size in less than a month. By starting with his own cultural knowledge and history with the village, and looking for simple steps towards what could be accomplished, Singh demonstrated the supply side push to address inchoate demand. Yearly droughts had already created inchoate demand for better access to water. But the village had not articulated a way to fulfill the demand, especially through an environmentally friendly solution. Singh's *actions* moved others to act, and the spread of those actions ended up creating the vision for and implementation of an environmentally friendly solution to the water problem that combined a variety of readily available technologies.

Although it was not his original intention, the network of Singh's organization grew into a new market a comprehensive process of community-based natural resource management. His techniques, now the dominant design for resolving water shortages in the region, including innovations in irrigation techniques, integration of respect and worship for natural resources with local customs, and leveraging urban youth as volunteers, have been adopted by over 90 other villages and have benefited as many as 42,000 families (Ashoka Case Study, 2006). We present this case study not as the final word in how social entrepreneurship happens, but as an existence proof of how it *could* happen as a process that transforms inchoate demand into dominant design through the application of innovative technology, as laid out in Table 8.1.

An incomplete journey – creating a dominant design of social entrepreneurship

Ashoka is creating new institutions through its efforts to correct inefficiency in the flow of capital to social entrepreneurs. An example is structuring distribution network for capital. Another is to engage major financial institutions to invest in the social sector. This is the focus of the Social Financial Services area of Ashoka, but not on a philanthropic basis. Instead, the organization is seeking to leverage the inchoate demand amongst the fragmented market of donors for a way to directly invest in social change. Arthur Wood describes the problem:

> Why are we doing this? From a funding perspective, one thing investors are very aware of is that there are 1.4 million 503c3s [tax-exempt organizations] in the United States alone. The problem with that is that it is an incredibly fragmented market; how do you know what is best practice on any particular area? The social capital market in the United States alone is $1.3 trillion dollars, but the shocking statistic is that only 3.8% of [503c3s] have revenues of larger than $10 million. So there is a capital market roughly the size of Spain or Italy, but that 3.8% includes universities and hospitals. That tells you that on the cutting edge of social issues, these organizations are incredibly fragmented.
>
> (Wood, A., interview, 2006)

This fragmentation is one cause of the inefficiency of the social sector; another is the lack diverse ways for donors to dedicate funds. Wood characterized the current social investment market as a range of 100% loss, grants and donations, and 5 to 6% traditional investment rates of return. 'I'm pretty appalling at math, but even I know that between minus 100 and plus 5 there is a range of positions on the graph,' he explained. 'Intuitively you know that economic efficiency is in that range, but we (the social sector) don't tend to look at it like that' (Wood, A., interview, 2006).

Thus, the current status of the social sector, from Ashoka's perspective, represents inefficiency and market failure. The organization began with harnessing the power of social entrepreneurship, but it has now evolved beyond that mission to address the institutional issues intrinsic within the classification of 'profit' and 'non-profit' enterprises. We can see that in this early stage, Ashoka is pushing to bring a new perception of philanthropy to the market place, not in response to a clear demand for 'social venturing', but based the belief that there is simply a better way to engage in social change. Wood described this belief as influencing Ashoka's strategy:

If you think of your private life there is a huge plethora of financial instruments. A paradox to the social market is that we know there are two players that will happily secure minus 100% investments in the market; they are high-net-worth individuals and super nationals.

(Wood, A., interview, 2006)

Ashoka is moving to evolve institutions of philanthropy on the belief that the current private donation and state solutions are not delivering the 100% premium. 'If you look at the effectiveness of social entrepreneurship, 80% of our Fellows are still doing this 5–10 years out, 50–60% of them have changed national policy, and 60% of them have had their ideas replicated. This (the replication) is very important and why we argue that social entrepreneurship is more effective than microfinance, because while microfinance is a one-off investment, social entrepreneurship is a long-term investment,' Wood said (Wood, A., interview, 2006).

Another point of evolution in the design of social venturing is around the description of social enterprises as 'non-profit'. Wood explains:

We have the firm view that what the citizen sector shouldn't do, and we very consciously use the phrase citizen sector, is to define what our sector does, which is huge, but what we *don't* do. The fact that we don't make a profit is not the most positive element to project what we do. We are trying to move away from this idea that we are defined by a unit of the tax code (non-profit) as opposed to saying 'How do you make a mission socially effective and targeted'.

(Wood, A., interview, 2006)

Because of this goal, a large part of Ashoka's mission has evolved into engaging major financial institutions to invest in social entrepreneurship. 'We believe the social sector represents the next great market after the middle-classes of China and India that everyone is so excited about at the moment,' Wood said, 'It's based on pure economics. What you've seen is a massive growth of these citizen organizations that gives you distribution into particular markets. On the social financial services side, what we seek to do is to engage major financial institutions to invest in this sector, not on the grounds of philanthropy, not on the grounds of CSR, but that there is a substantive business opportunity for them to make money' (Wood, A., interview, 2006).

'Why are we doing this? First of all the sector is huge, and the margins from a banker's perspective are around 40% right now. That ignores the opportunity cost of using senior management's time to actually try to raise money. So that frictional cost is even higher' (Wood, A., interview, 2006).

Ashoka is working to build sustainable, empowering social enterprise at a variety of levels other than the financial markets. As such, they are one group working to push a particular design, social venturing, to the marketplace. We can see that the inchoate demand for better tools for social changes has manifested itself in Ashoka's innovative approach, a combination of traditional venture capital with investment in social causes, but we cannot yet see if it will emerge as a dominant design.

Discussion and conclusion

We have found an interesting alignment between Geroski's work on the evolution of markets and a variety of examples from social entrepreneurship. We know that social problems occur as a result of a number of reasons. Within the current literature on social entrepreneurship, social issues are commonly viewed as market failure (Austin et al., 2006; Cohen and Winn, 2007). Our view is consistent with the Austrian school's view of market failures as drivers of entrepreneurial opportunities, and entrepreneurs as alert individuals in possession of knowledge of such market failures (Kirzner, 1979). However, by viewing the resolution of market failure as an opportunity for the *creation* of new of new products and services, we can focus on the *entrepreneurship* in social entrepreneurship.

Social issues create an opportunity for entrepreneurs, but only *ex-post* – the opportunity becomes real only when the dominant design actually comes to be. Understanding that there are social issues that need to be resolved is not enough; entrepreneurs have to *act* on inchoate demand to transform it into Geroski's 'first three minutes'. Everybody knows there is inchoate demand; everybody would like a cleaner environment and would want to see these market failures addressed, but what transforms these intuitions into Kirznerian opportunities for new markets is the *articulation* of the demand for particular products and services that consumers want to purchase and invest monetary or other resources in.

In sum, our multiple case analysis points to the efficacy of modeling the creation of new markets as an entrepreneurial process that transforms inchoate demand into a dominant design. However, the findings also point to several interesting overlaps with key ideas in current entrepreneurship research as well possible avenues for future work.

As a first step, we suggest more in-depth investigations into each of the cases above combined with more 'thick' descriptions of each step in the transformational process. Our analysis has necessarily been preliminary – a sort of 'existence proof' of the role of inchoate demand in driving some valuable new markets, especially within the domain of environmental issues. Such in-depth investigations would enable the development of tighter conceptual links between the qualitative data and several constructs of theoretical interest in entrepreneurship research that can provide 'legs' to the process of transforming inchoate demand into new markets. We see at least four potential candidates for such theoretical 'legs':

Schumpeterian New Combinations. The concept of applying new technology to existing products could explain the innovation journey required for dominant design. The Prius example shows the development of a new engine that was applied to an existing paradigm for basic car structure (Larson et al., forthcoming). The recurring waves of 'creative destruction' could be the sign that the current dominant design has overstayed it's welcome, as well as signaling the convergence of preferences for one design in the early evolution of markets, when multiple designs compete (Schumpeter, 1942).

Bricolage Processes. Bricolage refers to a problem-solving method using resources readily available, rather than setting out on a quest to seek new resources. Baker and Nelson describe the bricolage process as 'providing products and services that would otherwise be unavailable', thus creating products and markets where none existed (Baker and Nelson, 2005). How does bricolage help tap into inchoate demand to create new products and services in the social sector? Bricolage could be in an important technique in the social entrepreneur's arsenal as they engage in the process of building dominant designs. Laxman Singh's reliance on history and religious belief to motivate his 'water' could perhaps be modeled as an act of bricolage.

Exaptation. Exaptation, using things for which they were not originally designed, provides a specific explanatory mechanism in the evolution of new industries such as television (Dew et al., 2004). But exaptation could also be a potent explanation in the market for environmental solutions. Recycling, broadly construed, embodies the notion of putting things developed for one purpose to use in new ways. Designing coasters out of used compact discs can best be modeled as an exaptation rather than as a new combination or bricolage or conventional techniques of adaptation.

Effectual Logic. It is also possible to model the development of new ventures such as Method Home Products as the application an *effectual* logic to the problem of environmentally friendly cleaning products. (Sarasvathy, 2001). Effectual logic is best understood in contrast with the traditional, causal logic of entrepreneurship in which the entrepreneur gathers data on the relevant markets, engages in segmentation, and designs products to fit the needs of the selected segment. This obviously is inapplicable in the face of inchoate demand. Instead, an effectual entrepreneur who is not as concerned with predicting the future and prefers strategies of non-predictive control may have an advantage. Effectual entrepreneurs are willing to move into an undefined marketplace and to take an active role in its formation. In fact, effectual logic entails a dynamic process that spells out the creation of new markets that is almost immediately applicable to the transformation of inchoate demand into dominant design (Sarasvathy and Dew, 2005).

A further implication of our research, and the findings of overlap between the drivers of commercial ventures and the work of an organization like Ashoka, is that we may be supporting what Freeman terms the 'Separation Thesis' between business and ethics which holds that the 'discourse of business and the discourse of ethics can be separated so that sentences like "x is a business decision" have no moral content and "x is a moral decision" have no business content' (Freeman, 1994). We do not believe it is possible to delineate between the social and private mission of entrepreneurial endeavors. Inspired by Arthur Wood's rejection of the term 'non-profit' to describe Ashoka, in this chapter we have chosen to focus on the role of ethical, environmental consideration in the working of for-profit businesses, as well as in the work of Ashoka.

When we separate 'social entrepreneurship' away from the core of 'how opportunities to bring into existence "future" goods and services are discovered, created, and exploited, by whom and with what consequences' (Venkataraman, 1997: 120) are we implying that entrepreneurship is anti-social? Or, that entrepreneurship is generally bereft of social concerns? Our model offers a general way to understand the genesis of entrepreneurial ventures, and helps us understand how entrepreneurs can leverage the inchoate demand for a social good into creating products and services that enhance our ability to live.

We set out on this study with a view to focus scholarly attention on the 'entrepreneurship' in 'social entrepreneurship'. By focusing on what social entrepreneurs *do* rather than on what social entrepreneurship *is,* we have taken an important step in showing that social entrepreneurship is indeed *entrepreneurship.* But perhaps we would like to conclude with the more provocative argument that our analysis has also provided good evidence for the proposition that *all* entrepreneurship is, intentionally or otherwise, *social.*

References

Ashoka. 2006. http://www.ashoka.org (accessed on May 2010).

Ashoka Case Study. 2006. Environmental Innovations Initiative Case Studies: Laxman Singh and the Water Warriors of Laporiya. Available at: http://www.ashoka.org/casestudies (last visited May 2010).

Austin, J., Stevenson, H. and Wei-Skillern, J. 2006. Social and Commercial Entrepreneurship: Same, Different, or Both? *Entrepreneurship Theory and Practice,* **30**(1): 1–22.

Baker, T. and Nelson, R. 2005. Creating Something from Nothing: Resource Construction through Entrepreneurial Bricolage. *Administrative Science Quarterly,* **50**(3): 329–66.

Carson, R., Lear, L. and Wilson, E. O. 2003. *Silent Spring* (40th ed.). Boston: Houghton Mifflin.

Clifford, S. 2006. Running through the Legs of Goliath. *Inc,* **28**(2): 102–09.

Cohen, B. and Winn, M. I. 2007. Market Imperfections, Opportunity and Sustainable Entrepreneurship. *Journal of Business Venturing,* **22**(1): 29–49.

Council, T. S. A. 1937. Economic Preparedness in China and Japan. *Far Eastern Survey,* **6**(21): 235–46.

Davidson, D. 2001. *Subjective, Intersubjective, Objective.* New York and Melbourne: Oxford University Press.

Dean, T. J. and McMullen, J. S. 2007. Toward a Theory of Sustainable Entrepreneurship: Reducing Environmental Degradation through Entrepreneurial Action. *Journal of Business Venturing,* **22**(1): 50–76.

Dees, J. G. 1998. The Meaning of Social Entrepreneurship. Fuqua School of Business, Duke University, Center for the Advancement of Social Entrepreneurship (CASE), Durham, NC, 1–6.

Dew, N., Sarasvathy, S. D. and Venkataraman, S. 2004. The Economic Implications of Exaptation. *Journal of Evolutionary Economics,* **14**(1): 69–84.

Earl, P. E. and Potts, J. 2000. Latent Demand and the Browsing Shopper. *Managerial and Decision Economics,* **21**(3–4): 111–22.

Fainstein, S. S. and Fainstein, N. I. 1978. National Policy and Urban Development. *Social Problems,* **26**(2): 125–46.

Fowler, A. 2000. NGDOs as a Moment in History: Beyond Aid to Social Entrepreneurship or Civic Innovation? *Third World Quarterly*, **21**(4): 637–54.

Freeman, R. E. 1994. The Politics of Stakeholder Theory: Some Future Directions. *Business Ethics Quarterly*, **4**(4): 409–21.

Geroski, P. 2003. *The Evolution of New Markets*. Oxford: Oxford University Press.

Hibbert, S. A., Hogg, G. and Quinn, T. 2002. Consumer response to Social Entrepreneurship: The Case of the Big Issue in Scotland. *International Journal of Nonprofit and Voluntary Sector Marketing*, **7**(3): 288–301.

Hughes, P. and Luksetich, W. 2004. Nonprofit Arts Organizations: Do Funding Sources Influence Spending Patterns? *Nonprofit and Voluntary Sector Quarterly*, **33**(2): 203–20.

Kirzner, I. M. 1979. *Perception, Opportunity, and Profit*. Chicago, IL: University of Chicago Press.

Kirzner, I. M. 1997. Entrepreneurial Discovery and the Competitive Market Process: An Austrian Approach. *Journal of Economic Literature*, **35**(1): 60–85.

Knight, F. H. 1921. *Risk, Uncertainty and Profit* (Reprint ed.). Chevy Chase: Beard Books.

Larson, A. and O'Brien, K. Unpublished manuscript. Headwaters Strategy – Beyond Green Business Strategy.

Mair, J. and Martí, I. 2006. Social Entrepreneurship Research: A Source Of Explanation, Prediction, And Delight. *Journal Of World Business*, **41**(1): 36–44.

Mitchell, L. E. 2005. Structural Holes, CEOs, and Informational Monopolies: The Missing Link in Corporate Governance. *Brooklyn Law Review*, **70**(4): 1313.

Sarasvathy, S. D. 2001. Causation and Effectuation: Toward a Theoretical Shift from Economic Inevitability to Entrepreneurial Contingency. *Academy of Management. The Academy of Management Review*, **26**(2): 243–63.

Sarasvathy, S. D. and Dew, N. 2005. New Market Creation through Transformation. *Journal of Evolutionary Economics*, **15**(5): 533–65.

Schumpeter, J. A. 1942. *Capitalism, Socialism and Democracy* (6th ed.). Abingdon and South Yarra: Routledge and Palgrave Macmillan.

StartupNation.com. 2005. Taking a Fresh Look at an Old Product Category: Adam Lowry's Key Move.

Venkataraman, S. 1997. The Distinctive Domain of Entrepreneurship Research: An Editor's Perspective. In Katz, J. and Brockhaus, R. (eds), *Advances in Entrepreneurship, Firm Emergence, and Growth*, **3**: 119–38. Greenwich, CT: JAI Press.

Wiltbank, R., Dew, N., Sarasvathy, S. and Read, S. 2005. What to Do Next? The Case for Non-Predictive Strategy. *Strategic Management Journal*, **27**(10): 981–98.

Woodyard, C. 2006. Prius Finally Available without a Wait, www.usatoday.com. (accessed on 5 November 2006).

Yin, R. K. 2002. *Case Study Research: Design and Methods* (3rd ed.). Thousand Oaks, CA: SAGE.

York, J. G. 2007. Method: Sustainable Design for the Home as Corporate Strategy. Darden Business Publishing Case. Available at https://store.darden.virginia.edu/business-case-study/method-sustainable-design-for-the-home-as-corporate-strategy-191.

Zietlow, J. T. 2001. Social Entrepreneurship Managerial, Finance and Marketing Aspects. *Journal of Nonprofit and Public Sector Marketing*, **9**(1/2): 19–25.

Part III

Modelling the Social Venturing Process

9
Developing an Interactive Model of Social Entrepreneurship

Francesco Perrini and Clodia Vurro

Introduction

Social entrepreneurship (SE) has emerged as an important field of inquiry, spanning boundary lines across different disciplines, from social issues in management to entrepreneurship and strategic management. Over time, research and public policy-makers have come to believe that SE offers creative and innovative solutions to complex and persistent social problems through the adoption and implementation of entrepreneurial models of new venture creation.

Along with the growing interest in social entrepreneurship phenomenon per se, research and practice are still wondering how the overall development of the social sectors and their impact in terms of, with an social change can be fostered in concrete terms. In fact, despite widespread cross-boundary ferment, theoretical and empirical studies on entrepreneurial organizations specifically conceived to deal with complex social problems in an entrepreneurial way are still not in agreement about the definition of social entrepreneurship, the boundaries of its domain and what it hopes to achieve (Austin et al., 2006), mainly because it has been characterized by numerous manifestations across and within diverse social contexts, and by interests from very diverse research fields, from management to economics, from non-profit to public administration. As a result, social entrepreneurship is now at a promising stage of infancy, short on theory and definition but long on motivation and excitement about its potential.

Overall, although different in the way they define and analyze social entrepreneurship, extant contributions seem to converge on a view of social entrepreneurship as not limited to a particular empirical domain or to the well-established dichotomy between non-profit and for-profit organizations. Rather, what allows distinguishing the boundaries of social entrepreneurship is its focus on a different set of possibilities: innovative ways to initiate, create or sustain social change, prioritizing social value creation over economic value accumulation (Mair and Martì, 2006). Social entrepreneurship entails the integration of entrepreneurship and innovation in developing, and taking actions designed purposefully to stimulate a change in societal patterns starting from the identification of social disequilibria, namely a social opportunity. Born out of unsatisfied social needs, social entrepreneurial opportunities can result in new goods and services, organizing methods, markets or institutions to alleviate a defined social problem. However, the decision to exploit a social entrepreneurial opportunity is not tied exclusively to the expected value of its entrepreneurial profit, but, rather, to its potential to maximize social change and the improvement of social conditions – that is, the expected social value (Perrini, 2006). Thus, a realm of possibility results from a comparative assessment of its expected social value *versus* the economic viability of the overall project in terms of required resources, timing and alternatives.

Starting from these premises, this chapter explores how social entrepreneurial opportunities for creating 'future' social goods and services are discovered, developed and exploited. Our goal is to develop an interactive model of social entrepreneurship to guide future research in this field.

The material is organized as follows. First, we identify the roots of the debate on social entrepreneurship, reframing extant literature. Second, we define the domain of the social entrepreneurship construct. Third, we exploit the social entrepreneurship construct by looking at the main ways in which social entrepreneurship varies. Finally, we provide implications for future research.

The roots of an ongoing debate

The heterogeneity across and within diverse social contexts, the development of academic contributions within different domains (Weerawardena and Sullivan Mort, 2006) and the ambiguity implicit in the words 'social' and 'entrepreneurship' (Amit et al., 1993; Mair and Martì, 2006; Peredo and McLean, 2006; Shane and Venkataraman, 2000) have raised awareness about the opportunities of acting entrepreneurially within the social sectors, at the same time as blurring general understanding of the boundaries of social entrepreneurship.

To date, two parallel streams of research emerge from the analysis of the current literature in this field (Perrini, 2006): the *narrow view* and the *extended view* of social entrepreneurship. The first groups SE with the theories on the non-profit sector and organizations (Boschee, 1998; Cannon, 2000; Dart, 2004; Dees and Elias, 1998), with the accent on *entrepreneurism* as the shift of managerial competencies and market-based attitudes to non-profits in order to improve their operational efficiency and effectiveness. To explain further, rising costs, more competition for fewer donations and grants and increased rivalry from for-profit companies entering the social sector have fostered rivalry within the non-profit sector, compelling existing organizations to experiment with cautious management practices and new funding strategies (Newman and Wallender, 1978). To summarize: the narrow view of social entrepreneurship sees it as a non-profit, rational and strategically better response to a changed and challenged macro-situation resulting from the breakdown of welfare systems, increased financial pressure, increased costs in many areas of social sectors and decreased public and private grants and donations.

The extended view of social entrepreneurship, by contrast, considers SE to be a totally new, intersectorial field of research and application. In this interpretation, social entrepreneurship is not a matter of legal form – distinguishing simply among non-profits, for-profits and public sector organizations; rather, entrepreneurship, innovation, venturing and social orientation represent the basic ingredients of the social entrepreneurship 'formula' for alleviating social problems and catalyzing social transformation (Austin et al., 2006; Henton et al., 1997; Mair and Martì, 2006; Perrini, 2006; Thompson et al., 2000).

In an attempt to give autonomy to the overall discipline and prove the necessity of a new classification, most studies belonging to this view aim to identify the distinguishing traits of social entrepreneurship, starting from an understanding of what 'social entrepreneurship' implies and how it differs from business entrepreneurship. Accordingly, while the supremacy of social value creation is the distinctive feature of social entrepreneurship, explaining its 'S' dimension in the expression, the recognition of opportunities to create that value, the ability to take advantage of them, and the pressure to innovate explain the association with entrepreneurship (Peredo and McLean, 2006; Sullivan Mort et al., 2003; Weerawardena and Sullivan Mort, 2006) and underlie the 'E' dimension of the concept.

Social entrepreneurship research: setting boundaries

Overall, the literature pertaining to the narrow perspective on social entrepreneurship does not prove the necessity of a new classification.

If social entrepreneurship was considered a mere innovation within the non-profit sector, its innovativeness in dealing with complex social problems would not be considered (Johnson, 2000), and it would qualify simply as a process used by non-profits to become more businesslike. In other words, there tends to be little reflection on the notion of entrepreneurship and the potential for new meanings to surface. On the other hand, while authors who argue for the extended view of social entrepreneurship appear to understand the entrepreneurial nature of social entrepreneurship and its strong links to opportunity exploitation, self-sufficiency, and innovation, we believe this literature has not gone far enough in clarifying a clear, direct, and comprehensive definition of social entrepreneurship.

Although we believe that the diversity of social entrepreneurial phenomena should be taken into account in modeling social entrepreneurship, we argue that conceptualization is more than necessary in this phase of boundary-setting. Moreover, current research on the social entrepreneurship phenomenon has focused mainly on unitary dimensions – for example, preliminary or descriptive studies of social entrepreneurial opportunities, social entrepreneurs' characteristics, and types of social innovations – or on the interaction between one of these dimensions and the context of reference.

We argue that social entrepreneurship is much more than these individual parts, resting at the nexus of entrepreneurship, innovation and social issues, with the ultimate goal of improving social well-being and initiating, contributing to or guiding social change.

Different from previous contributions in this field of inquiry, and referring to the model of new venture creation introduced by Gartner (1985), we define social entrepreneurship as:

> A dynamic process which strives to exploit innovation designed explicitly to improve societal well-being, resulting from the interactions among (i) an individual dimension; (ii) an organizational dimension; (iii) an environmental dimension; and (iv) a process dimension that collectively initiate, guide or contribute to social change.

Entrepreneurship, innovation and social change represent the ingredients of the social entrepreneurship formula. The reminder of this section aims to better explain the definition proposed above and its different dimensions. Additionally, the reference to the Gartner model allows us to further clarify how social entrepreneurship and social entrepreneurship organizations can be distinguished in the current business landscape.

The individual dimension in the portrayal of the new social entrepreneur

Since the birth of entrepreneurship research, theories have associated a more person-centered perspective to the analysis of the specific traits of the entrepreneurial phenomenon, explaining entrepreneurship as a 'function of the types of people engaged in entrepreneurial activity' (Eckhardt and Shane, 2003: 334). Even though research on the portrayal of the entrepreneurs and on how to differentiate entrepreneurs from non-entrepreneurs (Gartner, 1985) is extremely heterogeneous, the studies share a sort of epic lens in describing these captains of industry. In fact, driven by, for example, particular personality traits or a particular background, the entrepreneur appears as the protagonist of the economic development, as the one who 'discovers, evaluates and exploits profit opportunities, taking into account risk, alertness to opportunity and the need for innovation' (Eckhardt and Shane, 2003).

Social entrepreneurship follows this trend, as it clearly emerges from the charismatic traits of the founder and leader of San Patrignano. Entrepreneurial aptitude and social orientation (Johnson, 2000) are both part of the social entrepreneur's portrait. The literature has associated to this category of entrepreneurs a certain risk-tolerance and a strong desire to control the surrounding environment (Prabhu, 1999). Social entrepreneurs are mainly innovators and, like their business counterparts, agents of change and drivers of social and economic progress (Dees and Elias, 1998; Leadbeater, 1997; Thompson, 2002), with a strong analytical capacity and problem-solving orientation.

The importance of the visioning ability clearly appears as the main driver of the social entrepreneurship process at the individual level. It is strictly tied to the characteristics of the entrepreneur, and to his/her willingness to enact that image of the future, acquiring the necessary resources and harnessing the support of other key people (Thompson et al., 2000).

At the same time, the vision is what shapes the mission or the purpose of the organization (Austin et al., 2006). The vision is embodied in all the characteristics of the SE organization and the decision it takes, the selection of staff included.

Equally important is social entrepreneurs' aptitude for networking and cooperation (Thompson, 2002). Because they operate in an intersectorial domain, there is a need to establish processes to safeguard against the loss of skills in an effort to connect and provide a continuous exchange and updating of information. The ability to build external relations still remains a typical trait of the social entrepreneur, who uses its own commitment to the mission to establishing legitimacy with different constituencies (Prabhu, 1999) and to enhancing visibility, since best practices still do not exist.

To sum up, we recognize two major distinguishing characteristics of the socially innovative entrepreneur. First is the vision that shapes a cause-driven social mission, which guides the social entrepreneur towards changing existing patterns in the society or the community of reference. Second is the field of action: social entrepreneurs insist on the social sector as change promoter in society; they pioneer innovation within the social sector through groundbreaking entrepreneurial ideas; they have the ability to build capacity and they concretely demonstrate the quality of the idea and measure social impacts – all with well-defined growth objectives.

The process dimension in the discovery and exploitation of an opportunity to innovate

The process dimension refers to the set of activities that the entrepreneur embraces to make its vision of the future a concrete organization, with its focus on the dynamics of discovery, evaluation and exploitation of opportunities (Shane and Venkataraman, 2000).

It is from the discovery of such opportunities and from the decision to exploit them that the entrepreneurial idea is developed, through a process of progressive interaction between the entrepreneur and its context of reference.

According to mainstream business entrepreneurship (Casson, 1982; Kirzner, 1997), to be called entrepreneurial, an activity must entail a discovery of new means–ends relationships that generate a different image of the future. Therefore, entrepreneurial opportunities represent the possibility of bringing into existence new goods, services, raw material and organizing methods that allow outputs to be sold at more than their cost of production. Improvements in the efficiency of existing goods and services do not constitute true entrepreneurial opportunity.

To date, researchers on social entrepreneurship have identified entrepreneurial opportunity as the major commonality between business and social entrepreneurship. However, social entrepreneurship stands out for focusing attention on a different set of possibilities: to be included in the social entrepreneurship domain, social entrepreneurial opportunities must be brought to bear on general or specific social targets – in other words, as with commercial entrepreneurial opportunities, social opportunities develop, apply or introduce new ideas, behaviors, products, services, processes or institutions; but, unlike their business counterpart, they are not the expression of a profit motive (Austin et al., 2006) but a way to contribute to the reduction of social burdens and thus initiate social change.

This is what explains a further radical difference between commercial and social opportunities. In business entrepreneurship, the exploitation of entrepreneurial opportunity is tied mainly to the expected value of the entrepreneurial profit. In other words, the decision to exploit and the choice of exploitation mode are linked to a sense of exclusivity and self-protection – the possibility to maintain the first-mover advantage as long as possible in order to preserve profit. As a result, the duration of the advantage must be increased by reducing the ability of others to 'imitate, substitute, trade for or acquire the rare resources required to drive down the surplus' (Shane and Venkataraman, 2000: 223).

Social entrepreneurship overturns this mechanism, placing its interest not primarily in achieving a competitive economic advantage, but in spreading the social innovation as widely as possible in order to maximize social change and the improvement of social conditions (Drayton, 2002).

Moreover, while the identification of social entrepreneurial opportunity is strictly related to the interaction between external factors (information corridors or factors that cannot be directly controlled by the single entrepreneur) and internal factors (previous experience both at the individual and organizational level, and the cognitive properties of the entrepreneur), as in the business entrepreneurship case (Shane and Venkataraman, 2000), the decision to exploit the opportunity is guided by the different nature of the social opportunity as explained above and so by the comparative assessment of the social expected value *versus* the economic viability.

In fact, as in the business case, social entrepreneurs do not detain or control all the necessary resources to launch the entrepreneurial organization. For this reason, the assessment of expected social value should be accompanied by a thorough analysis of the economic viability of the process in terms of the amount of required resources. In this sense, a good opportunity is one that is able to create adequate value in a way that justifies the entrepreneurial risk that the exploitation of the opportunity unavoidably implies. *Adequate* is defined, for example, in terms of the amount of capital to be invested, the timing of expected social returns, the risk of achieving results, the existing alternatives, the scalability and flexibility level and so on.

The environmental dimension

Even if the entrepreneurs have both the willingness and the abilities to enter the social entrepreneurship path, it is the environment in which they operate that will either kill or facilitate the process, in terms of both its ability to provide the required resources and the possibility to absorb the outcomes of the entrepreneurial activity. Regardless of considering the environmental component as given or shaped by the entrepreneurial actions, the presence of a supportive context of reference plays a crucial role in determining the success or failure of the social entrepreneurship process (Austin et al., 2006; Weerawardena and Sullivan Mort, 2006).

Literature on business entrepreneurship focuses on a list of variables that can affect the feasibility of the process of new venture creation, from the presence of venture capital to the availability of skilled human resources, including the proximity of suppliers and the structure of the supply chain, the role of market institutions and governments, the availability of complementary services, and so on.

In the case of social entrepreneurship three environmental factors appear to affect the process: the level of social, economic and political development; the development level of the social sector; the presence of supportive actors.

The first factor is the development level of social, economic, and institutional environment. This represents more a source of opportunity and entrepreneurial ideas than a constraint to the social entrepreneurship process, in that it is strictly related both to the presence of social gaps and to the level of social demand. Moreover, different development levels foster different kinds of innovative processes.

As explained by Alvord et al. (2004), in an exploratory study focused on the role of social entrepreneurship in context in which poor and marginalized group exist, innovation can take three main forms as a result of the social, political and economic conditions of the context in which it applies. The first, what they call building local capacity, refers to the possibility to exploit locally available resources, generally under-utilized. In this way, social entrepreneurship aims at giving autonomy to marginalized groups, allowing them to replicate autonomously the acquired knowledge base. The second kind of innovation is concerned with a process of adaptation of managerial practices, business models, products or services, in a way that fits the need of the community of reference. Examples are all those activities at the bottom of the pyramid (i.e. the pyramid represents the distribution of wealth across the planet, and the bottom includes all those that are at or below the poverty level) that aim to enhance poor communities' social, cultural and economic conditions (Prahalad, 2004). Finally, building a movement represents the third typology of innovation and relies on the assumption that giving political voice to marginalized groups can help them to increase social cohesion.

In some cases, especially in less developed countries where institutions are weak or nonexistent, innovation processes do not necessarily result in a new offering system or, more generally, in a new means–ends relationship; rather, the innovation can be the creation of a new institution or the transformation or deinstitutionalization of an existing institution. Again, the context of reference plays an important role in shaping the set of possibilities from which social entrepreneurship can develop.

The second environmental factor that can affect social entrepreneurship process is related to the previous one and corresponds to the structure of the competitive environment in which the organization begins to operate. In fact, even though they are innovators in the social sectors, organizations consistent with the social entrepreneurship concept operate in the same fields as public authorities and other third-sector organizations, such as non-profits. Since social entrepreneurship organizations are the latecomers it is quite obvious that their success depends on the strength of the other providers, on the resources and the characteristics of the welfare state, and on the state of development of the traditional third sectors.

The third element that has to be considered is the presence of a supportive environment. Given the newness that characterizes the social entrepreneurship phenomenon, the main reference is here to the financial and consulting service sectors and their ability to provide adequate financial assets and technical assistance to social entrepreneurship organizations. In order to overcome the misalignment between the needs of social entrepreneurs on one hand and the traditional financial sectors on the other, attention is extending to the role of social venture capital or venture philanthropy in supporting the diffusion of social entrepreneurship. To explain further, since the 1990s venture philanthropy has established itself as an alternative form of charitable giving based on venture capital principles applied to the first social entrepreneurship organizations (Porter and Kramer, 2002).

Additionally, social entrepreneurship feasibility is associated with the presence of a social network and the related possibilities for social entrepreneurs, to accumulate social capital (Sharir and Lerner, 2006), which is defined as the set of potential and actual resources deriving from relationships among individuals, networks and societies. As explained by Mair and Martí (2006), belonging to a social network can be relevant for social entrepreneurs both to have access to much more relevant information, resources and support, and to increase the general level of commitment to the social problem or the specific entrepreneurial initiative. At the same time, in situations in which the market for a particular social innovation is still absent, or the innovation concerns institutions, it is possible that the entrepreneur acts proactively, initiating the creation of an appropriate social network.

The organizational dimension

The exploitation of a social entrepreneurial opportunity inevitably involves the definition of an appropriate organizational setting that is crucial to predict the overall effectiveness of each social entrepreneurship initiative. There is considerable heterogeneity among organizational models selected by social entrepreneurs. They can be reframed into a continuum ranging from purely non-profit organizations (Dees and Elias, 1998) to purely for-profit organizations with a prominent social objective. This again emphasizes that social entrepreneurship can be pursued through various vehicles, and that the dichotomy of non-profit vs. for-profit is not the right way to distinguish between the social side and the business side of entrepreneurship (Peredo and McLean, 2006). Put it differently, social entrepreneurship can be found within or can span the non-profit, business and governmental sectors (Austin et al., 2006). Legal form in not paramount to the identification of social entrepreneurship boundaries; rather, one should move one step further and look at the dimensions according to which the choice between different forms is made.

Two aspects are critical in addressing organizational decisions: the scalability orientation and economic robustness.

Scalability orientation concerns social entrepreneurship organizations' aptitude to grow and to be replicated. It is relevant in this context because of the peculiar nature of social entrepreneurial opportunity, as explained above. Since its potential is evaluated in terms of expected social value, scalability is the criterion to keep in mind in the process of spreading social innovation as widely as possible and thus maximizing social change and the improvement of social conditions (Dees et al., 2004).

Four areas can be identified as relevant to sustain growth and enhance the ability of the organization to be replicated. The first one is *staff recruitment*, which includes formalization of specific processes like performance evaluation, selection and competence mapping. Second, recruitment has to be accompanied by the ability to manage *tradeoffs between quantity and quality*. Keeping in mind the objective of challenging a specific social burden (i.e. pursuing social change in a specific social sector), the dichotomy quantity versus quality appears to be shaped by the effectiveness in attaining the social mission, rather than mere economic results. However, all this passes through the definition of standard portfolio quality and the formalization of social performance indicators. Third, social entrepreneurship organization avoids growing before being *ready to sustain growth*. Only after small-scale tests have proved their success can growth and replication become viable opportunities.

Finally, growth is not possible without *interaction with the environment* of reference. The ability to create a supportive environment and to work in partnership with other organizations and institutions within the social sector are the two main organizational challenges in this critical area. Partnerships and networking can be important sources of efficiency, namely through shared facilities, services or activities, as well as the elimination of duplicative costs and excess capacity. At the same time, they are necessary to improve effectiveness, putting together complementary capabilities or enlarging the market or client base. Also, new expertise and increased bargaining power can result from the ability to establish fruitful partnerships. In fact, building networks and partnerships is critical for social entrepreneurship organizations if they are to establish legitimacy with multiple constituencies. In fact, the scarcity of models and acknowledged best practices, such that it is difficult to readily associate a unique meaning to social entrepreneurship and its specificities, makes it crucial to define a clear identity for the new organization to be recognized and distinguished both within and outside the boundary of the organization itself. In other words, the ambiguity of terms like *social value* or *social mission*, the necessity to balance that social mission with economic efficiency and the use of business tools, the multi-stakeholder nature and the collaborative approach problematize the process of legitimization within the context of reference.

Together with the scalability orientation, the second dimension to be considered in addressing the choice of an appropriate organizational setting is economic viability. One of the most important ways in which the entrepreneur can create value is by doing more with less. This is even more relevant for the social sector, in which lack of resources is a founding attribute. In this context, day-by-day operations require an explicit, balanced understanding of cost minimization and efficiency, and overall maximization of quality.

The assessment of efficiency and economic robustness goes hand in hand with the problem of measurability of results and balanced evaluation of social and economic outcomes. This issue is especially critical for social-purpose organizations in that they involve several different and crucial considerations. Values, for example, cannot be easily measured and often are tied to a long-term horizon. Significant diversity exists within each field of action and across different fields, in that each vision is highly community-based.

Since those considerations are case-specific, organizational arrangements should be chosen according to the ability of each format to mobilize needed resources, adopting an efficiency-based entrepreneurial orientation from the very beginning.

An interactive model of social entrepreneurship

Overall, it is possible to distinguish a number of different intervening factors affecting both the identification of an unfulfilled social need and its implementation through a formal organizational structure.

The identification of a social entrepreneurial opportunity arising from unfulfilled social needs is strictly related to the interaction between the state of the environmental context and individual characteristics. In fact, on the one side the extent to which the institutional context is developed, the presence of role models and the level of competition within that specific social sector affect the recognition of room for action, thus providing the impetus to behave entrepreneurially and innovate. On the other side, the individual characteristics of entrepreneurs, their previous personal and organizational experience with the problem to be addressed are what make sense of the inadequacy of the current situation and the existence of an entrepreneurial opportunity.

While the identification of social entrepreneurial opportunity is strictly related to the interaction between contextual factors and individual factors, as in the business entrepreneurship case (Shane and Venkataraman, 2000), the subsequent decision to exploit the opportunity is guided by the different nature of the social opportunity as explained above and so by the comparative assessment of the social expected value versus the economic viability.

As in the business case, social entrepreneurs do not retain or control all the necessary resources to launch the entrepreneurial organization. For this reason, the assessment of expected social value should be accompanied by a thorough analysis of the economic viability of the process in terms of the amount of required resources. In this sense, a good opportunity is one that is able of creating adequate value in a way that justifies the entrepreneurial risk that the exploitation of the opportunity unavoidably implies. Adequate is defined, for example, in terms of the amount of capital to be invested, the timing of expected social returns, the risk of achieving results, the existing alternatives, the scalability and flexibility level and so on.

Certainly, the effectiveness of opportunity exploitation in terms of potential to change society is strictly linked both to the extent to which the entrepreneurial process occurs in a supportive environment (resource providers and networks) and to the identification of an appropriated organizational setting, which informs subsequent exploitation. Both the stages of development of the organizational structure, in terms of procedure formalization and identification of the minimum efficient scale and success dimensions, and the existence or creation of a network of supportive actors and partners have to be considered.

The reasoning above boils down to the need for exploring social entrepreneurship not just as the integration between entrepreneurial mind-set, innovation and social change but also as a process of reciprocal interaction among the initiators of the process – the social entrepreneurs with their traits and motivations, the context in which the social entrepreneurship organizations develop, defined as the locus of opportunity identification and necessary resources, and the organizational setting through which activities are run – all this starting from the attempt to concretize the discovery and exploitation of a social entrepreneurial opportunity (Figure 9.1).

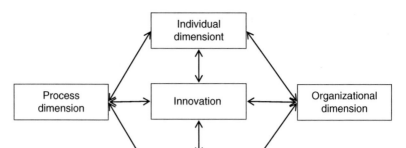

Figure 9.1   An interactive model of social entrepreneurship

Conclusion

Social entrepreneurship is surfacing an important path towards social change and social transformation. It is at the forefront of innovation and creativity within the social sector, in terms of groundbreaking potential and supportive contribution to the enhancement of societal well-being in initiating social change. Social entrepreneurship breaks up previous perspectives on social sectors, encompassing both profit strength and non-profit culture, with a strong orientation towards cooperation, participation and social cohesion. Social entrepreneurship sparks entrepreneurial activity on a different scale, based on sensitive and innovative social attitude, guided by a proactive concept of social change.

The value of this contribution lies in its attempt to develop a comprehensive, multi-dimensional framework as a further step in the process of boundary-setting and awareness-raising aimed at stimulating future research according to the critical areas identified and the links between them. In this sense, our model provides a template for systematically studying this new, fruitful domain of inquiry, and a basis for more empirical investigation in term of dimensions affecting the social entrepreneurial process. The lack of empirical studies can be considered as the most important missing element in social entrepreneurship research. We agree with Bruyat and Julien's view (2000) that we will not understand the phenomenon of social entrepreneurship if we do not consider each single element of the discourse (the entrepreneur, the project, the environment, the organization), as well as the links between them over time. We suggest that entrepreneurship scholars focus their efforts on the nexus of entrepreneurial opportunities, enterprising individuals or teams, and modes of organizing within the overall context of a dynamic environment.

Although social entrepreneurship is a new field of inquiry, still largely phenomenon-driven, in the last ten years research spanning from social issues in management to entrepreneurship and strategic management has devoted increasing attention to the phenomenon per se, corroborating the relevance of the subject and the presence of a cross-border interest in it.

SE is at the forefront of innovation and creativity within the social sector, breaking up previous perspectives on social sectors and encompassing both profit strength and non-profit culture, with a strong orientation towards cooperation, participation and social cohesion. Social entrepreneurship sparks entrepreneurial activity on a different scale, based on sensitive and innovative social attitude, guided by a proactive concept of social change. Social entrepreneurship is certainly not a zero-sum game but rather a win-win exchange process with the environment and its constituencies, a constant and precarious equilibrium between economic sustainability and the ability to pursue a social vision superior to the creation of economic value and sustained by it.

References

Alvord, S. H., Brown, L. D. and Letts, C. W. 2004. Social Entrepreneurship and Social Transformation. *Journal of Applied Behavioral Science*, **40**(3): 260–82.

Amit, R., Glosten, L. and Muller, E. 1993. Challenges to Theory Development in Entrepreneurship Research. *Journal of Management Studies*, 30(5): 815–34.

Austin, J., Stevenson, H. and Wei-Skillern, J. 2006. Social and Commercial Entrepreneurship: Same, Different or Both? *Entrepreneurship Theory and Practice*, 30(1): 1–22.

Boschee, J. 1998. *What does it take to be a Social Entrepreneur?* Minneapolis, MN: National Centre for Social Entrepreneurs.

Bruyat, C. and Julien, P. A. 2000. Defining the Field of Research in Entrepreneurship. *Journal of Business Venturing*, 16(2): 165–80.

Cannon, C. M. 2000. Charity for Profit: How the New Social Entrepreneurs are Creating Good by Sharing Wealth. *National Journal*, 16: 1898–904.

Casson, M. 1982. *The Entrepreneur. An Economic Theory*. Totowa, NJ: Barnes and Noble.

Dart, R. 2004. The Legitimacy of Social Enterprise. *Nonprofit Management & Leadership*, **14**(4): 411–24.

Dees, J. G. and Elias, J. 1998. The Challenges of Combining Social and Commercial Enterprise. *Business Ethics Quarterly*, 8(1): 165–78.

Dees, J. G., Battle Anderson, B. and Wei-Skillern, J. 2004. Scaling Social Impact: Strategies for Spreading Social Innovation. *Stanford Social Innovation Review*, 1(4): 24–32.

Drayton, W. 2002. The Citizen Sector: Becoming as Entrepreneurial and Competitive as Business. *California Management Review*, 44(3): 120–32.

Eckhardt, J. T. and Shane, S. A. 2003. Opportunities and Entrepreneurship. *Journal of Management*, 29(3): 333–49.

Gartner, W. B. 1985. A Conceptual Framework for Describing the Phenomenon of New Venture Creation. *Academy of Management Review*, 10(4): 696–706.

Henton, D., Melville, J. and Walesh, K. 1997. The Age of Civic Entrepreneur: Restoring Civil Society and Building Economic Community. *National Civic Review*, 6(2): 149–56.

Johnson, S. 2000. *Literature Review on Social Entrepreneurship*. University of Alberta: Canadian Center for Social Entrepreneurship.

Kirzner, I. 1997. Entrepreneurial Discovery and the Competitive Market Process: An Austrian Approach. *The Journal of Economic Literature*, 35(1): 60–85.

Leadbeater, C. 1997. *The Rise of the Social Entrepreneur*. London: Demos.

Mair, J. and Martì, I. 2006. Social Entrepreneurship Research: A Source of Explanation, Prediction, and Delight. *Journal of World Business*, 41(1): 36–44.

Newman, W. H. and Wallender, H. W. 1978. Managing Not-for-Profit Enterprises. *Academy of Management Review*, 3(1): 24–31.

Peredo, A. M. and McLean, M. 2006. Social Entrepreneurship: A Critical Review of the Concept. *Journal of World Business*, 41(1): 56–65.

Perrini, F. 2006. *The New Social Entrepreneurship: What Awaits Social Entrepreneurial Ventures?* Cheltenham, UK: Edward Elgar.

Porter, M. E. and Kramer, M. R. 2002. The Competitive Advantage of Corporate Philanthropy. *Harvard Business Review*, 80(12): 57–68.

Prabhu, G. N. 1999. Social Entrepreneurial Leadership. *Career Development International*, 4(3): 140–45.

Prahalad, C. K. 2004. *The Fortune at the Bottom of the Pyramid: Eradicating Poverty through Profits*. Upper Saddle River, NJ: Wharton School Publishing.

Shane, S. and Venkataraman, S. 2000. The Promise of Entrepreneurship as a Field of Research. *Academy of Management Review*, 25(1): 217–26.

Sharir, M. and Lerner, M. 2006. Gauging the Success of Social Ventures Initiated by Individual Social Entrepreneurs. *Journal of World Business*, 41(1): 6–20.

Sullivan Mort, G., Weerawardena, J. and Carnegie, K. 2003. Social Entrepreneurship: Towards Conceptualization. *International Journal of Nonprofit and Voluntary Sector Marketing*, 8(1): 76–88.

Thompson, J. 2002. The World of the Social Entrepreneur. *The International Journal of Public Sector Management*, 15(2): 412–32.

Thompson, J., Alvy, G. and Lees, A. 2000. Social Entrepreneurship: A New Look at the People and the Potential. *Management Decision*, 38(5): 328–38.

Weerawardena, J. and Sullivan Mort, G. 2006. Investigating Social Entrepreneurship: A Multidimensional Model. *Journal of World Business*, 41(1): 21–35.

10
Emerging Social Entrepreneurship: Exploring the Development Process

Simone Maase and Kees Dorst

Introduction

Social entrepreneurs are change promoters in society; they pioneer innovation through the entrepreneurial quality of an innovative idea, their capacity-building aptitude, and their ability to demonstrate the quality of the idea and to measure social impacts (Perrini and Vurro, 2006). Drayton (2006) defines social entrepreneurs as men and women developing system-changing solutions that address the world's most urgent social challenges. Valuable knowledge has been developed about how social entrepreneurs recognize opportunities in society and how intentions to start a social enterprise are formed (Mair and Noboa, 2006; Robinson, 2006). Others focused on the organizational aspects of the social enterprise and sought to identify patterns predicting or leading to successful social entrepreneurship (Alvord et al., 2004; Cramer, 2003; Desa and Kotha, 2006; Mulgan, 2006a). The social entrepreneurs of the cases explored in this study are citizens with an innovative idea for solving a social problem, but without an existing organization backing them. Research (Alvord et al., 2004; Bornstein, 2004; Meroni, 2007) shows that there are numerous examples of citizens developing social ventures and collaboration networks successfully. Studying these initiatives is important because they provide an opportunity;

> to learn from their common success factors and to be alerted to cross-cutting obstacles they encountered. It will help us to develop, initiate and test new policies, aimed at enabling and empowering individuals or 'creative communities' to do better and to do more.
>
> (Meroni, 2007: 5)

A starting point for this study has been the growing number of initiatives by individuals and small groups of citizens who develop and implement solutions to social problems (Gerometta et al., 2005; Meroni, 2007). In this study we focus on the development process of the emerging social enterprise. Using Mintzberg's (1976: 246) definition of a process, we set out to explore seven examples of emerging social entrepreneurship initiated by citizens.

> A process is a set of actions and dynamic factors with a beginning and an end.
>
> (after Mintzberg, 1976)

The aim of this study is to explore and describe the development process of emerging social entrepreneurship. We seek to identify patterns of actions and to relate them to the literature on social innovation and social entrepreneurship. We do not focus here on dynamic factors that might be at play and influence the process.

This chapter consists of six sections. The first introduces the central theme. The second summarizes three processes derived from literature on social innovation and social entrepreneurship. In the third section we describe the materials and methods used in this study. The fourth section presents the results of both within and cross-case analysis. In the fifth we discuss how the results of this study link back to the processes, themes and propositions derived from literature. We identify differences and similarities between our cases of emerging social entrepreneurship and literature. In section six we draw final conclusions and set an agenda for future research.

Processes of social innovation and social entrepreneurship

The literature on social innovation and social entrepreneurship describes processes related to emerging social entrepreneurship. The cases explored in this study are considered to be seeds of social innovation and social entrepreneurship. Many of these cases develop into small or medium-sized enterprises (SMEs) or foundations with a primary social goal. The social entrepreneur provides a product or service fulfilling a social need. The next subsection describes a process of social innovation and deals with processes described in social entrepreneurship literature. The phases and related propositions and themes from the authors of these bodies of literature are summarized in Table 10.1.

Table 10.1   Phases described in social innovation and social entrepreneurship processes

Social innovation Mulgan (2006b)	Social entrepreneurship Robinson (2006)/Mair and Noboa (2006)	Technology social ventures Desa and Kotha (2006)
1 Generating ideas by understanding needs and identifying potential solutions	Opportunity-identification and intention-formation	Idea/Opportunity stage
	'Theme 1: Successful social entrepreneurs will identify opportunities in social and institutional contexts they believe they understand.'	*'Prop 1a: The social entrepreneur's social networks and past experience will predict sources of opportunity recognition for TSVs.'*
2 Developing, prototyping, and piloting ideas *'Statement: Progress is often achieved more quickly through turning the idea into a prototype and then galvanizing enthusiasm for it.'*	Opportunity evaluation and exploration *'Theme 2: Successful social entrepreneurs will consider social and institutional factors when evaluating opportunities to create social ventures.'*	Prototype/Founding stage *'Activities and results: Seed funding Seed pitch Seed evaluation'*
3 Assessing, scaling up, and diffusing good ideas *'Statement: this phase requires skilful strategy and coherent vision, the ability to marshal resources and support, and to identify key points of leverage.'*	Opportunity pursuit	Growth stage *'Prop 4: As TSV evolves from the idea/opportunity stage to the venture growth stage new stakeholders reshape the identity and mission of the social venture.'*
4 Learning and evolving		

Social innovation

Social innovation in the field of political and social science is often related to innovative solutions for poverty alleviation or social exclusion (Alvord et al., 2004; Gerometta et al., 2005). Other researchers refer to social innovation when describing processes of behavioral change or social trends. Although we believe that the term social innovation applies to both strands of research, for our study the concept of social innovation as described by Mulgan (2006a) provides a valuable theoretical background. Mulgan defines social innovation as referring to new ideas that work in meeting social goals. A somewhat narrower definition proposed by Mulgan (2006a: 8) is social innovation as

> [i]nnovative activities and services that are motivated by the goal of meeting a social need and that are predominantly developed and diffused through organizations whose primary purposes are social.

Mulgan (2006a) seeks to describe similarities and differences between social and business innovation. One of the challenges both business and social innovation face is to survive the often long phase when revenues are negative. Methods to speed up this period designed for business innovation are, for example, faster prototyping and the use of rigorous milestones against which funds are released. Another similarity is that successful growth is only possible if innovations really do meet needs. To develop and spread they need the support of people with resources – investors, co-developers and purchasers. Patterns of social innovation that differ from business innovation deal with motives, patterns of growth, critical resources and the judging of success (Mulgan, 2006a). Three phases in the social innovation process are defined and summarized in Table 10.1.

Social entrepreneurship

In the literature, various processes related to emerging social entrepreneurship have been described. Three processes related to our subject of study are intention-formation (Mair and Noboa, 2006), the process of navigating social and institutional barriers (Robinson, 2006), and the evolution of technology social ventures (Desa and Kotha, 2006). The phases as described for these processes are summarized in Table 10.1.

Intention-formation

The start of the social enterprise is inherently linked to the formation of an intention to create it (Katz and Gartner, 1988; Mair and Noboa, 2006). Mair and Noboa propose a model that describes how the intention to start a social enterprise is formed. Intention-formation is an essential phase in the process of starting a social enterprise and cannot be missing in our exploration of the development process of social enterprises. Nevertheless, our study will not focus on this phase in detail.

Navigating social and institutional barriers

Robinson (2006) emphasizes the process of navigating social and institutional barriers in relation to the markets or communities the entrepreneur wants to impact. He relates the successfulness of social entrepreneurs to their ability to execute and navigate. He further explores the social and institutional barriers and defines three themes for action: identification and discovery, evaluation, and addressing the barriers. The phases he distinguishes are summarized in Table 10.1.

Technology social ventures

The third process we think relevant to our study and which should be addressed here is the process of the evolution of technology social ventures described by Desa and Kotha (2006). Technology social ventures combine technological innovation and the fulfillment of social needs in a way that is financially sustainable. The cases we focus on in this study are providers of products and services. They are not technology-driven solutions themselves, but in most cases a product is developed together with a service. In technology social ventures the technology is in most cases implemented in a product or service fulfilling a social need, which makes it interesting to compare the evolution process of technology social ventures with the process experienced by emerging social enterprises.

Table 10.1 summarizes the processes for social innovation and social entrepreneurship according to Mulgan, Mair and Noboa, Robinson, and Desa and Kotha. When the processes are arranged in parallel, similarities become apparent. The first phase in both the process of social innovation and social entrepreneurship describes the action of developing an idea. All three perspectives address a phase of prototyping, piloting and evaluation. Mulgan (2006b: 152) states that 'progress is often achieved more quickly through turning the idea into a prototype or pilot and then galvanizing enthusiasm for it, than by formal market research or desk analysis'. Both the social innovation and social entrepreneurship perspectives mention the importance of evaluating the idea and setting up a pilot or pitch in the second phase. The third phase is characterized by implementation, consolidation, scaling up and the growth of the innovation. Only in the social innovation process is a fourth phase of learning and evolving mentioned. The overview of phases along which the innovation process takes place will serve as an anchor point for our exploration and cross-analysis of cases of emerging social entrepreneurship. This body of literature does not inform us in detail about how the social entrepreneur moves from one phase to another. Propositions, themes and statements give direction. These propositions and themes are included in Table 10.1 and will be discussed and linked to our research results in the discussion section of this chapter.

Method and material

This study seeks to identify phases and patterns in the development process of emerging social entrepreneurship. One of the propositions described in Alvord et al. (2004) is that successful social enterprises are often founded by leaders with the capacity to work with and to build bridges among very diverse stakeholders. Emerging social entrepreneurs face the challenge of developing both the solution addressing the social need and a network of collaborating partners simultaneously. The grassroots origin of the cases in our study implies a complex process, as organizational structure, partnerships and the product or service all have to be developed from scratch. This leads to the following research question:

> How do emerging social entrepreneurs develop their idea into a working solution and simultaneously create partnerships and an organizational structure?

To explore the process of development replication logic requires applying a multiple case design (Yin, 2003). For this study the process approach is preferred above the variance approach because the former is especially suitable to explore and explain what is actually happening in the empirical world (Langley, 1999). To make sense of the data gathered, we combine aspects of the narrative and visual mapping strategy. The narrative approach is used as a preliminary step aimed at preparing a chronological overview of what happened over time. Visual mapping will be used to compare and identify patterns in the process of development. The material will be structured fixing our attention on time, events and orderings. To provide sufficient material to generate patterns this study includes seven cases (Eisenhardt, 1989; Langley, 1999). In order to be able to cross-compare we selected five cases that have appeared to be successful in their development so far. Two less successful cases were added to the study for contrast.

We selected seven cases that are potential seeds of social innovation and start-ups of social entrepreneurship in the Netherlands. All cases have the following characteristics:

- The idea was conceived by an individual or small group of individuals.
- Intention-formation had taken place. Each initiator was taking visible action to generate resources, build the organizational structure and find partners.
- The idea included both an innovative solution to a social problem and the launch of a new product or service.
- No organizational structure existed at the start: the initiators started the case as citizens without any organizational structure or support.

Four cases were selected from the database of GreenWish, a Dutch foundation supporting initiators of grassroots cases for sustainable development. GreenWish support can involve connecting an initiative to potential partners, helping to write a project or business proposal, and fundraising. Three cases caught our attention through the media.

In studying cases of emerging social entrepreneurship it is hard to determine whether the developed solution solves the social problem successfully. For this exploration the execution of a pilot in cooperation with a number of partners is set as the indicator for success.

The information about the cases was gathered during two meeting with the initiators of each case. The first meeting consisted of a structured interview. The questionnaire focused on the history of the case and the development process the case had gone through so far. The interview and reporting format used for this first interview was derived from the formats used in the EMUDE research activity aimed at gathering and reporting cases of social innovation (Maase and Dorst, 2007; Meroni, 2007). Adjustments were made to expand the interview with questions asking for current challenges the initiators were facing. The first interview was executed by a team of two students following the bachelor course at our faculty. The within-case data analysis (Eisenhardt, 1989) consisted of a standard descriptive format and a system organization map representing the organizational form of each case. A second meeting with the initiators of each case focused on future development. This meeting took place within two to four weeks after the first interview and was set up in a workshop-like format. The starting point for the second encounter was to create, with the case initiators and potential partners, a solution to a current challenge in the development of the case. This challenge was derived from the analysis of the results of the first interview and discussed with the initiator beforehand. In the workshop the system organization map was discussed with the initiator in regard to its accurateness and errors were adjusted to the current organizational situation. Both the student team and the researcher were present at the workshop. All interviews and workshops took place between September 2006 and January 2007. The workshop was recorded in mp3-format for detailed analysis afterwards. Table 10.2 provides a brief description of the key innovation of each case, indicating both the social problem addressed by the solution and the product or service.

Table 10.2 Cases and their key innovations

CASE	Key innovation
TVE	A lunchtime school 'restaurant' combining the training of future cooks, reintegrating jobless parents, training kids about healthy food and providing high quality lunch at primary schools.
OEPS	A beach pavilion for leisure based on both ecologically and socially sustainable principles providing space for training and education of students of secondary schools. Simultaneously the beach and surrounding dune area are developed to become an ecological zone. Providing education on ecology, sustainable energy etc. for schoolchildren is also part of the initiative.
WDBH	A website for various stakeholders in the chain of job trading to exchange information for finding and providing a job closer to home. Primer focus is to connect people (employees) who want to switch or change jobs in order to reduce their travel distance and time.
RAG	To create work for a significant number of people at the lower end of society in developing countries by producing fashionable products locally and selling them in Europe, the US and Australia.
MMM	High-end fashion label, locally produced by homeless women in the Netherlands. Each piece of clothing includes a piece of old, re-used fabric or other clothing material.
TAS	A sphere-shaped transparent container at supermarkets for consumers to place in plastic shopping bags, enabling direct re-use by consumers, significantly reducing plastic waste.
TVO	TVO aims to provide knowledge and optimism through contact with nature. Workshops (re-)connecting people to nature and its resource capacity will be part of the initiative.

Results

Phases in the development of emerging social entrepreneurship

Based on the interviews and case descriptions we set up the timeline for each case. The starting point of a case was defined as the moment the initiator started to share the idea. In other words: the initiator stated goals and intentions to the outer world. Cases found themselves in different phases of development at the moment of the interview. For a cross-case comparison we aligned the starting points of the cases to one point in time (Figure 10.1).

Based on analysis of our data and the cross-case timeline comparison we recognized three phases or specific sets of actions: solution development, pilot and growth. Below we describe the actions and results of these phases as we saw them developing.

Solution development

The development process in the cases we studied starts with a period of solution development. The initiator discusses the idea with various people in his or her social network and starts to formulate it in either a business plan or project proposal. In most cases, organizations outside the social network are also approached. The social entrepreneur starts by first contacting organizations he or she thinks are essential to cooperate with and that can provide necessary resources. This phase is characterized by a fuzzy and iterative approach in which the preliminary idea is elaborated in detail. Contacts between the social entrepreneur and potential partners are informal. Four out of seven cases contacted GreenWish in this phase.

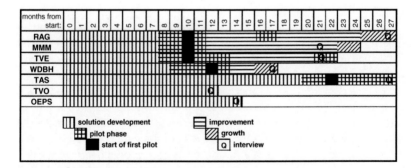

Figure 10.1   Case timelines with aligned starting points

Pilot

Five out of seven cases reach the pilot phase within two years from the starting point. Four cases organized a pilot within one year. The pilot phase is characterized by finding partners with whom to set up a pilot. Contacting partners, as in the solution development phase, is an iterative process. The initiator repetitively discusses the idea with potential partners. The actions of the first part of this phase resemble the actions of the solution development phase, but the purpose is slightly different. In the solution development phase the discussion focuses on gathering information, identifying potential partners and refining the idea. In the pilot phase the initiator seeks to get the potential partner's commitment to collaborate. The main result of the pilot phase is running the pilot itself, which encompasses the solution in real life. For this the commitment and contribution of partners is necessary.

Improvement

After the pilot phase evaluation takes place and actions are taken to improve the solution. In some cases this phase is interwoven with the pilot phase. In either approach, this is an iterative process, where adjustments are made to the organizational structure and the product or service.

Growth phase

The growth phase consists of building the final network structure for continuous operation. Because only one of the cases in our study reached this stage at the moment we investigated the cases, we will not elaborate on this phase here.

Establishment of partnerships

The key innovations (Table 10.2) of all seven cases implied the establishment of a network of partners. The cases in this study did not originate in existing organizations, and the intended solutions all required collaboration with various sectors in society to make the solution work. In the cases explored, we distinguished the following functional purposes of partnerships, in random order: to provide funding, to provide part of the service, to supply the product or necessary material, to promote the solution, to provide labor, to provide consultancy on both the organization and content development, and to use the product/service system. In our cross-case analysis we arranged the cases along a 'time to pilot' axis, in ascending order (Table 10.3). We looked for patterns between

Table 10.3 Case data: comparing "time to pilot" with "number of partners" and "sectors involved"

CASE	Entrepreneur's professional context	Organization on 01012007	Collaboration network	Time to pilot in months	NR of partners involved in pilot
RAG	Industrial product designer	SME	Intra-sector	10	7
MMM	Director of care institute + communication consultant	Foundation	Multiple-sector	10	7
TVE	Product stylist	Foundation	Multiple-sector	10	11
WDBH	Marketing manager	SME	Inter-sector	12	7
TAS	Event organiser	Foundation	Inter-sector	22	8
TVO	Artist	Artist	Multiple-sector	? >12	?
OEPS	Unknown	Foundation	Multiple-sector	? >14	?

'time to pilot', the number of partners involved in the pilot and number of societal sectors involved.

One might expect that the more partners are involved in the pilot, the more time it takes to get to the start of a pilot. Comparing the cases, we see that this relationship appears to be true if we exclude case technology social ventures, which represent an exception. Such ventures were able to establish collaboration with 11 different partners within one year from start-up. The data in Table 10.3, however, does not reveal that the initiator of technology social ventures had already established relationships with potential partners before starting the initiative. (The initiator had worked on another project that gave her the social network facility needed to set up the social enterprise pilot.)

The cases in our study established partnerships with various societal sectors. One case developed partnerships with organizations from only one societal sector (RAG). The other cases all developed partnerships with two or more societal sectors. Comparing the 'time to pilot' with the number of different sectors involved (intra, inter, multiple sector partnerships) we expect growing complexity from intra via inter to tri-sector partnerships to be positively related to 'time to pilot'. Table 10.3 does not clearly confirm this. Two cases (technology social ventures, MMM) established multiple-sector partnerships within ten months. Two other cases (WDBH, TAS) developed multiple-sector partnerships using

12 and 22 months. The RAG case needed ten months for establishing partnerships with organizations from one sector only. This leads to the assumption that other factors influencing the time to pilot are at play.

Almost all initiators at some point in the interview indicated they had experienced difficulties in finding committed partners for their initiatives. Although the initiator of technology social ventures managed to get to a pilot in ten months from start-up, she said:

> It's very difficult to find the right person to forward your idea in an organization. Once I found someone who was enthusiastic and promised to help, after some time that person had changed jobs and my proposal got lost. I lost a lot of time waiting.

Another frustrating aspect for emerging social entrepreneurs is the experienced 'slowness of bureaucracy'. Initiator WDBH claimed:

> Everybody I talk to is very enthusiastic about the idea, I even discussed it with people at the highest level of one of our national ministries, but I've been waiting for months now to receive an answer. I just do not understand why it takes so much time to take a decision. I keep calling them again and again. Meanwhile I just go on...

The quotations above indicate there are dynamic factors at play in the development process which frustrate the creation of partnerships and the setting up of a pilot scheme. In this study we did not focus on these dynamic factors. Our exploration describes the set of actions and phases of the development process of emerging social entrepreneurship.

Discussion

The aim of this research was to explore the development process of cases of emerging social entrepreneurship in order to find an answer to the question

> How do emerging social entrepreneurs develop their idea into a working solution, and simultaneously create partnerships and an organizational structure?

Based on the timeline of development of seven cases and inspired by literature on social innovation and social entrepreneurship, four main phases were distinguished and described in the results section. In the discussion below we link the results back to propositions, statements and themes in literature, which are related to the phases of the development process. We refer to the work of Desa and Kotha, Robinson, and Mulgan (2006a and 2006b).

Opportunity recognition and solution development by emerging social entrepreneurs

Desa and Kotha (2006) explored the evolution of new technology social ventures. Described in the same book is Robinson's study (2006) of six social ventures in which he explores the issues of identification of the social entrepreneurial opportunities. We want to discuss Desa and Kotha's first proposition: 'the social entrepreneur's social networks and past professional experience predicts sources of opportunity recognition for technology social ventures', and also Robinson's first theme: 'successful social entrepreneurs will identify opportunities in social and institutional contexts they believe they understand'. Analyzing the social and institutional context of the initiators of our cases, in three cases (MMM, TVE and RAG) the initiators had professional experience or a social network that was of value for the development of the solution. Four case initiators entered completely new fields – for example, a marketing manager in a big firm who started his own business to provide a solution to the traffic jam problem (WDBH),and a freelance organizer of big music events who works on promoting re-use of plastic bags (TAS). Citizen social innovators do not seem to be aware or care whether they understand the social and institutional barriers. Their social context informs them about an opportunity. Their personal drive to change something for the better in all cases leads to the start of the initiative. Initiators do not identify opportunities per se within the social and institutional context they believe to understand. They identify opportunities in social and institutional contexts they want to change or contribute to, informed by their social context. Their personal drive and enthusiasm creates the force which sets them off to start a fuzzy, 'trial and error'-like process of elaborating the solution and looking for partners. While doing so they encounter and learn about the social and institutional barriers related to their idea. Perseverance and personal skills seem to be the main factors leading to the success of a case. On the other hand, the 'trial and error'-like approach causes a lot of frustration with the social entrepreneurs in our study. Although it is impossible to make up for missing experience it would be valuable for the starting entrepreneur to understand the social and institutional barriers as soon as possible. A more systematic approach of the solution development phase might reduce the level of frustration and speed up the establishment of partnerships. Especially in the less successful cases, TVO and OEPS, it is clear that the entrepreneurs were not at the start aware of the social and institutional barriers.

In addition to this neither had a clear picture of what the solution should look like. The initiator of OEPS stated in the interview:

> It doesn't matter to me what the final result will look like or who wants to join, as long as it is going to contribute to the learning of young people.

To date, this initiator has enthused a lot of potential partners but a pilot has not yet started up. Bringing clarity to the solution could improve communication with potential partners.

Establishing partnerships

Intra-, inter- and multiple-sector partnerships in emerging social entrepreneurship

Austin (2006) emphasizes the need for the analysis of collaboration networks as a form of social entrepreneurship. He proposes to conduct research on how to create social purpose networks most effectively. Our exploration discussed below relates to this research question. We expected the dimension 'time to pilot' to be positively related to the number of sectors that are necessary for the emerging social enterprise to operate. We expected social enterprises in need of a multiple-sector collaboration network to take considerably longer to set up a pilot than inter- and intra-partnerships, because of the increasing complexity of multiple-sector networks. Four of the seven cases aimed to develop multiple-sector networks. Cross-comparing the seven cases we found that two cases (MMM and TVE) developed the multiple-sector network relatively fast and started a pilot within one year. Cases RAG and WDBH developed intra- and inter-sector networks in about the same amount of time (within one year after start; Table 10.3). Two cases that also aimed to establish multiple-sector networks did not manage to get to the pilot phase within one year (TVO and OEPS). It seems, therefore, there are other factors at play in the partnership process influencing the time to pilot. One factor is access to a relevant social network. The initiator of case TVE had previously collaborated with other people trying to develop a comparable social enterprise. The experience and contacts developed in this previous activity created the opportunity to quickly elaborate the second initiative towards the pilot phase. Simiarly, the past professional experience of one of the initiators of MMM gave direct access to a network. In addition, all cases that developed a pilot within one year had a clear idea of the product or service solution from the start. Other factors may have been at play but are not described here.

Partners' involvement in solution development

Desa and Kotha's proposition describes four states:

> As the TSV evolves from the idea/opportunity stage to the venture growth stage new stakeholders reshape the identity and mission of the social venture.

In our cases stakeholders are approached in the first two phases of the development process. Both the product/service and the collaboration network are developed simultaneously. The emerging social entrepreneur reacts to the input and demands of potential stakeholders by reshaping the initial idea. A mutual negotiation takes place between the goal of the social entrepreneur and the contribution a potential partner is willing to make. For our study, the 'reshaping' of the identity of the venture not only took place in the growth phase, but also in the solution development and pilot phase. The successful social entrepreneur (MMM, RAG, TVE, and WDBH) showed both flexibility and leadership in encounters with potential partners. Another phenomenon of partners' involvement we observed was that the social entrepreneur organized meetings with a number of potential partners. The initiator of case TVE organized a session inviting all kinds of potential partners from various sectors in society to discuss the idea for the social enterprise. At the end of this meeting the initiator asked the attendants to express their commitment. According to the initiator of TVE this meeting contributed to the fast set-up of a pilot. In one of our interviews she said:

> I discussed the idea with a lot of people whom I thought would be interested to join the initiative. Almost everybody was enthusiastic, but after a few months still nobody wanted to commit. I decided to organize a dinner inviting all these potential partners. Without this gathering I think the [establishment of the] school-restaurant would not have taken place yet.

Both access to a network of potential partners, as, for example, provided by the Dutch association GreenWish, and setting up collaborative sessions with potential partners seem to enhance the development of the solution and partnership network.

Collaboratively piloting emerging social enterprises

Mulgan (2006b: 152) states:

> Social innovation may be helped by formal market research or desk analysis, but progress is often achieved more quickly through turning the idea into a prototype or pilot and then galvanizing enthusiasm for it.

Setting up an embryonic organization and concentric development are proposed as tools because social innovations can require several attempts before they work. Analysis of our cases shows that all cases go through a pilot phase. Enthusiasm and commitment to collaborate has to be established in order to create the embryonic organization. The answer to the question how to do this remains unanswered in the literature on social innovation referred to. Questions like 'How to collaboratively develop the solution?', 'How to involve potential users and partners in the early development phases?', and 'How to evaluate and adapt the pilot results?' arise. We propose to integrate the theoretical framework of product development to social entrepreneurship. Sixty years of research within this field provides an extensive body of knowledge, resulting in manuals describing methods and tools to optimize the development process of products and product/service systems (Buijs and Valkenburg, 1996; Roozenburg and Eekels, 1995; Ulrich and Eppinger, 1995; VDI 2221, 1985). Early research after the product development process focused on the process taking place in single organizations and multidisciplinary teams within one organization. Recently the field started to widen its focus. Interesting strands of research for emerging social entrepreneurship are collaborative design (Scrivener, 2006) and research after the development of solution-oriented partnerships (Manzini et al., 2004). Tools and methods have been developed to design collaboratively involving partners and users in design activities, to visualize the collaboration network, and to assess the system.

Conclusions

In this study we explored the development process of seven emerging social enterprises. We sought to identify patterns and phases in the process and to describe them. The challenge an emerging social entrepreneur faces is to simultaneously develop the content of the solution and a collaboration network. We distinguished four phases in the development of the solution: the solution development phase, the pilot phase, the improvement phase, and the growth phase. Propositions and themes described in the body of literature on social entrepreneurship and social innovation were discussed for their relevance to emerging social entrepreneurship. We came to the following three observations.

First, initiators do not identify opportunities per se within the social and institutional context they believe to understand. They identify opportunities in social and institutional contexts they want to change or contribute to. In many cases emerging social entrepreneurs are not aware of social and constitutional barriers related to their ideas resulting in a fuzzy and 'trial and error'-like approach in the solution development phase. A more systematic approach of the solution development phase might reduce frustration and speed up the establishment of partnerships.

Second, multiple-sector collaboration networks for emerging social entrepreneurship do not necessarily take longer to develop than intra- or inter-sector collaboration networks. Other factors seem to be at play that influence the time needed to prepare and start the pilot.

Third, in emerging social entrepreneurship initiated by citizens, partners start to influence the identity and structure of the social venture already in the first two phases of the development process. Both the product or service and the collaboration network are developed simultaneously and in some cases collaboratively. Organizing collaborative sessions with potential partners seems to enhance the development of the solution and contribute to the establishment of partnerships. To the best of our knowledge, questions like 'How to collaboratively develop the solution?', 'How to involve potential users and partners in the early development phases?' and 'How to evaluate and adapt the pilot results collaboratively?' are not answered in literature. A new theoretical framework might provide answers, although from a different angle. Another field of research we think could inform the development process of social entrepreneurship is that of product development. This field builds on about 60 years of research tradition, which has resulted in a thorough description of the product development process and the development and evaluation of numerous tools and methods to guide and improve the process. The solution development and the pilot phases in particular have been subjects of extensive research (Lawson, 2006). Tools to generate and develop ideas, especially together with potential users or partners (Manzini et al., 2004) might be of value for the emerging social entrepreneur to enhance the establishment of partnerships and to navigate effectively the social and institutional barriers. In the pilot and improvement phase the application of design evaluation tools involving the users of the newly developed product service system might contribute to a thorough evaluation and provide convincing arguments for new stakeholders to get involved in the growth phase. The field of collaborative design can contribute to the development of methods and tools for the establishment of partnerships for emerging social entrepreneurship.

Our research leaves unanswered the question how exactly these tools and methods will contribute, but our aim is to further explore the potential of design methods and tools for emerging social entrepreneurship in the future.

References

Alvord, S. H., Brown, L. D. and Letts, C. W. 2004. Social Entrepreneurship and Societal Transformation: An Exploratory Study. *Journal of Applied Behavioral Science*, **40**(3): 260–82.
Austin, J. E. 2006. Three Avenues for Social Entrepreneurship Research. In Mair, J., Robinson, J. and Hockerts, K. (eds), *Social Entrepreneurship*, 3: 22–33. Basingstoke: Palgrave Macmillan.
Buijs, J. and Valkenburg, R. 1996. *Integrale Productontwikkeling*. Utrecht: Lemma.
Bornstein, D. 2004. *How to Change the World, Social Entrepreneurs and the Power of New Ideas*. New York: Oxford University Press.
Cramer, J. 2003. *Ondernemen met hoofd en hart – duurzaam ondernemen: praktijkervaringen*. Assen: Koninklijke van Gorcum.
Desa, G. and Kotha, S. 2006. Ownership, Mission and Environment: An Exploratory Analysis into the Evolution of a Technology Social Venture. In Mair, J., Robinson, J. and Hockerts, K. (eds), *Social Entrepreneurship*, **11**: 155–79. Basingstoke: Palgrave Macmillan.
Drayton, B. 2006. Everyone A Changemaker – Social Entrepreneurship's Ultimate Goal. *Innovations – Technology, Governance, Globalisation* (Winter 2006). MIT Press with Harvard University and George Mason University. Available at http://www.ashoka.org (accessed May 11.2007).
Eisenhardt, K. M. 1989. Building Theories from Case Study Research. *Academy of Management Review*, **14**(4): 532–50.
Gerometta, J., Häussermann, H. and Longo, G. 2005. Social Innovation and Civil Society in Urban Governance: Strategies for an Inclusive City. *Urban Studies*, **42**(11): 2007–21.
Katz, J. and Gartner, W. B. 1988. Properties of Emerging Organizations. *Academy of Management Review*, **13**(3): 429–41.
Langley, A. 1999. Strategies for Theorizing from Process Data. *Academy of Management Review*, **24**(4): 691–710.
Lawson, B.R. 2006. *How Designers Think* (4th edn). Oxford: Architectural Press.

Maase, S. J. F. M. and Dorst, C. H. 2007. Exploring the (co)-creation of Sustainable Solutions. *International Journal of Environmental, Cultural, Economic, and Social Sustainability*, 2(6): 5–13.

Mair, J. and Noboa, E. 2006. Social Entrepreneurship: How Intentions to Create a Social Venture are formed. In Mair, J., Robinson, J. and Hockerts, K. (eds), *Social Entrepreneurship*, 8: 121–36. Basingstoke: Palgrave Macmillan.

Mair, J., Robinson, J. and Hockerts, K. 2006. *Social Entrepreneurshp*. Basingstoke: Palgrave Macmillan.

Manzini, E., Collina, L. and Evans, S. 2004. *SolutionOoriented Partnership – How to Design Industrialised Sustainable Solutions*. Cranfield Bedfordshire: Cranfield University.

Meroni, A. 2007. Creative Communities – People Inventing Sustainable ways of Living. Milan: Edizioni Poli Design.

Mintzberg, H. 1976. The Structure of 'Unstructured' Decision Processes. *Administrative Science Quarterly*, 21(2): 246–75.

Mulgan, G. 2006a. *Social Innovation, What it is, Why it Matters and How it can be Accelerated*. London: The Young Foundation.

Mulgan, G. 2006b. The Process of Social Innovation. *Innovations – Technology, Governance, Globalisation*, 1(2): 145–61.

Perrini, F. and Vurro, C. 2006. Social Entrepreneurship: Innovation and Social Change across Theory and Practice. In Mair, J., Robinson, J. and Hockerts, K. (eds), *Social Entrepreneurship*, 5: 57–86. Basingstoke: Palgrave Macmillan.

Robinson, J. 2006. Navigating Social and Institutional Barriers to Markets: How Social Entrepreneurs Identify and Evaluate Opportunities. In Mair, J., Robinson, J. and Hockerts, K. (eds), *Social Entrepreneurship*, 7: 95–120. Basingstoke: Palgrave Macmillan.

Roozenburg, N. F. M. and Eekels, J. 1995. *Product Design: Fundamentals and Methods*. Chichester: Wiley.

Scrivener, S. A. R. 2006. Editorial. *CoDesign*, 2(3): 123–25.

Ulrich, K. T. and Eppinger, S. D. 1995. *Product Design and Development*. New York: McGraw-Hill.

VDI 2221, 1985. *VDI 2221 – Methodik zum Entwickeln und Konstruieren technischer Systeme und Producte*. Düsseldorf: VDI-Verlag.

Yin, R. K. 2003. Case Study Research – Design and Methods. Applied Social Research Methods Series Volume 5 (3rd edn). Thousand Oaks, CA: Sage.

Part IV

Strategic Perspectives in Social Entrepreneurship

11
Strategic Partnerships: Results from a Survey of Development Trusts in the UK

Helen Haugh, MariaLaura Di Domenico and Paul Tracey

Introduction

It is now generally acknowledged that all organizations operate in a relational context (Oliver, 1990), and the trend for more partnerships, either within or between sectors, is well established (Googins and Rochlin, 2000; Gray, 2000). The majority of social enterprises that operate in the UK are small and their capacity to generate social value is constrained by the low level of resources that they either own or control. A strategy for gaining access to more resources, and therefore enhancing their capacity to generate greater economic and social value, is through working in partnership with other organizations, either in the public, private or social sector.

This chapter presents the results from a survey of partnerships in which at least one of the partners is a development trust (a type of community-led social enterprise). Data was gathered from 94 development trusts in the UK. The study is guided by four research questions:

1) *To what extent do social enterprises work in partnership with other organization?*
2) *Why do they work in partnership?*
3) *What are the resource implications of partnerships?*
4) *And what are the disbenefits of partnerships?*

The chapter is presented as follows. The next section presents the context of the research and reviews the theoretical frameworks that have previously been employed to examine partnerships. The methodology of our study is then described, followed by our results and discussion.

In the conclusion we summarize the answers to the research questions that guided the study, and outline how we intend to develop our work in the future.

Partnerships and social enterprise

The strategy of working in partnership has become very popular, and many organizations create partnerships for a wide range of reasons. This rise in interest has been accompanied by a proliferation of terms used to describe the practice of working closely with another firm. These include collaboration, strategic alliance, inter-organizational relations and joint venture, as well as the more loose arrangement of a network. This has meant that the study of partnerships is very inclusive, and draws on several key theoretical frameworks.

Partnerships are built on relationships characterized by 'relatively enduring transactions, flows, and linkages that occur among or between an organization and one or more organizations in its environment' (Oliver, 1990: 241). Thus a partnership involves one or more organizations, something of value is exchanged between the partners, and it should endure beyond discrete exchanges or single transactions. Inherent in this arrangement is the presence of trust between partners which serves to lubricate transactions and facilitate the smooth exchange of resources. In our research a partnership is defined as a two-way exchange or sharing of material or immaterial resources between two organizations with the aim of maximizing social, economic or political benefits and minimizing social, economic or political costs for both organizations.

Partnerships can be categorized in terms of the relative position of each partner in the value chain, and by the economic sector of the partners. Vertical partnerships link organizations that either precede or succeed each other in the value chain, as when a public sector organization contracts with a social enterprise to deliver pre-employment services to clients. Horizontal partnerships link organizations in the same set of value chain activities, as when several social enterprises that provide similar services agree to work together. Partnerships may involve partners in the same sector (Das and Teng, 1999; Kanter, 1994) or between sectors (Googins and Rochlin, 2000), as between private and public sectors (Grimshaw et al., 2002; Hodge, 2004; Trafford and Proctor, 2006), the private sector and social economy (Arsenault, 1998; Austin, 2000; Rondinelli and London, 2003), or public sector and social economy (Kapucu, 2006; Schwartz, 2001; Waddock, 1988).

The typical structure of an economy presents opportunities for partnerships between firms in the same sector or from other sectors. The private sector consists of corporations and entrepreneurs motivated by self-interest, pursuing wealth creation and profit maximization. They are in business to earn profits and generate acceptable financial returns to stockholders (Rondinelli and London, 2003). Operating alongside the private sector is the public sector, which provides goods and services for consumption by society and those unable to access private sector suppliers. The traditional view of a mixed economy has been institutionalized into the two sectors described. However, it is well known that a host of organizations that aim to generate value and yet are neither profit-making nor statutory also operate in a mixed economy: these organizations and associations are collectively referred to as the social economy (Westlund, 2003). They play an important role in providing solutions to social issues at community level and generate the additional benefits of building social cohesion and social capital (Amin et al., 1999, 2002; Williams, 2003). Social capital is embedded in relationships between individuals and although difficult to define, measure and attribute, is both an antecedent and an outcome of relationships built on trust between parties (Knorringa and van Staveren, 2007; Nooteboom, 2007).

The defining characteristics of organizations in the social economy are that they are independent and do not distribute profits to those with an ownership interest in them. They operate in many industry sectors and deliver a range of services, for example, culture and recreation, education and research, health, social care, environmental management and recycling, housing, religion, and regeneration; and also include associational activities, such as unions, and trade and professional associations.

Within the social economy, social enterprises are distinctive as they differ from grant-dependent organizations that rely for their income on government grants, donations and member or user fees (DiMaggio and Anheier, 1990). Social enterprises pursue market-based strategies to generate independent income. They are 'market-driven, client driven, self-sufficient, commercial, or business-like' (Dart, 2004: 414). They combine the private sector's capacity for wealth creation, the public sector's service ethos, and the social economy's values of community participation and local capacity-building.

When two organizations from the same sector work together, although they have differences between them, they will share a common sectoral heritage. However, when organizations from different sectors work together, they will face difficulties arising from institutional differences in language, culture and values (Googins and Rochlin, 2000; Sagawa and Segal, 2000). Lack of knowledge of one sector about another sector, and the traditional adversarial relationships between sectors, means that partnerships between social enterprises and organizations in the private or public sectors is likely to be difficult (Dudley, 2000), and hence resources will be needed to overcome barriers to efficiency and effectiveness.

The relative power of each partner influences the process and content of the partnership. This creates a potential barrier when the two partners differ in size in that the power relationship between the partners is likely to be imbalanced. The differences in power lead to fear that the smaller partner may lose autonomy and be unduly influenced by the larger partner. As the majority of social enterprises are small, one of the disadvantages of working in partnership across sectors is that they tend to surrender their autonomy to the stronger partner and in doing so lose control over their mission (Dudley, 2000).

Thus although partnerships have the potential to generate benefits for the partners, and create additional social value for society, their creation and management also incurs costs and may produce negative outcomes, such as loss of autonomy and mission drift. In order to take account of this, our research strategy ensured that respondents reported both the positive and negative aspects of working in partnership.

Conceptual framework

The analysis of partnerships has drawn on several well-established theories in the social sciences (Kumar and Nti, 1998; Oliver, 1990; Varadarajan and Cunningham, 1995). In our research we draw upon resource dependence theory, strategic motivation theory, collaborative advantage, organizational learning, and legitimacy theory to investigate the extent, motivation, costs and disbenefits of partnerships in which one of the partners is a social enterprise.

The two main tenets of resource dependence theory are that few organizations are self-sufficient with respect to critical resources and that all firms are heterogeneous and possess asymmetric abilities to develop and acquire resources (Pfeffer and Salancik, 1978). The lack of self-sufficiency leads firms to depend on other firms to expand their resource portfolio. The creation of partnerships is one way of managing resource dependence since they are a vehicle for bringing additional resources into the firm. Thus, for example, when a social enterprise agrees to work in partnership with a public sector organization to deliver health services to clients, they will earn income from the trading contract between them. Thus resource dependence theory supports the proposition that the motivation for establishing a partnership with another organization is to acquire resources.

Strategic motivation theory proposes that the rationale for a firm's strategy is to enhance its competitive position (Kogut, 1988). The strategic purpose of organizations in the social economy is to create social value (Austin et al., 2006). Thus, when a social enterprise agrees to work in partnership with a corporation, as when Ben and Jerry's agrees a social franchise arrangement to create jobs for the long-term unemployed in a 'partnership', this enables the social enterprise to help more people return to work. The theory of strategic motivation supports the proposition that a social enterprise will work in partnership with another firm if this will enable it to achieve its strategic objectives.

In addition to achieving their strategic objectives, an important benefit from working in partnership is that it enables a firm to achieve more than it would be able to achieve when working alone: the total social value added is greater than would have been achieved by both partners working independently. Thus, when two social enterprises that offer similar services agree to work together, they generate additional benefits in terms of economies of scale and scope. The theory of collaborative advantage (Huxham, 1993) supports the proposition that a social enterprise will work in partnership with another firm if the benefits of doing so exceed those that could be generated individually by each partner.

The motivation to work in partnership is also explained by the opportunity to exchange knowledge and learn from partners (Doz and Hamel, 1998). Much organizational knowledge is tacit, and embedded in the rites, rituals and routines of the organization. The enduring nature of partnerships and the opportunities they create for social exchange ensures that time is available for interpersonal interaction in which organizational knowledge is transferred between the partners. For social enterprises the achievement of financial sustainability is fundamental to their survival and is a skill they could learn from organizations in the private sector. Thus organizational learning theory supports the proposition that a social enterprise will work in partnership with other firms in order to gain knowledge from its partner.

Finally, engaging in partnerships enables a social enterprise to gain legitimacy to operate from its association with the actions and reputation of the partner. Legitimacy, or societal approval to operate and exercise authority (Dowling and Pfeffer, 1975), in turn brings benefits through raising the profile of the organization and facilitating access to resources. A partnership might add value by enhancing the reputation and raising the profile of the social enterprise with external stakeholders. The benefits can be mutual – corporations might pursue a strategy of partnering with the social economy as a tool to enhance its corporate social responsibility profile (Rondinelli and London, 2003). Legitimacy theory supports the proposition that a social enterprise will work in partnership with other firms if doing so will enhance its legitimacy to stakeholders.

Partnerships therefore have the potential to add value by increasing the resources of the social enterprise, enabling them to achieve their strategic objectives and deliver more than could be achieved by working alone; creating opportunities for knowledge exchange and learning; and enabling partners to achieve legitimacy with different stakeholder groups. A strategy of working in partnership can be operationalized by seeking partners either within the same sector or from another sector.

Key research themes

Extent of partnership activity

There is a great deal of rhetoric surrounding the extent of partnership working which has not been challenged; in particular, partnerships involving organizations in the social economy are largely unexamined (Googins and Rochlin, 2000). In our study, we analysed the number of partnerships, the position of the partners in the value chain, and the sector of the partners.

Motives for working in partnership

Explanations for creating and sustaining partnerships have proposed a wide range of motives to explain why a firm would work in partnership with another organization. Our literature review identified four main motives, each of which add value to the partners: to increase income, to achieve the objectives of the social enterprise, to improve knowledge and expertise, and to enhance legitimacy and raise the profile of the social enterprise. The motivation to engage in partnership working was examined by asking respondents to identify the benefits they attributed to working in partnership. The aim of this question was to enable us to identify the value that partnerships add to the social economy.

Resource implications of partnerships

The creation and management of an agreement to work in partnership has resource implications for both partners. The establishment of the partnership will require additional resources, separate from the existing costs and overheads of each partner. We examined the resource implications of partnerships by asking respondents to identify the resources invested in establishing and managing these relationships.

Disbenefits of partnerships

As well as incurring additional costs, partnerships are likely to face problems that impact on the efficiency and effectiveness of the agreement to work together. We examined the disadvantages of working in partnership by asking respondents to identify the costs and disbenefits of establishing and managing partnerships.

Methodology

There is as yet no comprehensive list of social enterprises in the UK. Although there are many trade associations that include social enterprises in their membership, many of these include ventures that are also dependent on grants and philanthropy. To ensure that we gathered data from social enterprises that are committed to achieving financial sustainability from trading, our sample frame was the membership of the Development Trusts Association (DTA) in the UK.

The first development trusts in the UK were created in the 1970s, and their origins are rooted in the community development corporations that emerged in deprived areas of the US in the 1960s. Development trusts aim to encourage and facilitate social, economic and/or environmental regeneration through the provision of a range of community-centred services, such as building restoration, managed workspace, pre-employment support and training, childcare, recycling services, and community transport. Each has a strong geographical identity and serves multiple communities of interest (DTA, 2006). Development trusts are independent organizations and aim to achieve financial sustainability through asset-based development, trading, and service delivery contracts.

Data was gathered from respondents in a questionnaire that was sent to all members of the DTA. Thus our findings provide a detailed view of partnerships for a specific type of social enterprise, and are not generalizable to all social enterprises. However, our results do provide a base for conceptualizing the social economy.

Data collection

Following good survey practice guidelines (Dillman, 1978, 1999), data collection was carried out according to a number of discrete stages. To begin, permission to send the survey to the membership of the DTA was secured from the Association and a letter of introduction was sent to the chief executive (or equivalent senior manager) of each member. The letter explained the aims and process of the research. This was followed by an e-mail to each member seeking their commitment to participate in the survey. Subsequently, a second e-mail was sent to all members in which the link to the online questionnaire was given. All potential respondents were provided with the full names and contact details of the researchers. Those members who did not want to complete the survey were able to deselect themselves from participating in the research. Three weeks after inviting respondents to complete the online questionnaire, e-mail reminders were sent to all remaining non-respondents.

Results

Of the 301 questionnaires distributed, 107 (35.5%) responses were received after the above stages of data collection were complete. Some 13 (partially completed responses) were unusable because of incomplete data, resulting in 94 (31.2%) usable responses. This represents a good response rate compared with similar studies on dyadic alliances (John, 1984).

Respondent profile

The survey was distributed to senior personnel in each development trust and the respondents were chief executives (40.4%), managers (24.5%), and directors (12.8%). The majority of respondents had been employed by their organization for between one and five years (52.1%). This is followed by those employed for between five and ten years (25.5%), and finally those with more than ten years' employment (11.7%). We were therefore confident that respondents were knowledgeable about the motivations, resource implications, and challenges that their organization encountered when working in partnership. In addition, the previous employment of respondents was in the private sector

(23.4%), the public sector (27.7%), and the social economy (31.9%). This shows that there is movement by executives at senior level between sectors, and this may impact on their willingness to engage in cross-sector partnerships.

Organizational profile

Most of the sample had been established for more than one year (93.6%). The majority of ventures were between one and less than five years old (37.2%), followed by between five and less than ten years (30.9%), and 25.5% had been established for more than ten years. Thus most of the development trusts surveyed had had time to develop and implement successful strategies, and where partnerships are concerned, sufficient time to create and establish relationships with partnering organizations.

The size of each development trust was measured by employment and turnover. Most of the ventures are small and employed fewer than ten full-time staff (73.4%), and only 4.3% employed more than 40 full-time staff. This endorses the view that the structure of the social economy in the UK is polarized between many small and few large organizations. Although 21.3% did not employ any part-time staff or volunteers (24.5%), 63.8% of ventures employed between one and ten part-time staff, and 33% included volunteers in their workforce. This again endorses the general assumption of the pluralistic nature of the social enterprise workforce.

In relation to turnover, 89 respondents provided detailed information about their income. The results show that in the previous full trading year, 24.5% of respondents earned less than £100,000, and 13.4% earned more than £1 million. The majority of ventures (33%) earned between £100,000 and £400,000. Very few respondents were dependent on one source of income: trading (3.3%), grants (5.6%), and private sector sponsorship (1.12%). Thus, although they aim to achieve financial sustainability from trading, the reality is that most combine income from several sources, including trading, grants, sponsorship, donations and investments.

Some 20.2% of respondents had yet to develop an income stream from trading, whereas 15.7% earned more than 75% of their income this way. The importance of relationships with the public sector is endorsed by the finding that more than 40% of respondents received 75% of their income from the public sector. In contrast, income from sponsorships and donations were not important sources of income for the majority of respondents (not received by 72.2% and 63.6% of respondents respectively). Therefore, although they manage several income streams, the most important sources are the public sector, and the least important sources are sponsorship and donations. This endorses the rejection by social enterprises of grant dependency and pursuit of independent sources of income from service delivery contracts and trading.

Bi-variate analysis of annual income by source of income found that as the size of the organization increases, the proportion of income generated from trading increases. This is an encouraging result as it shows that growth is being achieved through increases in independent income. Moreover, the results showed that as the size of the organization increases, the proportion of income derived from public sector grants decreases. For example, organizations with a turnover of less than £100,000 derived 70.61% of their annual income from public sector grants compared with 47.9% for those earning over £1 million. This shows that the largest are more actively involved in trading in the market place and are thus likely to be more sustainable in the long term.

Extent of partnership activity

Of the respondents, 58.5% were involved in at least one dyadic partnership, and of these 81.8% had partnerships with more than one organization. Respondents were asked to complete the questionnaire in relation to the dyadic partnership they considered to be the most significant for their organization. The most important partnerships nominated by respondents were with the public sector (43.6%), the social economy (43.6%) and the private sector (12.7%). The majority of partnerships are vertical trading agreements in which the social enterprise is either a supplier of services to, or provides services on behalf of, their partner. Thus cross-sector partnerships were more important than same sector partnerships, and involved the contractual delivery of services in exchange for income.

Data was gathered about the duration, or intended duration, of the most important partnership as specified by the respondent. The majority (92.7%) reported that the duration of the partnership was longer than one year. Of these, 41.8% stated that it was ongoing and not time-limited. This confirms that the important partnerships were enduring relationships between the two parties.

Analysis of previous employment of the respondent when compared with the sector of their most important partner organization was conducted to explore the extent of path dependence in partnerships. Our

Table 11.1 Previous employment and partner sector

Respondent sector	Partner sector		Non-profit	Total
	Public	**Private**		
Public	8	0	5	13
Private	5	2	4	11
Non-profit	7	3	10	20
Other	4	2	3	3

N = number of respondents.

data relates to only 53 respondents and hence correlation analysis is not possible. However, the results do indicate that previous employment might influence choice of partner (Table 11.1); this would be interesting to explore with a larger data set.

Data was gathered about the initiation of the partnership. Of the respondents, 52.7% reported that they had initiated their most important partnership, 25.4% had been initiated by the partner, and 20% reported that their most important partnership had been initiated by a third party. This suggests that the networks are important sources of potential partners and are therefore a valuable strategic resource for the organization.

Four main motivations to work in partnership were examined. Respondents were asked to rate the benefits of their most important partnership for their own organization, and also to comment on the benefits of the arrangement to their partner (Table 11.2).

The results show that the most important motive for working in partnership is the strategic aim of attaining the objectives of the development trusts and the partner. This is followed by the opportunities

Table 11.2 Motives for working in partnership

Motive	Benefit to development trust (in %)	Benefit to partner (in %)
Facilitate attainment of key organizational objectives	90.9	87.0
Improve knowledge, learn and gain expertise	81.8	64.8
Gain legitimacy and raise profile of own organization	83.6	68.2
Increase income	69.1	31.5

for gaining knowledge and expertise, and raising the profile of the venture. The ability to increase the income of the venture from working in partnership is important, yet less so than the opportunity to achieve strategic objectives. In relation to the motivation of the partner, the opportunity to increase income was not rated as highly, suggesting that the financial benefits of partnerships are also less important than the strategic benefits. For all partnerships between the sample and the private sector, bi-variate analysis of sector and motive found that the benefit of the partnership in terms of raising the profile of the private sector partner was a motivating factor.

Respondents were asked to evaluate the effectiveness of their most important partnership in relation to communication between partners, partner involvement, community involvement, the availability of financial resources and progress towards achieving the objectives of the partnership, the development trusts, and the partner organization. The responses (Table 11.3) show that with the exception of financial resources, respondents evaluated the partnership highly. This is endorsed by the correlation of responses between the questions.

Table 11.3 Evaluation of the partnership by the development trust

	Mean	Std. Dev.	1	2	3	4	5	6	7
1. Levels of communication with partner organization	3.96	0.93	1.00						
2. Involvement of partner organization	3.86	1	0.63	1.00					
3. Involvement of community	3.79	0.96	0.35	0.17	1.00				
4. Availability of adequate financial resources	2.86	1.13	0.38	0.31	0.36	1.00			
5. Progress towards key objectives of the partnership	3.76	1.08	0.52	0.43	0.36	0.41	1.00		
6. Progress towards key objectives of the social enterprise	3.8	1.03	0.55	0.39	0.45	0.45	0.68	1.00	
7. Progress towards key objectives of the partner	4.07	0.78	0.32	0.19	0.40	0.42	0.57	0.64	1.00

Respondents were asked about the costs that had been incurred in setting up the partnership. Financial or capital investment costs were incurred by 43.7% of firms. However, 30.9% reported that they had not incurred any direct financial costs. This is a surprising finding that may be explained by the absorption of partnership costs into the total costs of the social enterprise. Costs relating to the secondment of staff to create and manage the partnership had been incurred by 30.9% of social enterprises. Thus some respondents did not calculate the costs of their most important partnership, and it is therefore likely that they were absorbed into the total costs of the venture. This might be a reflection of the fact either that the cost and accounting systems of respondents is not adequate enough to separate costs of different partnerships, or that partnerships are not viewed by the firm as a distinct activity with their own cost centre.

A quarter of respondents had not carried out any market research into the need for and viability of the partnership prior to its creation. This shows that, although most ventures had assessed the strategic and financial implications of their most important partnership, a minority had not and had therefore acted opportunistically.

The managerial arrangement for the partnership defines the remit, processes and procedures of the arrangement, and an effective arrangement will enhance its legitimacy (Kumar and Nti, 1998). In terms of the management and coordination of the partnership, a combination of formal reporting mechanisms (69%) and informal exchanges (58.2%) were adopted by the ventures. Some 45.5% of ventures employed individual(s) who were devoted solely to managing the partnership.

Thus the findings concerning costs and management of the partnership are not conclusive, suggesting that some respondents create and manage partnerships as specific cost centres with their own staff, whereas others absorb their costs and management into the general running of their organization. Therefore, the approaches to working in partnership vary between formal strategic management, administration and control, to opportunistic, informal and less rigorous procedures.

Disbenefits of partnerships

The greatest disadvantages of partnerships for both the respondent and the partner were related to staff and other resource constraints (52.7% and 30.9% respectively) (Table 11.4). Although it was anticipated that difficulties would arise as a result of differences in culture and values

Table 11.4 Disbenefits of partnerships

Disbenefit	Development trust (%)	Partner (%)
Staff/other resource constraints	52.7	30.9
Financial/capital costs	30.9	21.8
Loss of autonomy	18.2	20
Clash in ethos/key objectives with partner organization	18.2	12.7

between the partners, this was mentioned by relatively few respondents (18.2% and 12.7%).

Respondents were asked to evaluate the level of power in decision-making held by their organization, and to comment on the perceived balance of power between partners. As most development trusts in the sample were small, it was anticipated that the partner organization would exert most power over decisions concerning the partnership. However, most respondents reported that both organizations held equal power in decision-making (50.9%), and the remainder were equally divided between the development trust holding more power (23.6%) and the partner being the most powerful (23.6%). Thus, despite the disadvantages of size, most partnerships were associated with equitable distribution of power in decision-making. This is further supported by the responses concerning autonomy: it was anticipated that this would be lost by partners when working together. This is an interesting finding which, despite the large numbers of small organizations in the sample, does not reflect issues of power difference, loss of autonomy or a diluting of the social mission of the social enterprise (Dudley, 2000). Smaller partners are thus not unduly influenced by their partner, and the data indicates that each partner is able to influence or determine strategic objectives to serve their interests (Cook and Emerson, 1978). The partnerships were thus found to be based upon mutually beneficial patterns of co-operation that drew on the expertise of the partners.

Perceptions of partnerships

All respondents (n = 94) were asked to evaluate the benefits and disbenefits of partnerships. Thus we are able to compare responses of those who have adopted a strategy for partnerships, and those who have not (Table 11.5).

Table 11.5 Perceptions of partnerships

		No partnership strategy	Partnership strategy
Ability to deal with	Mean	3.47	3.98
community based issues	Std. Dev.	0.65	0.77
	P(T <= t)two-tail	0.006*	
Ability to include different	Mean	3.52	3.92
stakeholders in	Std. Dev.	0.83	0.68
decision-making	P(T <= t)two-tail	0.035*	
Ability of partners to reach	Mean	3.08	3.5
consensus	Std. Dev.	0.63	0.85
	P(T <= t)two-tail	0.027*	
Autonomy when partnering	Mean	2.48	2.96
with public sector	Std. Dev.	0.53	1.07
	P(T <= t)two-tail	0.018*	
Autonomy when partnering	Mean	2.8	3.11
with private sector	Std. Dev.	0.61	1.04
	P(T <= t)two-tail	0.129	

*Significant at the 0.05 level.

The mean, standard deviation, two-tailed T test and the p value have been calculated. All results are significant (0.05 level), with the exception of autonomy when collaborating with the private sector. Table 11.4 shows that development trusts that have adopted a strategy of partnering are more positive than those that have not about the ability of the partnership to deal with community-based issues, to include different stakeholders, to reach a consensus between partners, and to retain autonomy when partnering with the public and private sectors. The findings from the survey do not, however, support the less favourable perceptions of partnerships held by those respondents who have not implemented strategic partnerships.

Conclusion

The aim of the research was to investigate partnerships involving social enterprises. Despite the rhetoric of increased partnerships in the social economy, and the many case studies of good practice that have been published, the lack of previous quantitative research led us to carry out a survey in which the sample frame was the membership of the DTA.

The majority of development trusts were small in terms of employment and turnover, and 58.5% were involved in partnerships. Thus they are more likely to be engaged in partnerships than not. Most of the partnerships were with either the public sector or organizations in the social economy, and incidence of partnerships between development trusts and the private sector was relatively low. Most respondents were positive about the benefits of working in partnership, and appreciated their role in achieving the objectives of the partners, enhancing learning, and raising the profile of the organization. Thus the driving force behind partnership working was strategic, rather than resource-dependent.

However, in common with smaller firms in the for-profit sector, the small size of most development trusts means that few resources are ever surplus to requirements. A partnership strategy has resource implications in terms of creating and managing relationships. Most respondents adopted a combination of formal and informal management and administration of the partnership. For some respondents, the costs associated with their most important partnership were not calculated separately and were absorbed into the costs of the venture. This means that an accurate cost-benefit analysis cannot be carried out, and hence it is not possible to calculate the financial sustainability of implementing a partnership strategy.

Although a strategy of working in partnership has the potential to increase access to resources, achieve objectives and raise the profile of the organization, working in partnership generally requires compromises to be agreed and decisions made in the best interests of the partnership, rather than the individual partners. The generally perceived loss of autonomy that is assumed to arise in partnerships was found to be less important than the human and other resources, and financial and capital resources required by the partnership.

To conclude, our survey has provided an overview of partnerships involving development trusts in the UK. Our subsequent research builds on these insights by gathering qualitative data from informants working for both partner organizations in ten case studies of same-sector and cross-sector partnerships involving social enterprises. The case studies will draw on resource dependence theory, social exchange theory and power relations to provide a deeper understanding of the inter-organizational processes associated with creating and managing partnerships in which one of the partners is a social enterprise. This will enable us to hear the voices of both parties involved in partnerships and with them explore the deeper, processual aspects of creating and managing relationships between partners.

References

Amin, A., Cameron, A. and Hudson, R. 1999. Welfare at Work? The Potential of the UK Social Economy. *Environment and Planning A*, **31**(11): 2033–51.

Amin, A., Cameron, A. and Hudson, R. 2002. *Placing the Social Economy*. London: Routledge.

Arsenault, J. 1998. *Forging Nonprofit Alliances*. San Francisco: Jossey Bass.

Austin, J. 2000. *The Collaboration Challenge*. San Francisco: Jossey Bass.

Austin, J. E., Stevenson, H. and Wei-Skillern, J. 2006. Social Entrepreneurship and Commercial Entrepreneurship: Same, Different, or Both. *Entrepreneurship Theory and Practice*, **30**(1): 1–22.

Cook, K. and Emerson, R. 1978. Power, Equity and Commitment in Exchange Networks. *American Sociological Review*, **43**(5): 721–39.

Dart, R. 2004. The Legitimacy of Social Enterprise. *Nonprofit Management & Leadership*, **14**(4): 411–24.

Das, T. K. and Teng, B. S. 1999. Managing Risks in Strategic Alliances. *Academy of Management Executive*, **13**(4): 50–62.

Dillman, D. 1978. *Mail and Telephone Surveys: The Total Design Method*. New York: Wiley.

Dillman, D. 1999. *Mail and Internet Surveys: The Tailored Design Method*. New York: Wiley.

DiMaggio, P. and Anheier, H. 1990. The Sociology of Nonprofit Organizations and Sectors. *Annual Review of Sociology*, **16**(1): 137–59.

Dowling, J. and Pfeffer, J. 1975. Organizational Legitimacy: Social Values and Organizational Behaviour. *Pacific Sociological Review*, **18**(1): 122–36.

Doz, Y. and Hamel, G. 1998. *Alliance Advantage: The Art of Creating Value through Partnering*. Boston, MA: Harvard Business School Press.

DTA 2006. *Development Trusts Association Annual Membership Survey*. London: DTA.

Dudley, L. 2000. Searching for a Collective Ethos in Inter-Organizational Relationships. *International Journal of Organizational Theory and Behaviour*, 3(3&4): 479–502.

Googins, B. K. and Rochlin, S. A. 2000. Creating the Partnership Society: Understanding the Rhetoric and Reality of Cross-Sectoral Partnerships. *Business and Society Review*, **105**(1): 127–44.

Gray, B. 2000. Assessing Inter-Organizational Collaboration. In Faulkner, D. and De Rond, M. (eds), *Cooperative Strategy – Economic, Business, and Organizational Issues*, : 243–61. Oxford: Oxford University Press.

Grimshaw, D., Vincent, S. and Willmott, H. 2002. Going Privately: Partnership and Outsourcing in UK Public Services. *Public Administration*, **80**(3): 475–502.

Hodge, G. A. 2004. The Risky Business of Public-Private Partnerships. *Australian Journal of Public Administration*, **63**(4): 37–49.

Huxham, C. 1993. Pursuing Collaborative Advantage. *Journal of the Operational Research Society*, **44**(6): 599–611.

John, G. 1984. An Empirical Investigation of Some Antecedents of Opportunism in a Marketing Channel. *Journal of Marketing Research*, **21**(3): 278–89.

Kanter, R. B. 1994. Collaborative Advantage: The Art of Alliances. *Harvard Business Review*, **72**(4): 96–108.

Kapucu, N. 2006. Public-Nonprofit Partnerships for Collective Action in Dynamic Contexts of Emergencies. *Public Administration*, 84(1): 205–20.

Kogut, B. 1988. Joint Ventures: Theoretical and Empirical Perspectives. *Strategic Management Journal*, 9(4): 319–32.

Knorringa, P. and van Staveren, I. 2007. Beyond Social Capital: A Critical Approach. *Review of Social Economy*, 65(1): 1–9.

Kumar, R. and Nti, K. O. 1998. Differential Learning and Interaction in Alliance Dynamics: A Process and Outcome Discrepancy Model. *Organization Science*, 9(3): 356–67.

Nooteboom, B. 2007. Social Capital, Institutions and Trust. *Review of Social Economy*, 65(1): 29–53.

Oliver, C. 1990. Determinants of Inter-Organizational Relationships: Integration and Future Directions. *Academy of Management Review*, 15(2): 241–65.

Pfeffer, J. and Salancik, G. 1978. *The External Control of Organizations: A Resource Perspective*. New York: Harper Row.

Rondinelli, D. A. and London, T. 2003. How Corporations and Environmental Groups Cooperate: Assessing Cross-Sector Alliances and Collaborations. *Academy of Management Executive*, 17(1): 61–76.

Sagawa, S. and Segal, E. 2000. *Common Interest, Common Good: Creating Value through Business and Social Sector Partnerships*. Boston: Harvard Business School Press.

Schwartz, R. 2001. Collaborating with the Third Sector – Problem or Solution: Lessons from the Israeli Experience. *International Journal of Public Administration*, 24(11): 1127–31.

Trafford, S. and Proctor, T. 2006. Successful Joint Venture Partnerships: Public-Private Partnerships. *International Journal of Public Sector Management*, 19(2): 117–29.

Varadarajan, R. P. and Cunningham, M. H. 1995. Strategic Alliances: A Synthesis of Conceptual Foundations. *Journal of the Academy of Marketing Science*, 23(4): 282–96.

Waddock, S. A. 1988. Picking Powerful Partners for Social Progress. *Business and Society Review*, Winter88, 64: 20–4.

Westlund, H. 2003. Social Economy and Employment – The Case of Sweden. *Review of Social Economy*, 61(2): 163–82.

Williams, C. 2003. Developing Community Involvement: Contrasting Local and Regional Participatory Cultures in Britain and their Implications for Policy. *Regional Studies*, 37(5): 531–41.

12
A Resource-Based View of Value Creation in Social Purpose Business Ventures

Nathalie Moray and Robin Stevens

Introduction

Social entrepreneurship has become a global phenomenon that employs innovative approaches to addressing social issues with the aim to improve benefits for society. Academic interest in the topic has mainly focused on practitioner events and teaching, and it is only recently that social entrepreneurship has become subject to rigorous academic analysis. The rise of social entrepreneurship as a topic of interest is related to an increasing societal and political consensus about the fact that organizations need to address social issues, questioning the narrow focus on profit maximization that has traditionally been put forward by economists (Margolis and Walsh, 2003). This trend has put social responsibility of business or 'triple bottom line' objectives (people, profit and planet) as one of the priorities at different levels of policy-making.

Academics have looked at this from two broad perspectives. First, the widely established business and society literature has investigated issues as broad as corporate social responsibility, business ethics, sustainable development, corporate social performance, stakeholder management and corporate citizenship (Antal and Sobczak, 2004). The common denominator of this research stream is the expectation that organizations in general – and established firms in particular – should consider how they interface with their societal environment or manage challenging social problems (Carroll, 1991; Wood, 1991). Second, a research stream has emerged within the management and entrepreneurship literatures, looking at entrepreneurial activity as a source of social value creation (e.g. Christie and Honig, 2006). Social entrepreneurship has been on the rise in recent decades (Austin et al., 2006; Peredo and

Chrisman, 2006; Peredo and McLean, 2006), informed by the generally accepted notion that entrepreneurial activity positively affects economic development and growth (e.g. Acs and Audretsch, 1990; Ireland et al., 2003). The concept originated from the non-profit sector, where entrepreneurial initiatives were increasingly seen as alternative funding schemes as public funding decreased substantially (Dees, 1998; Emerson, 2003; Fowler, 2000; Mort et al., 2003; Weerawardena and Mort, 2006). To date, most researchers acknowledge that social entrepreneurship is entrepreneurship with an embedded social purpose, creating social value (e.g. Christie and Honig, 2006; Peredo and McLean, 2006, Peredo and Chrisman, 2006), through the recognition and exploitation of entrepreneurial opportunities (e.g. Austin et al., 2006; Mair and Martí, 2006), not being limited to a particular judical/organizational form (e.g. Mair and Martí, 2006).

However, academics and policy-makers still know very little about the process of value creation of social entrepreneurs. Addressing this gap, this chapter builds a resource-based theory of value creation that can be used as a point of departure for explanatory empirical studies. The chapter unfolds along the following lines. First, we offer a succinct overview of the literature that has focused on the social responsibility of business. Second, we suggest studying this phenomenon in 'social purpose business ventures', since this type of firm can be seen as operating on the cross borders of the economic realm and the social realm. Third, we conceptualize 'value creation' and build a resource-based theoretical model for better understanding the process of value creation in social purpose business ventures. More specifically, we discuss the theoretical constructs social mission, business model and social performance. We close with suggestions for further research and the main contributions to the literature.

Literature on the social responsibility of business

In the last decade, academics have increasingly shown interest in the social responsibility of business with its focus on 'triple bottom line' objectives (people, profit and planet). The widely established business and society (B&S hereafter) literature has investigated issues as broad as corporate social responsibility (CSR hereafter), business ethics and stakeholder theory, and studied how companies are expected to become socially committed (Scherer and Palazzo, 2007). The common denominator of this research stream is the expectation that firms should consider how they interface with their societal environment or manage challenging social problems (Carroll, 1991; Wood, 1991). In a seminal article, Carroll (1979) presented a continuum on which firms can be potentially positioned in terms of their ethical stance towards what they consider as their responsibility. Corporate social responsibility refers to the specific actions that organizations undertake to move beyond their economic and legal responsibilities, addressing ethical issues and potentially embracing philanthropic actions. The presence of discretion is a key issue as many corporate activities that further social welfare are mandated by law (Barnett, 2007). McWilliams and Siegel (2001) adhere to this view and refer to corporate social responsibility as 'the actions that appear to further some social good, beyond the interests of the firm, required by law'. Although definitional agreement is increasing, there is no consensus about the basic assumption that corporate social responsibility is indeed a responsibility of firms beyond their wealth generating function (Aguilera et al., 2007; Barnett, 2007). The main argument against corporate social responsibility is that expending limited resources on social issues necessarily decreases the competitive position of a firm by unnecessarily increasing its cost (Barnett, 2007). Although this perspective has dominated curricula of business schools and the thinking of managers for years (Brickson, 2007), corporate social responsibility has been moving towards a mainstream business practice (Godfrey and Hatch, 2007; Porter and Kramer, 2006). Pressure on firms to engage in CSR has increased over the last three decades (Aguilera et al., 2007; Campbell, 2007; Jenkins, 2006; McWilliams and Siegel, 2000, 2001; Porter and Kramer, 2006). As a result, established firms awoke to it only after being surprised by public responses to issues they had not previously thought were part of their business responsibilities (Porter and Kramer, 2006). More recently, academics and policy-makers have also gained interest in how SMEs can integrate corporate social responsibility practices in their day-to-day business activities (e.g. Jenkins, 2006; Murillo and Lozano, 2006).

Scholars studied corporate social responsibility from different theoretical angles such as institutional theory (Campbell, 2007), stakeholder theory (Brickson, 2007), the resource-based view (Russo and Fouts, 1997), multilevel theory (Aguilera et al., 2007), and social movement theories (Den Hond and De Bakker, 2007). However, empirical research is often conflicting, potentially pointing to measurement issues (McWilliams et al., 2006). Exemplary for this debate is the research on the link between corporate social responsibility and corporate social performance (Marquis et al., 2007). Some studies indicate no relationship (e.g. Aupperle et al., 1985; McWilliams and Siegel, 2000), some a positive (e.g. Russo and Fouts, 1997) and some a negative relationship (e.g. McWilliams and Siegel, 2001; McWilliams et al., 2006), which shows an inconsistency in the results.

Whereas corporate social responsibility emerged in a corporate context (e.g. Brickson, 2007; Porter and Kramer, 2006), social entrepreneurship originated from the not-for-profit sector (Dees, 1998; Emerson, 2003; Fowler, 2000; Mort et al., 2003; Weerawardena and Mort, 2006). More specifically, social entrepreneurship is seen as a response to diminishing government involvement in the economy and society (e.g. Den Hond and De Bakker, 2007; Nicholls, 2006; Perrini and Vurro, 2006; Sharir and Lerner, 2006; Sullivan, 2007) and extended rapidly to the private and public sector.

Although the corporate social responsibility literature and the social entrepreneurship literature share a primary interest in the creation of social value, their fundamental assumptions are distinct: socially responsible companies are those whose primary goal is profit (Carroll, 1999), whereas social entrepreneurs emphasize social value and economic value creation as a necessary condition to ensure (financial) viability (Dorado, 2006; Schuler and Cording, 2006).

The question of what exactly encompasses 'social entrepreneurship' has been a main topic of interest to date. Both the locus of social entrepreneurship and the levels of analysis it potentially embraces has been subject of study.

First, the locus of social entrepreneurship is argued to consist of three broad perspectives (Mair and Martí, 2006). The first perspective posits that social entrepreneurship resides in a not-for-profit context (Mort et al., 2003). On the one hand this perspective involves efficient non-profit management, bringing market-based skills and business expertise to the non-profit sector, and the US approach to 'social enterprise' (Nyssens, 2006) on the other. In this view, social enterprises are viewed as an innovative response to the funding problems of non-profit organizations, which are finding it increasingly difficult to solicit private donations and government and foundation grants (Dees, 1998). The second perspective views social entrepreneurship as the socially responsible practice of commercial businesses and overlaps to a large extent with the literature on corporate social responsibility. The third perspective views social entrepreneurship as a means to tackle social problems and catalyze social transformation, irrespective of the for-profit or not-for-profit status of the organization (Mair and Martí, 2006). More specifically, social entrepreneurship is a process involving the innovative use and combination of resources to pursue opportunities to catalyze social change and/or address social needs (Mair and Martí, 2006). The European perspective on 'social enterprises' (DTI, 2007; Nyssens, 2006; Vidal, 2005) can be positioned within this perspective, referring to organizations with an explicit aim to benefit the community, initiated by a group of citizens and in which the material interest of capital investors is subject to limits. Social enterprises also place a high value on their autonomy and on economic risk-taking related to ongoing socio-economic activity (Nyssens, 2006). In practice, however, researchers often take a narrower view of the concept of 'social enterprise', limiting social enterprises to the social economy in general (Nyssens, 2006) and 'work integrating social enterprises' (WISEs) in particular (e.g. Campi et al., 2006; Delaunois and Becker, 2001; Hulgard, 2006). WISE's are profit businesses that seek to help poorly qualified unemployed people, who are at risk of permanent exclusion from the labor market, return to work and to society in general through productive activity (Vidal, 2005).

Next to the discourse about the locus of social entrepreneurship, the field embraces individual, organizational, and inter-organizational levels of analysis. Whereas definitions of social entrepreneurship typically refer to processes at the (inter)organizational level, definitions of social entrepreneurs focus on the founder of the initiative (Mair and Martí, 2006). The individual social entrepreneur is referred to as a 'change maker' (Sharir and Lerner, 2006), acting upon an opportunity and gathering resources to exploit it. Most empirical work is limited to explorative cases or qualitative field studies, focusing on the characteristics of the process of social entrepreneurship (e.g. Anderson et al., 2006; Sharir and Lerner, 2006; Waddock and Post, 1991). Entrepreneurship is concerned with the discovery and exploitation of profitable opportunities focusing on the process of firm creation encompassing issues such as generating promising ideas, resource mobilization, firm organizing, and market making (Eckhardt and Shane, 2003; Shane and Venkataraman, 2000). To date, most researchers acknowledge that social entrepreneurship is 'entrepreneurship with an embedded social purpose, creating social value' (e.g. Christie and Honig, 2006; Peredo and Chrisman, 2006; Peredo and McLean, 2006), through the recognition and exploitation of entrepreneurial opportunities (e.g. Austin et al., 2006; Mair and Martí, 2006), not limited to a particular judical/organizational form (e.g. Mair and Martí, 2006).

Studying social purpose business ventures

Both the B&S and the social entrepreneurship literature have looked at organizations addressing social issues from different perspectives and in a variety of contexts. Conceptually, both fields have contributed to our understanding of particular contexts in which social engagement can operate. However, to date, the corporate social responsibility literature lacks empirical studies focusing particularly on how small and medium-sized businesses act 'responsibly' (Jenkins, 2006; Murillo and Lozano, 2006). Concurrently, social entrepreneurship research is in need of empirical research that moves away from descriptive case studies and that is conceptually clear about the particular (sub)population of 'social entrepreneurs' it wants to study. We focus on social purpose business ventures, defined as *a firm in the entrepreneurial stage, with an explicit social mission, financed at least 50% by private investors, which achieves sustainability through trading*. We develop our arguments below.

First, there is a general consensus that social entrepreneurship is an *'entrepreneurial activity that primarily serves a social objective'* (Austin et al., 2006; Peredo and Chrisman, 2006; Peredo and McLean, 2006), making the social mission the central and defining characteristic (Dees, 1998; Tracey and Jarvis, 2007). Social purpose business ventures share a mission for realizing social value, rather than personal and shareholder wealth, which is the key driver for commercial entrepreneurial activity. Although a clear definition of what constitutes a 'social mission' is lacking, there is agreement that 'social missions' have in common *'the desire to benefit society or to contribute to the welfare or well-being in society'* (Mort et al., 2003; Peredo and Mclean, 2006).

Second, at least part of the working (start) capital comes from private sources (other than subsidies/gifts/grants). With this criterion we wish to capture these firms that are able to mobilize private money (e.g. bank loan, equity financing etc.). Additionally, following DTI's (2007) definition of social enterprise, the firms should achieve sustainability through trading. According to this view, trading viability, social aims and social ownership are the distinguishing features of these firms (e.g. Tracey and Jarvis, 2007). Trading is seen as the selling of services or products. Nyssens (2006) adheres to this perspective and argues that social enterprise is *'a continuous activity, producing and selling goods and/or services'*.

Third, borrowing from lifecycle models of organizations (typically ranging from three to nine phases, e.g. Gersick, 1994; O'Rand and Krecker, 1990), we focus on the entrepreneurial stage. This stage is marked by early innovation, little structure and planning and the search for appropriate business model(s). Kazanjian and Rao (1999), for example, sampled relatively young technology-based new ventures (mean age of 6.7 years) to study capability creation. The firms had to be created within the last 15 years, in order to capture their developmental character as new, emerging organizations provide a unique opportunity to assess how and why capabilities develop. In a similar fashion, Sapienza et al. (2006) and Zott and Amit (2007) sampled relatively young entrepreneurial firms to study internationalization and business model.

Similar approaches have been adopted by other researchers, typically focusing on a particular type of 'social enterprise'. Hockerts (2006) for example, claims that a *'social purpose business venture's'* – main purpose of existence is to create external social benefits through the establishment of a for-profit business. In the same vein, Dorado (2006) documents about 'social entrepreneurial ventures' while Strothotte and Wüstenhagen (2005) look at 'social entrepreneurial enterprises'. The population-level conceptualization developed in this paper adds to these contributions in that (1) it can be operationalized in a number of indicators, which potentially increases external validity, and (2) it leaves room for different judical forms, which is the dominant perspective among social entrepreneurship scholars today.

Theoretical framework for studying value creation in social purpose business ventures

For gaining understanding in the process of value creation in social entrepreneurial firms we start from 'value creation' as a central concept and use resource-based theory constructs for studying the process of value creation: the social mission, the business model and social performance.

Value creation is a central concept in the management and organization literature (Lepak et al., 2007) as the primary pursuit of business is creating and maintaining value (Sirmon et al., 2007; Wheeler et al., 2003). Kang et al. (2007) define value as the difference between benefits derived and costs incurred, which results in a greater level of appropriate benefits than target users currently possess (Sirmon et al., 2007). In this context, Bowman and Ambrosini (2000) argue that a distinction is needed between 'use value' and 'exchange value'. 'Use value' is subjectively assessed by the (potential / target) customers, which can refer to the individual, group / organization or society level (Lepak et al., 2007). Target users can be customers in the traditional sense, displaying willingness to pay for the value offered, and / or 'clients' that are bene-fiting from the value created by the firm. This is in line with Strothotte and Wüstenhagen (2005), who take the notion of 'customer value' to determine where economic value is created in social entrepreneurial enterprises. 'Customers' are broadly defined as potential users of the products and services. 'Exchange value' or 'economic value' refers to the total exchange value offered by customers (i.e. what the firm gener-ates financially) and is realised at the point of sale. Other authors have looked at value creation from a sustainable development perspective (Figge and Hahn, 2005; Hahn et al., 2007). From this point of view, companies create value in the light of the tradeoff between the use of scarce resources on one hand and the production of goods and services on the other.

Social value as such has not been subject to rigorous theorizing. In general terms, Peredo and Mclean (2006) define social value as contributing to the welfare or well-being in a given community.

Using the resource-based view to study value creation

The resource-based view (RBV hereafter) of the firm is an influential framework for understanding strategic issues (Alvarez and Busenitz, 2001; Barney, 2001) and is increasingly used by entrepreneurship schol-ars (Ireland et al., 2003). The basic argument of the RBV is that internal, firm-specific (valuable, rare, inimitable and non-substitutable) resources and capabilities lead to a competitive advantage (Colbert, 2004; Lei et al., 1996; Maritan, 2001), provide the basis of superior firm perfor-mance (Lado et al., 2006; McWilliams et al., 2006; Ray et al., 2004) and lead to value creation (Amit and Zott, 2001). From this perspec-tive, Sirmon et al. (2007) argue that the resource-based view explains the process of value creation. We sequentially build a theoretical model integrating three constructs for gaining understanding in the pro-cess of value creation in social purpose business ventures: the social mission, business model and social performance. The central argu-ment is that the business model concept addresses the issue of how value is created, referring to the process underlying the exploitation of the social mission and the achievement of particular performance levels.

Social mission

Researchers have adopted the 'social mission' as a key dimension of what characterizes social entrepreneurship (Austin et al., 2006; Mort et al., 2003; Peredo and McLean, 2006; Seelos and Mair, 2005). Clearly, a social entrepreneur has a theoretical assumption about how it wishes to create value, which is often reflected in the core mission and values of the organization. However, researchers are aware about the fact that the extent to which a firm adheres to a social mission is often a matter of relative priority, where goals related to profit realization on one hand and social value on the other operate on a continuum and often interplay (Mair and Martí, 2006; Peredo and McLean, 2006). Mission statements could be a potential point of departure for studying the 'degree' of social orientation that social purpose business ventures firms display. Mission statements are usually considered as the cornerstone of every company's strategy formulation exercise and as essential component of planning systems in large organizations (e.g. O'Gorman and Doran, 1999). However, research is inconclusive about the relationship between the mission statement and performance (Sidhu, 2003; Bartkus et al., 2006). Some scholars conclude that there is no association (O'Gorman and Doran, 1999; Pearce and David, 1987; Sidhu, 2003) while Bartkus et al. (2006) is more careful, suggesting that 'most elements in mission statements are not associated with firm performance'. A concurrent approach to learn about the degree to which social purpose business ventures adhere to a social mission is investigating 'organizational goals' that can generally be associated with doing business, such as profitability, sales growth, product/service superiority, generating value for eventual acquisition and stability and longevity of the firm (Autio et al., 2000), adding generating social value to the list. In a pilot study of work integrating social enterprises (Stevens and Moray, 2008), we find that the social goal is significantly more important than other goals in the organization (amounting to a mean score of 36 on 100 points to be divided over 6 organizational goals), which points to the potential usefulness of this measure in social purpose business ventures (see Table 12.1).

Finally, Carroll's (1979) perspective on what entails *corporate social responsibility* also provides insight in the degree to which social purpose business ventures adhere to a social mission. For evaluating the extent to which firms move beyond their economic and legal responsibilities Aupperle et al.'s (1985) operationalization of economical, legal, ethical and philanthropical actions can be used. Looking at 'orientation toward social responsibility', rather than performance (Ruf et al., 1998), the measurement tool has been used successfully by numerous scholars (e.g. Agle et al., 1999; Ibrahim et al., 2008).

Table 12.1   The relative importance of different organizational goals

	N	Min	Max	Sum	Mean	Std. Dev.
Maximizing profitability	42	0	40	431	10.26	12.28
Maximizing sales growth	42	0	40	553	13.17	13.30
Maximizing product/ service superiority	42	0	30	311	7.40	8.64
Maximizing value for eventual acquisition	42	0	20	80	1.90	5.05
Maximizing stability and longevity of the firm	42	0	80	1327	31.59	18.17
Maximizing social value	42	0	100	1498	35.67	23.34

Valid N (listwise): 42.

F-test: $p < 0.001$.

Wilcoxon test for pairs: $p < 0.001$ (except stability and longevity of the firm = not significant).

Business model

Following the social mission, each social purpose business venture develops a revenue model and structure of how its products and/or services will reach the end customer so as to create value, which is generally referred to as business model (Amit and Zott, 2001; Wüstenhagen and Boehnke, 2008). Despite the widespread use in industry and the acknowledgement that each firm needs a fitting business model to be effective (Perrini and Vurro, 2006), 'business models' are rarely studied in academic research. Although there are as many definitions as there are proponents of the term (e.g. Bonaccorsi et al., 2006; Margretta, 2002; Mahadevan, 2000; Morris et al., 2005; Timmers, 1998; Venkatraman and Henderson, 1998; Zott and Amit, 2007), most definitions refer to how and where organizations create 'value' (Lai et al., 2006; Wüstenhagen and Boehnke, 2008) and theorize using resource-based view concepts such as assets, resources and performance. For example, Lai et al. (2006) offer a typological definition based on two dimensions: type of assets involved (i.e. what products or services have been created for appropriation) and type of rights being sold (i.e. how value is appropriated). They consider four types of assets: physical, financial, intangible and human, which are in line with the types of resources as defined by

Barney (1991). Additionally, they delineate four types of asset rights: creator, distributor, landlord and broker. Further, Alt and Zimmerman (2001) distinguish six generic elements of a business model: the mission, structure, processes, revenues, legal issues and technology. More conceptually, Mahadevan (2000) states that a business model is a unique blend of the value stream for the business partners and the buyers, the revenue stream, and the logistical system.

Authors have argued that analyzing the business model requires an understanding of the strategic capabilities of the firm (Miller, 2003; Seelos and Mair, 2007; Teece et al., 1997), and an analysis of the value chain (Porter, 1985; Woiceshyn and Falkenberg, 2008). First, the strategic capability of a firm refers to the ability to perform at a level required to survive and prosper and is underpinned by the resources (Barney, 1991) and competences (Hamel and Prahalad, 1990) of the firm. Seelos and Mair (2007) refer to a business model as a set of capabilities that is configured to enable value creation consistent with either economic or social strategic objectives. Harrison and Miller (1999) argue that understanding the strategic capability is based on a profound understanding of the competitive environment, the resource base and potential of the firm, and the values that engender commitment from stakeholders to the organization's goals. Second, the value chain is argued to be an important element in the business model (Calia et al., 2007). Value chain analysis is argued to consist of four major factors (Porter, 1985):

- defining the nature of the external market the organization serves;
- identifying the particular products or services that are at the heart of the firm's existence;
- identifying the critical activities that are needed to deliver the products or services to the customer / client; and
- determining the value created by these activities.

Porter's value chain framework has been the accepted language for analyzing the logic of firm-level value creation. However, researchers have looked for alternative routes for analyzing the 'value chain' in a non-manufacturing context. Stabell and Fjeldstad (1998), for example, have explored the value shop model to analyze how non-routine problem-solving processes facilitate value creation. Woiceshyn and Falkenberg (2008) elaborated the model by looking at the underlying resources that firms need for problem solving.

Social performance

Social entrepreneurship scholars have lamented that there is a substantial lack of research in top-tier journals that demonstrate the social performance of organizations (Mair et al., 2006; Margolis and Walsh, 2003). However, two related aspects have been the subject of academic attention. First, some authors have focused on the problem of non-profit organizations and mission-driven organizations to measure their performance (Lingane and Olsen, 2004; Sawhill and Williamson, 2001; Wood, 1991). Sheehan (1996), for example, concluded that although most non-profit organizations in the sample had a clear mission statement, only 14% claimed to collect reliable measures of mission impact. Non-profit organizations have increasingly turned to traditional business models to improve their effectiveness and efficiency. In some areas, such as strategic planning, marketing and organizational development, this has proven useful. This is not the case for the measurement of the extent to which social value is created since relatively tangible and quantifiable measures such as financial indicators, market share and customer satisfaction cannot be relied on to measure social performance (Austin et al., 2006; Lingane and Olsen, 2004; Sawhill and Williamson, 2001).

Second, authors looked at corporate social performance which is defined by Wood (1991: 693) as

> a business organization's configuration of principles of social responsibility, processes of social responsiveness and policies, programs and observable outcomes as they relate to the firm's societal relationships.

According to this view, social outcomes are divided into three types: the social impact, the programs an organization use to implement socially responsible activities and the policies in place to deal with social issues. Researchers that have looked at the social impact of businesses paid attention to assessment devices such as social indicators, social reporting and accounting, the social balance sheet and social return on investment (Lingane and Olsen, 2004; Pearce, 2005; Wood, 1991). More specifically, it has been argued that for measuring the social impact of an organization the linkage between the (social) mission, goals, strategies and programs is crucial (Sawhill and Williamson, 2001; Kaplan, 2001). If the mission is not clearly defined, it is hard to develop meaningful measures of social impact. Sawhill and Williamson (2001) suggest that defining measurable goals is effective to assess the social impact of an organization. This is in line with Lepak et al. (2007), arguing that the source and target of value creation need to be clear to understand how value is created at the firm level. A 'double' or 'triple bottom line' approach is central to interpreting social venture outcomes (Nicholls, 2006). Emerson (2006) strengthens this argument by stating that for understanding value creation in social ventures, we need to track the 'blended return': the financial (exchange value), the social and environmental performance (use value).

Further research and contribution

We have developed a theoretical framework for addressing the question of how value is created in social purpose business ventures. We conceptualize this particular subpopulation of social entrepreneurs as firms in the entrepreneurial stage, with an explicit social mission, financed at least 50% by private investors, which achieve sustainability through trading.

Research that aims at empirically investigating this model in social purpose ventures will have to address a number of challenges. First, building on the operational definition of a social purpose business venture, a sample frame should be constructed that represents this theoretical population. We have identified a number of strata in which our theoretical population can be identified. These lists will be subject to telephone screening on the measures we have developed for assessing our operational definition, in order to remove 'false positives'. More specifically, we are constructing a database that compiles lists of

- people and environmental oriented cooperative firms;
- entrepreneurial firms that meet the criteria for being a work integrating social enterprise;
- firms active in the social economy (which do not belong to the previous strata);
- the investment portfolio's of social investors; and
- firms which received the legal statute of 'venture with a social objective' by the federal government.

Each of these lists has been constructed by experts in the field (strata 1, 3, 4) or is a database that has been constructed following a policy measure (strata 2 and 5). Second, the constructs we propose in this chapter are subject to rigorous operationalization to ensure construct validity. For some constructs a number of useful existing validated measures will prove to be useful (e.g. Autio et al., 2000 for 'organizational goals'; Aupperle et al., 1985 for orientation towards social responsibility), for other constructs, new multi item measures will have to be developed and pretested (e.g. the measurement of use value and exchange value).

At least three contributions to the literature can be mentioned. First, the B&S literature has largely overlooked small businesses and entrepreneurial firms in how they address social issues, especially at the level of 'discretionary' activities. Although interest for social responsibility issues in SMEs is increasing, the research developed today does not specifically focus on entrepreneurial entities that have a social mission as their dominant 'value proposition'. Second, the social entrepreneurship literature is in need for an empirical study that moves away from exploration to theory-based hypothesis testing research in a context where the entrepreneurial character of social value creation is most prominent. We argue that for an elaborate empirical study we need to achieve unit homogeneity by focusing on one well-defined (sub)population of organizations. We do this by gearing our research efforts to social purpose business ventures defined earlier. Third, we contribute to theory by constructing a framework for gaining understanding in the process of value creation in social purpose business ventures. Taking a resource-based perspective, we argue that investigating the social mission–business model–social performance nexus will provide valuable insight in how these firms balance their economic and social value creating activities, given their initial social value proposition and potentially resulting in different performance levels.

References

Acs, Z. and Audretsch, D. 1990. *Innovation and Small Firms*. Cambridge, MA: MIT Press.

Agle, B. R., Mitchell, R. K. and Sonnenfeld, J. A. 1999. Who Matters to CEOs? An Investigation of Stakeholder Attributes and Salience, Corporate Performance and CEO Values. *Academy of Management Journal*, **42**(5): 507–25.

Aguilera, R. V., Rupp, D. E., Williams, C. A. and Ganapathi, J. 2007. Putting the S Back in Corporate Social Responsibility: A Multilevel Theory of Social Change in Organizations. *Academy of Management Review*, **32**(3): 836–63.

Alt, R. and Zimmerman, H. 2001. Preface: Introduction to Special Section – Business Models. *Electronic Markets*, **11**(1): 3–9.

Alvarez, S. and Busenitz, L. 2001. The Entrepreneurship of Resource-Based Theory. *Journal of Management*, **27**(6): 755–75.

Amit, R. and Zott, C. 2001. Value Creation in e-Business. *Strategic Management Journal*, **22**(6/7): 493–520.

Anderson, R. B., Dana, L. P., and Dana, T. E. 2006. Indigenous Land Rights, Entrepreneurship, and Economic Development in Canada: 'Opting-in' to the Global Economy. *Journal of World Business*, **41**(1): 45–55.

Antal, A. B. and Sobczak, A. 2004. Beyond CSR: Organizational Learning for Global Responsibility. *Journal of General Management*, 30(2): 77–98.

Aupperle, K. E., Carroll, A. B. and Hatfield, J. D. 1985. An Empirical Examination of the Relationship Between Corporate Social Responsibility and Profitability. *Academy of Management Journal*, 28(2): 446–63.

Austin, J., Stevenson, H. and Wei-Skillern, J. 2006. Social and Commercial Entrepreneurship: Same, Different or Both? *Entrepreneurship Theory and Practice*, 30(1): 1–22.

Autio, E., Sapienza, H. J. and Almeida, J. G. 2000. Effects of Age at Entry, Knowledge Intensity, and Imitability on International Growth. *Academy of Management Journal*, 43(5): 909–24.

Barney, J. 1991. Firm Resources and Sustained Competitive Advantage. *Journal of Management*, 17(1): 99–120.

Barney, J. 2001. Resource-Based Theories of Competitive Advantage: A Ten-Year Retrospective on the Resource-Based View. *Journal of Management*, 27(6), 643–50.

Barnett, M. L. 2007. Stakeholder Influence Capacity and the Variability of Financial returns to Corporate Social Responsibility. *Academy of Management Review*, 32(3): 794–816.

Bartkus, B., Glasman, M. and McAfee, B. 2006. Mission Statement Quality and Financial Performance. *European Management Journal*, 24(1): 86–94.

Bonaccorsi, A., Giannangeli, S. and Rossi, C. 2006. Entry Strategies under Competing Standards: Hybrid Business Models in the Open Source Software Industry. *Management Science*, 52(7): 1085–98.

Bowman, C. and Ambrosini, V. 2000. Value Creation Versus Value Capture: Towards a Coherent Definition of Value in Strategy. *British Journal of Management*, 11(1): 1–15.

Brickson, S. L. 2007. Organizational Identity Orientation: The Genesis of the Role of the Firm and Distinct forms of Social Value. *Academy of Management Review*, 32(3): 864–88.

Calia, R., Guerrini, F. and Moura, G. 2007. Innovation Networks: From Technological Development to Business Model Reconfiguration. *Technovation*, 27: 426–32.

Campbell, J. L. 2007. Why Would Corporations Behave in Socially Responsible Ways? An Institutional Theory of Corporate Social Responsibility. *Academy of Management Review*, 32(3): 946–67.

Campi, S., Dufourny, J. and Gregoire, O. 2006. Work Integration Social Enterprises: Are they Multiple-Goal and Multi-Stakeholder Organizations? In Nyssens, *Social Enterprise*, 29–49.

Carroll, A. 1979. A Three-Dimensional Conceptual Model of Corporate Performance. *Academy of Management Review*, 4(4): 497–505.

Carroll, A. B. 1991. The Pyramid of Corporate Social Responsibility: Toward the Moral Management of Organizational Stakeholders. *Business Horizons*, 34(4): 39–48.

Carroll, A. B. 1999. Corporate Social Responsibility: Evolution of a Definitional Construct. *Business & Society*, 38(3): 268–95.

Christie, M. and Honig, B. 2006. Social Entrepreneurship: New Research Findings. *Journal of World Business*, 41(1): 1–5.

Colbert, B. A. 2004. The Complex Resource-Based View: Implications for Theory and Practice in Strategic Human Resource Management. *Academy of Management Review*, **29**(3): 341–58.

Dees, G. J. 1998. Enterprising Nonprofits. *Harvard Business Review*, **76**(1): 54–67.

Delaunois, P. and Becker, E. 2001. Luxembourg: Work-Integration Social Enterprises in an Emerging Third Sector. In Borgzage, C., Dufourny, J. *The Emergence of Social Enterprise*, 182–91. Routledge: London and New York.

Den Hond, F. and De Bakker, F. G. A. 2007. Ideologically Motivated Activism: How Activist Groups Influence Corporate Social Change Activities. *Academy of Management Review*, **32**(3): 901–24.

Dorado, S. 2006. Social Entrepreneurial Ventures: Different Values so Different Process of Creation, No? *Journal of Developmental Entrepreneurship*, **11**(4): 319–43.

DTI, 2007. *Researching Social Enterprise*. Department of Trade and Industry: London. Available at http://www.sbs.gov.uk.

Eckhardt, J. T. and Shane, S. 2003. Opportunities and Entrepreneurship. *Journal of Management*, **29**(3): 333–49.

Emerson, J. 2003. The Blended Value Proposition: Integrating Social and Financial Returns. *California Management Review*, **45**(4): 35–51.

Emerson, J. 2006. Moving ahead Together: Implications of a Blended Value Framework for the Future of Social Entrepreneurship. In Nicholls, *Social Entrepreneurship*, 391–406.

Figge, F. and Hahn, T. 2005. The Cost of Sustainability Capital and the Creation of Sustainable Value by Companies. *Journal of Industrial Ecology*, **9**(4): 47–58.

Fowler, A. 2000. NGDO's as a Moment in History: Beyond Aid to Social Entrepreneurship or Civic Innovation. *Third World Quarterly*, **21**(4): 637–54.

Gersick, C. 1994. Pacing Strategic Change: The Case of a New Venture. *Academy of Management Journal*, **37**(1): 9–45.

Godfrey, P. and Hatch, N. 2007. Researching Corporate Social Responsibility: An Agenda for the 21st Century. *Journal of Business Ethics*, **70**: 87–98.

Hahn, T., Figge, F., and Barkemeyer, R. 2007. Sustainable Value Creation among Companies in the Manufacturing Sector. *International Journal Environmental Technology and Management*, **7**(5/6): 496–512.

Hamel, G. and Prahalad, C. 1990. The Core Competences of the Corporation. *Harvard Business Review*, **68**(3): 79–91.

Harrison, R. and Miller, S. 1999. The Contribution of Clinical Directors to the Strategic Capability of the Organization. *British Journal of Management*, **10**: 23–39.

Hockerts, K. 2006. Entrepreneurial Opportunity in Social purpose Business Ventures. In Mair, J., Robinson, J. and Hockerts, K. (eds), *Social Entrepreneurship*, **10**: 142–54. Basingstoke: Palgrave Macmillan.

Hulgard, L. 2006. Danish Social Enterprises: A Public-Third Sector Partnership. In Nyssens, *Social Enterprise*, 50–9.

Ibrahim, N. A., Haword, D. P. and Angelidis, J. P. 2008. The Relationship Between Religiousness and Corporate Social Responsibility Orientation: Are there Differences between Business Managers and Students? *Journal of Business Ethics*, **78**(1–2): 165–74.

Ireland, D., Hitt, M., and Sirmon, D. 2003. A Model of Strategic Entrepreneurship: The Construct and its Dimensions. *Journal of Management*, **29**(6): 963–89.

Jenkins, H. 2006. Small Business Champions for Corporate Social Responsibility. *Journal of Business Ethics,* **67**(3): 241–56.

Kang, S., Morris, S. and Snell, S. A. 2007. Relational Archetypes, Organizational Learning, and Value Creation: Extending the Human Resource Architecture. *Academy of Management Review,* **32**(1): 236–56.

Kaplan, R. S. 2001. Strategic Performance Measurement and Management in Non-Profit Organizations. *Nonprofit Management & Leadership,* **11**(3): 353–70.

Kazanjian, R. and Rao, H. 1999. Research Note: The Creation of Capabilities in New Ventures – A Longitudinal Study. *Organization Studies,* **20**(1): 125–42.

Lado, A., Boyd, N., Wright, P. and Kroll, M., 2006. Paradox and Theorizing within the Resource-Based View. *Academy of Management Review,* **31**(1): 115–31.

Lai, R., Weill, P. and Malone, T. 2006. Do Business Models Matter? MIT Sloan Working Paper no. 4615-06, MIT Sloan School of Management. Available at: http://seeit.mit.edu/Publications/DoBMsMatter7.pdf.

Lei, D., Hitt, M. A. and Bettis, R. 1996. Dynamic Core Competences through Meta-Learning and Strategic Context. *Journal of Management,* **22**(4): 549–69.

Lepak, D. P., Smith, K. G. and Taylor, M. S. 2007. Value Creation and Value Capture: A Multilevel Perspective. *Academy of Management Review,* **32**(1): 180–94.

Lingane, A. and Olsen, S. 2004. Guidelines for Social Return on Investment. *California Management Review,* **46**(3): 116–35.

Mahadevan. B. 2000. Business Models for Internet-Based E-commerce: An Anatomy. *California Management Review,* **42**(4): 55–69.

Mair, J. and Martí, I. 2006. Social Entrepreneurship Research: A Source of Explanation, Prediction, and Delight. *Journal of World Business,* **41**(1): 36–44.

Mair, J., Robinson, J. and Hockerts, K. 2006. *Social Entrepreneurshp.* Basingstoke: Palgrave Macmillan.

Margretta, J. 2002. Why Business Models Matter. *Harvard Business Review,* **80**(5): 86–92.

Margolis, J. and Walsh, J. 2003. Misery Loves Companies: Rethinking Social Intiatives by Business. *Administrative Science Quarterly,* **48**(6): 268–305.

Maritan, C. 2001. Capital Investment as Investing in Organizational Capabilities: An Empirically Grounded Process Model. *Academy of Management Journal,* **44**(3): 513–31.

Marquis, C., Glynn, M. A. and Davis, G. F. 2007. Community Isomorphism and Corporate Social Action. *Academy of Management Review,* **32**(3): 925–45.

McWilliams, A. and Siegel, D. 2000. Corporate Social Responsibility and Financial Performance: Correlation or Misspecification? *Strategic Management Journal,* **21**(5): 603–9.

McWilliams, A. and Siegel, D. 2001. Corporate Social Responsibility: A Theory of the Firm Perspective. *Academy of Management Review,* **26**(1): 117–27.

McWilliams, A., Siegel, D. and Wright, P. 2006. Corporate Social Responsibility: Strategic Implications. *Journal of Management Studies,* **43**(1): 1–18.

Miller, D. 2003. An Asymmetry-Based View of Advantage: Towards an Attainable Sustainability. *Strategic Management Journal,* **24**(10): 961–96.

Morris, M. Schindehutte, M. and Allen, J. 2005. The Entrepreneur's Business Model: Toward a Unified Perspective. *Journal of Business Research,* **58**(6): 726–35.

Mort, G. S., Weerawardena, J. and Carnegie, K. 2003. Social Entrepreneurship: Towards Conceptualisation. *International Journal of Nonprofit and Voluntary Sector Marketing*, 8(1): 76–88.

Murillo, D. and Lozano, J. M. 2006. SMEs and CSR: An Approach to CSR in their Own Words. *Journal of Business Ethics*, 67(3): 227–40.

Nicholls, A. 2006. *Social Entrepreneurship. New Models of Sustainable Social Change.* New York: Oxford University Press.

Nyssens, M. 2006. *Social Enterprise. At the Crossroads of Market, Public Policies and Civil Society.* London and New York: Routledge.

O'Gorman, C. and Doran, R. 1999. Mission Statements in Small and Medium-Sized Businesses. *Journal of Small Business Management*, 37(4): 59–66.

O'Rand, A. and Krecker, M. 1990. Concepts of the Life Cycle: Their History, Meanings, and Uses in the Social Sciences. *Annual Review of Sociology*, 16: 241–61.

Pearce, J. A. and David, F. 1987. Corporate Mission Statements: The Bottom Line. *Academy of Management Executive*, 1(2): 109–16.

Pearce, J. 2005. *Social Enterprise in Anytown.* London: Calouste Gulbenkian Foundation.

Peredo, A. and Chrisman, J. 2006. Toward a Theory of Community-Based Enterprise. *Academy of Management Review*, 31(2): 309–28.

Peredo, A. and McLean, M. 2006. Social Entrepreneurship: A Critical Review of the Concept. *Journal of World Business*, 41(1): 55–65.

Perrini, F. and Vurro, C. 2006. Social Entrepreneurship: Innovation and Social Change across Theory and Practice. In Mair, J., Robinson, J. and Hockerts, K. (eds), *Social Entrepreneurship*, 5: 57-86. Basingstoke: Palgrave Macmillan.

Porter, M. 1985. *Competitive Advantage: Creating and Sustaining Superior Performance.* New York: Free Press.

Porter, M. and Kramer, M. 2006. Strategy & Society: The Link Between Competitive Advantage and Corporate Social Responsibility. *Harvard Business Review*, 84(12): 78–92.

Ray, G., Barney, J. and Muhanna, W. 2004. Capabilities, Business, Business Processes, and Competitive Advantage: Choosing the Dependent Variable in Empirical Tests of the Resource-Based View. *Strategic Management Journal*, 25(1): 23–37.

Ruf, B. M., Muralidhar, K. and Paul, K. 1998. The Development of a Systematic, Aggregate measure of Corporate Social Performance. *Journal of Management*, 24(1): 119–33.

Russo, M. and Fouts, P. 1997. A Resource-Based Perspective on Corporate Environmental Performance and Profitability. *Academy of Management Journal*, 40(3): 534–59.

Sapienza, H. J., Autio, E., George, G. and Zahra, S. A. 2006. A Capabilities Perspective on the Effects of Early Internationalization on Firm Survival and Growth. *Academy of Mangement Review*, 31(4): 914–33.

Sawhill, J. C. and Williamson, D. 2001. Mission Impossible? Measuring Success in Nonprofit Organizations. *Nonprofit Management & Leadership*, 11(3): 371–86.

Seelos, C. and Mair, J. 2005. Sustainable Development, Sustainable Profit. *European Business Forum*, 20: 49–53.

Shane, S. and Venkataraman, S. 2000. The Promise of Entrepreneurship as a Field of Research. *Academy of Management Review*, 25(1): 217–26.

Sharir, M. and Lerner, M. 2006. Gauging the Success of Social Ventures Initiated by Individual Social Entrepreneurs, *Journal of World Business*, **41**(1): 6–20.

Sheehan, R. 1996. Mission Accomplishment as Philanthropic Effectiveness: Key Findings from the Excellence in Philanthropy Project. *Nonprofit and Voluntary Sector Quarterly*, **25**(1): 110–23.

Scherer, A. G. and Palazzo, G. 2007. Toward a Political Conception of Corporate Responsibility: Business and Society seen from a Habermasian Perspective. *Academy of Management Review*, **32**(4): 1096–120.

Schuler, D. A. and Cording, M. 2006. A Corporate Social Performance-Corporate Financial Performance Behavioral Model for Consumers. *Academy of Management Review*, **31**(3): 540–58.

Seelos, C., and Mair, J., 2007. Profitable Business Models and Market Creation in the Context of Deep Poverty: A Strategic View. *Academy of Management Perspectives*, **21**(4): 49–63.

Sidhu, J. 2003. Mission Statements: Is it Time to Shelve them? *European Management Journal*, **21**(4): 439–446.

Sirmon, D. G., Hitt, M. A. and Ireland, R. D. 2007. Managing Firm Resources in Dynamic Environments to Create Value: Looking inside the Black Box. *Academy of Management Review*, **32**(1): 273–92.

Stabell, C. B. and Fjeldstad, O. D. 1998. Configuring Value for Competitive Advantage: On Chains, Shops, and Networks. *Strategic Management Journal*, **19**: 413–37.

Stevens, R. and Moray, N. 2008. Exploring the Mission of Social Entrepreneurial Firms. Forthcoming, Journal of Enterprising Communities.

Strothotte, T. G. and Wüstenhagen, R. 2005. Structure of Sustainable Economic Value in Social Entrepreneurial Enterprises. In Vinig, G. T., and Van der Voort, R. C. W. (eds), *Research on Technological Innovation and Management*, vol. 9: *The Emergence of Entrepreneurial Economics*, 85–94. Oxford: Elsevier.

Sullivan, D. M. 2007. Stimulating Social Entrepreneurship: Can Support from Cities make a Difference? *Academy of Management Perspectives*, **21**(1): 77–8.

Teece, D. J. Pisano, G. and Shuen, A. 1997. Dynamic Capabilities and Strategic Management. *Strategic Management Journal*, **18**(7): 509–33.

Timmers, P. 1998. Business Models for Electronic Markets. *Electronic Markets*, **8**: 3–8.

Tracey, P. and Jarvis, O. 2007. Toward a Theory of Social Venture Franchising. *Entrepreneurship Theory and Practice*, **31**(5): 667–85.

Venkatraman, N. and Henderson, J. 1998. Real Strategies for Virtual Organizing. *Sloan Management Review*, **40**: 33–48.

Vidal, I. 2005. Social Enterprise and Social Inclusion: Social Enterprises in the Sphere of Work Integration. *International Journal of Public Administration*, **28**: 807–25.

Waddock, S. A. and Post, J. E. 1991. Social Entrepreneurs and Catalytic Change. *Public Administration Review*, **51**(5): 393–401.

Weerawardena, J. and Mort, G. S. 2006. Investigating Social Entrepreneurship: A Multidimensional Model. *Journal of World Business*, **41**(1): 21–35.

Wheeler, D., Colbert, B. and Freeman, R. E. 2003. Focusing on Value: Reconciling Coproate Social Responsibility, Sustainability and a Stakeholder Approach in a Network World. *Journal of General Management*, **28**(3): 1–28.

Woiceshyn, J. and Falkenberg, L. 2008. Value Creation in Knowledge-Based Firms: Aligning Problems and Resources. *Academy of Management Perspectives*, **22**(2): 85–99.

Wood, D. 1991. Corporate Social Performance Revisited. *Academy of Management Review*, **16**(4): 691–718.

Wüstenhagen, R. and Boehnke, J. 2008. Business Models for Sustainable Energy. In Tukker, A., Charter, M., Vezzoli, C., Sto, E., Andersen, M. M. (eds), *System Innovation for Sustainability 1. Perspectives on Radical Changes to Sustainable Consumption and Production (SCP)*, 85–94. Sheffield: Greenleaf.

Zott, C. and Amit, R. 2007. Business Model Design and the Performance of Entrepreneurial Firms. *Organization Science*, **18**(2): 181–99.

13
The Functions of Performance Measurement in Social Entrepreneurship: Control, Planning and Accountability

Alex Nicholls

Introduction

Today, systems of performance measurement (metrics) are central to all organizational strategy and operations (Austin, 1996; Rousseau, 2006). Metrics are costly but valuable since they offer the tantalizing prospect of capturing complex situations in an apparently objective and impartial fashion to minimize risk and maximize return. Metrics offer internal actors in an organization the tools with which to assemble the data that allow them to control processes and make effective decisions. For external actors metrics allow performance assessments to be made that drive efficient resource allocation and build an argument for (or against) society granting the organization a mandate to operate by creating (or destroying) perceptions of its accountability and legitimacy. Metrics now pervade society on a trajectory that began with the establishment of consistent reporting practices in the private sector (Hopwood, 1983) and that now encompasses the public sector (Bevan and Hood, 2006; Osbourne and Gaebbler, 1992) and, increasingly, the third sector too (Paton, 2003). Today metrics are a defining feature of our modernity (Giddens, 1990). Indeed, there has never before been so much focus on measurement across the industrialized world (Power, 1994a, 1994b).

However, research into the sociology of accounting as an institutional practice has reminded us that the objectivity and impartially of metrics and their reporting context is open to contestation (Hopwood, 1978, 1983). The assumed objectivity of metrical data is exploded when its role within power structures and hierarchies is revealed (Power, 1994a, 1994b, 2003). Similarly, key insights into the processes behind the origin of particular reporting standards demonstrate how politics, history and culture all shape metrics in context and that, therefore, the data they produce is always contingent (Hopwood et al., 1994; Loft, 1994). When assessing the role and meaning of metrics it is, consequently, critical to consider not only what is the unit of analysis being measured, but also why, and for whom. Such a historical-contextual analysis helps to reveal the limits and the opportunities of measurement systems and their concomitant data sets.

In business the main systems of performance measurement and reporting have become established in accounting standards via a combination of common practice and regulation that has evolved largely over the last hundred years (Hopwood, 1983; Hopwood and Miller, 1994). The universal unit of performance measurement is financial and accounting conventions have stabilized over time to support the production of regular, comparative and longitudinal data (see Miller, 1994). In the public sector, welfare economics (Arrow, 1951; Chipman and Moore, 1978; Feldman, 1980; Little, 1950; O'Connell, 1982) has developed to inform public expenditure decision-making with quantitative analysis and has supported a trend within New Public Management for more evidence-based policy (Bevan and Hood, 2006; Hood, 1991). Since the 1980s market economics has also entered the mainstream of public policy discourse (see, for example, LeGrand, 2003; LeGrand and Bartlett, 1993).

However, in the third sector there are neither established units of *social* performance measurement nor regulatory and accounting conventions by which such data can be given comparative meaning (Clotfelter, 1992; DiMaggio and Anheier, 1990; Edwards and Hulme, 1995, 1996; Forbes, 1998). This is largely because of the perceived difficulty in establishing the relationship between complex input factors (grants, volunteers, market income, social capital, etc.) and the social outputs that represent the mission objectives of such organizations. However, such assumptions are being challenged by a new generation of third sector organizations that are evolving more rigorous systems of performance measurement that enhance accountability as part of their mission to bring about systemic change in failing social and environmental contexts. The work of such organizations has increasingly become known as social entrepreneurship (Alvord et al., 2004; Dees, 1994, 1998a, 1998b; Leadbeater, 1997; Light, 2008; Nicholls, 2004, 2006, 2008a).

This chapter explores the use of metrics as a defining feature in a sample of ideal-type socially entrepreneurial organizations. First, the chapter suggests that social entrepreneurship can be identified by three elements – sociality, innovation, and market orientation – and that each of these relates to a particular use of metrics in establishing performance and impact (Nicholls and Cho, 2006). Next, the chapter draws upon perspectives from the sociology of accounting to develop a theoretical model of three categories of metrics that can be applied to practice in social entrepreneurship. After a brief discussion of methodology, a survey of 41 socially entrepreneurial organizations is analysed by means of the theoretical model and a series of research questions addressed. Conclusions suggest some emergent challenges inherent in the current functions of metrics in social entrepreneurship.

Social entrepreneurship and performance measurement

It has been suggested that we live today in an 'audit society' (Power, 1994b) organized around complex, data intensive, command and control structures designed to reduce risk and embed authority (Beck, 1992; Giddens, 1990: Taylor-Gooby, 2004, 2006). Certainly, the twentieth century witnessed an extraordinary rise in the spread and influence of measurement systems, first in the institutionalization of accounting standards in the commercial sector (Miller, 1994) and then with the rise of New Public Management and the drive towards evidence-based policy in public welfare economics and government strategy (Hood, 1991). New data collection technologies and the rise of neo-liberal market ideology fuelled this growth to which regulation then gave normative value (Harvey, 2007). However, until recently, the influence of new systems of measurement has been less apparent, and often contested, in the third sector (Dart, 2004; Emerson, 1999; Kendall and Knapp, 2000; Paton, 2003; REDF, 2000).

Whilst the social accounting movement has succeeded in (re)connecting financial performance with its social and environmental context over the last decade (Elkington, 1997; Gray, 2002) the pace of change in the performance and impact measurement appropriate for charities, non-governmental organizations (NGOs), and social purpose businesses has been far slower (for an overview of social metrics see Nicholls, 2008b, 2009). For example, charity regulation in the UK remains largely unchanged from its original eighteenth-century model (see, for example, Connolly and Hyndman, 2000) and debates around the performance measurement and accountability of NGOs are fiercely contested and, as yet, largely unresolved (Edwards and Hulme, 1995, 1996; Jacobs, 2006). However, with the rise of social entrepreneurship a new model of highly accountable, performance-driven social purpose organizations is emerging (Nicholls, 2008a; Nicholls and Cho, 2006).

Social entrepreneurship is the product of individuals, organizations and networks that challenge conventional structures by addressing failures – and identifying new opportunities – in the institutional arrangements that currently cause the inadequate provision, or unequal distribution, of social and environmental goods (Dees, 1994, 1998a, 1998b; Light, 2008; Nicholls, 2008a). Social entrepreneurship aims to be more effective – and, in some cases, more efficient – in addressing such 'institutional voids' than the existing organizational structures and arrangements. More specifically, social entrepreneurship has been defined as any action that displays three key characteristics, each of which has implications for enhanced performance measurement: sociality, innovation and market orientation (Nicholls and Cho, 2006).

The notion of 'sociality' encompasses the context (i.e. operational sector), process (i.e. employment practices, supply chain management, financial model, etc.) and/or set of outputs (that which can be measured) that fit with normative notions of the public benefit (i.e. goods or services that are non-rivalled and non-excludable: meaning that consumption of the good/service by one individual does not reduce the availability for others and that no one can be excluded from accessing the good/service). Sociality drives the mission objectives and strategy of all social entrepreneurship and provides the anchor for all management decision-making ahead of, for example, profit maximization. The need to identify and capture 'deadweight' mission outputs and impacts inherent in the notion of sociality provides the first driver for the more metricized model of social organization represented in social entrepreneurship. Theoretical antecedents in contexts as varied as welfare economics (that provides a well-established template for the measurement of the efficiency and effectiveness of the provision of public goods), management consultancy, and venture capital are combining to build a metrical architecture bespoke to social entrepreneurship that is finding expression in the emergent infrastructure around the field demonstrated in such organizations as New Philanthropy Capital, Bridgespan, the European Venture Philanthropy Association and others. A consequence of this has been the development of a range of new metrics designed to account for the complex outputs and processes of the field. These range from the general and indicative (triple bottom line accounting: Elkington, 1997) via the qualitative (social reporting: see

Nicholls, 2008b, 2009) to the specific and quantitative (social return on investment: Emerson, 1999).

Capturing social impact is, perhaps, most straightforward in Type 1 social entrepreneurship – namely social enterprises (social purpose organizations that also generate commercial income) – when there is a direct correlation between financial and social performance in terms of value creation (however, see Emerson, 2003, for an argument against such an analytic dichotomy). For example, in the case of Fair Trade (Nicholls and Opal, 2005), the larger the commercial market grows, the more social benefit is created. However, such measurement is less clear-cut in Type 2 social entrepreneurship that focuses on social innovation rather than social enterprise (see Boschee, 2003; Dees, 2003, for the debate concerning the two types of social entrepreneurship; also see Mulgan, 2007). This leads to the second boundary characteristic of social entrepreneurship, innovation.

Innovation in social entrepreneurship indicates the creation of new ideas and models that address social or environmental issues. Socially entrepreneurial innovation can be manifested in three ways: in new product and service development (institutional innovation); in the use of existing goods and services in new – more socially productive – ways (incremental innovation); in reframing normative terms of reference to redefine social problems and suggest new solutions (disruptive innovation). Identifying innovation – of whichever type – is a comparative process of analysis between existing models and institutional arrangements and new options and opportunities. The credibility of the innovation element of social entrepreneurship also requires a measurement component – namely, evidence of what is new and different in the socially entrepreneurial proposition. Without this evidence a social project cannot legitimately lay claim to being entrepreneurial. However, building performance measurement systems to capture and quantify innovation is notoriously difficult. For example, despite a long-standing recognition of the economic value of innovation by government and business there is still no definitive policy approach or strategic model of how to generate and sustain such innovation over time (Mulgan, 2007). Social entrepreneurship faces the same challenge to demonstrate its claims to innovation. Part of the solution to this problem to date has been to build heroic narratives around social entrepreneurs that serve to mythologize and 'celebrate' their achievements as extraordinary and, therefore, by inference, new. Such a socially entrepreneurial myth becomes self-fulfilling as social innovators self-identify with the model. The active involvement of both grant makers (Skoll Foundation) and network builders (Ashoka, Schwab Foundation) has added vital resources to this process as well as building its internal logic and stock of stories. Nevertheless, hard evidence of innovation can remain elusive.

The final defining characteristic of social entrepreneurship, market orientation, builds on the distinctive features of sociality and innovation noted above and, as a consequence, is the key defining factor of social entrepreneurship. Sociality and innovation have always been present in the third sector, but performance-driven accountability has typically been absent (Edwards and Hulme, 1995, 1996). This is largely due to the legitimacy 'surplus' historically accorded by society to charities, NGOs, and voluntary and community organizations (Jepson, 2005; Lister, 2003; Nicholls, 2008b; Suchman, 1995). In other words, the societal value of such organizations was taken as largely self-evident because of their public mission focus and non-distribution requirement (DiMaggio and Anheier, 1990). As a consequence, stated social mission and organizational form have traditionally acted as proxies for the efficiency and effectiveness of their operations, leaving the latter typically untested. The perceived difficulties inherent in measuring comparative social performance have supported this consensus.

The market orientation of social entrepreneurship confronts these assumptions around the third sector by exhibiting a performance-driven, competitive, outlook that drives greater accountability and co-operation across sectors. Social enterprises specifically address conventional commercial markets (for example, the Furniture Resource Centre in Liverpool, UK), but in general social entrepreneurship broadens the conception of a 'market' beyond the merely neo-liberal to suggest that markets establish exchange value and to re-embed conceptions of the market into their sociological and anthropological contexts (Etzioni et al., 1992; Nicholls and Young, 2008; Offer, 2007; Young, 2006). Market orientation in social entrepreneurship includes ideas of reciprocity and the common-good – the Economy of Regard (Offer, 2007) – as well as the rational, utility maximizing individual typified in one aspect of Adam Smith's work (Sutherland, 2008: but see, Haakonssen, 2002, for a different view). Thus, socially entrepreneurial market orientation is based on realizing values as well as value (Young, 2006). For example, the work of Bunker Roy in the Barefoot College, based in northern India, acknowledges the centrality of community and cooperation whilst also relentlessly innovating in pedagogic and developmental systems. Similarly, Apopo in East Africa harnesses local fauna (trained indigenous rats) to address a major social problem – the presence of landmines across rural areas.

Market orientation demands greater – and more socially embedded – performance measurement from social entrepreneurship. In tandem with these new metrics, larger conversations about the structure of accountability and performance measurement have also been evident in development NGOs (for example the BOND, 2006), environmental organizations (Jepson, 2005) and foundations (Edwards and Hulme, 1995, 1996: for a summary see Nicholls, 2008b, 2009). Common to all these initiatives is a concern with improving the relevance and reliability of impact measurement as well as developing more transparent reporting. The move towards greater market orientation (as defined here) in social purpose organizations is, therefore, at the heart of the new metrics of social entrepreneurship.

Given the importance of a variety of new metrics to social entrepreneurship, this chapter will explore the functions of new systems of performance measurement in this field. The assumption will be made that such new metrics are key indicators of social entrepreneurship – integral to the legitimacy of its sociality, innovation and market orientation. Therefore, the primary research question considered here is as follows: to what extent is social entrepreneurship characterized by its performance measurement approaches?

The next section develops a theoretical model of the strategic functions of metrics in social entrepreneurship that is then explored further based on empirical survey data. In order to analyse the complex performance measurement context of social entrepreneurship – multiple stakeholders, contingent data, fluid accounting systems – the theoretical approach used here is derived from accounting as social and institutional practice.

Performance measurement as social and institutional practice

As has been noted above, in the past 20 years there has been a sociological and neo-institutionalist turn in the study of accountancy and reporting practices. From this perspective, accounting is a social and institutional practice that is 'intrinsic to, and constitutive of, social relations, rather than derivative or secondary' (Miller, 1994:1). Hopwood (1983), Miller (1994), and Power (1994a, 1994b, 2003) amongst others, have pioneered new thinking in this field that has re-embedded performance measurement and reporting in its sociological context to reveal it as a culturally and historically situated phenomenon that is less about process integrity and more about context and meaning. Miller (1994) identified three interrelated lines of research within accounting as social and institutional practice: first, accounting as a transformative technology – or 'way of intervening' – that translates qualities into quantities at both the micro (the introduction of organizational structures such as cost centres or decision-making mechanisms such as return of investment) and the macro (the monetization of all value creation) levels; second, the rationales, languages, and meanings within accounting that shape particular epistemologies; third, a combination of the first and second that considers how the calculative methodologies of accounting make complex organizational processes 'knowable' and, thus, shape the economic discourses around them. Underpinning each of these lines of research are fundamental questions concerning the origin, context and influence of accounting as practice.

Such research is particularly open to multidisciplinary analysis. Miller (1994) identified three important theoretical and methodological approaches: ethnography that focuses on the meanings and perceptions of actors who develop and use accounting techniques and systems in different cultural contexts; political economy that explores conflicting interests and power dynamics in the creation and deployment of accounting; organizational theory (particularly neo-institutionalism) that considers how accounting systems, narratives, and myths act as structural influences on organizational shape and form. Power (1994a) demonstrated the latter in his discussion of how the symbolic aspect of audit has become more powerful than its conclusions, with the perverse effect that process transparency becomes undesirable.

Underpinning accounting as social and institutional practice are questions concerning how and why performance measurement and reporting is constructed particularly as this affects what is reported, in what way, and at whose behest. In this context, performance measurement and reporting can be seen as the product of power dynamics and hierarchies of knowledge. When such an analytic lens is applied to performance measurement in organizations three categories of metrics emerge. The issue of the unit of analysis (what is being measured) is reflected in *control metrics*. The issue of the purpose of metrics (why a particular measurement system is being applied) is reflected in *planning metrics*. Finally, the issue of the audience of metrics (for whom the data is being assembled) is reflected in *accountability metrics*. In order to address the question of to what extent social entrepreneurship is characterised by its performance measurement approaches each of the three categories is now considered in more detail.

Control metrics correspond to Miller's (1994) conceptualization of accounting as transformative technology: they are designed to assess operational systems effectiveness – typically via comparative analyses of input, process and output data – so as to maximize the efficiency with which resources are deployed. This can be at the project, organization, or sector level. Control metrics represent the 'what' of performance measurement and reporting. Typical examples of such metrics are; return on investment; profit and loss accounts; full cost accounting. The control metrics data are considered to be objective and are usually given a quantitative, often financial, value. The audience for control metrics is usually outside the organization, though they may also play a part in internal planning (see below). As a consequence, such data are open to comparative analysis typically via markets. Control metrics are also often the subject of regulation, since, for at least a century, governments have assumed that publicly available control metric data drives organizations towards enhanced societal impacts.

In social entrepreneurship, control metrics relate to the sociality of the organization and focus on assessing and justifying its performance in terms of the context, process and outputs of its actions. Context metrics report on – and thus legitimate – the public or environmental benefit generated by the organization. The best-established example of this is the annual report filed in many territories by charities, community interest companies and other tax privileged groups that aim to demonstrate their contribution to the public good. Process metrics are particularly relevant to social firms that deliver their mission through the selection of the marginalized target populations for employment and training and ethical retailers/wholesalers whose social mission relates to improving labour practices and working conditions, as well as to reconfiguring the distribution of economic rents more fairly across supply chains. Output metrics attempt to quantify the mission achievements of the social entrepreneurial organization in a range of units of analysis from simple throughput to more complex outcomes and externalities. Output metrics are also often related to input factors to gauge levels of efficiency in terms of resource allocation and operational performance, for example in the social return on investment model (SROI). A second area of research in this chapter concerns the role of control metrics in social entrepreneurship, in particular the extent to which they are used to legitimate the social mission.

Planning metrics correspond to Miller's (1994) notion of accounting as rationale and myth: they are used to build a strategic language through which diverse operational issues can be consolidated into a model of the organization now and in the future: they represent the 'why' of performance measurement and reporting. Such a language defines the organization, captures its core competences and competitive position, and thus allows new strategic options to be developed from current activities and context. Planning metrics typically synthesize quantitative and qualitative measures to generate creative strategic choice-making going forward. Such metrics build representative pictures of a range of futures often in the form of the two-by-two matrices beloved of management consultants. They also combine and interpret existing data as future scenarios and opportunities. This is a process that may involve deconstructing or decontextualizing extant data so that it can be used in new ways to inform strategic thinking. Planning metrics often take the form of heuristics and alternative epistemological structures rather than measurement systems in a conventional sense. Typical examples attempt to measure and map: pathways to technological invention; co-creation processes; long-tail economics (see Mulgan, 2007). This is an emergent field of metrics whose potential may be huge, but is still largely unrealized (see for example BP's scenario planning methodologies).

In social entrepreneurship planning metrics relate strongly to its second defining feature, innovation. Clearly, most strategic planning encompasses innovation as *change*, but in the case of social entrepreneurship strategic planning acts as *defining rationale*. Such planning metrics can reframe issues to open up new strategic directions or contribute to the creative destruction typical of entrepreneurial thinking, but they also provide they cultural material with which social entrepreneurs frame themselves, their organizations, and the problems they address. Across all three types – institutional innovation, incremental innovation, and disruptive innovation – social entrepreneurs relentlessly seek out new and better models of change to enhance the effectiveness of their mission objectives. Planning metrics allows social entrepreneurs to innovate a model of a future that is better than today. This aspect of metrics in social entrepreneurship extends the research focus further. In this case the research analysis concerns how social entrepreneurship uses planning metrics to innovate its social mission.

Finally, *accountability metrics* represent the 'for whom' of performance measurement and reporting. Accountability metrics combine Miller's (1994) transformative technologies of accounting – they marshal complex situations into comprehensible data – with its rationale building dimension, since they also provide a justification for organizational action. Such metrics provide stakeholders within and without the organization with a means of making a judgement on the fit between how it should act and how it does act or, at least, on their perceptions of these two variables. Accountability metrics data do not usually take the form of financial – or even quantitative – values, but are rather expressed in more qualitative terms that aim to capture the structures, processes, and quality of engagements with stakeholders. Such data often reflects local and cultural factors. Typical examples of such metrics are: stakeholder surveys and consultations; shareholder meetings; transparency and openness in reporting processes. Accountability metrics data is often subjective, hard to capture, and highly contingent. Governments do not typically use regulation to intervene in accountability metrics, though industry standards and self-regulation (for instance the Ethical Trading Initiative) have emerged over the past ten years in some countries.

Within social entrepreneurship, accountability metrics frame its market orientation in terms of a mission focus on beneficiaries, their needs and the effectiveness of innovative interventions to address these needs. Whilst it was noted above that market orientation in social enterprise includes accountability to external market actors (investors, customers, government), across the whole spectrum of social entrepreneurship performance measurement is calibrated first to the social mission and to the beneficiaries embedded within the mission. This leads to the final focus of analysis in this research, namely how social entrepreneurship uses accountability metrics to embed its beneficiaries in its social mission.

This section has suggested that there are three theoretical categories of metrics addressing the 'what', 'why' and 'for whom' epistemologies of performance measurement and reporting: control metrics; planning metrics; accountability metrics. It has also been suggested that each of these manifests itself in social entrepreneurship and that they map against the three defining features of this form of action (see Table 13.1). A series of research questions have been proposed here to explore the extent to which social entrepreneurship is characterized by its performance measurement approaches. After a brief discussion of

Table 13.1 Performance measurement in social entrepreneurship

Epistemology	Category of metric	Social entrepreneurship context	Strategic focus
What is being measured?	Control	Sociality	Social return on investment
Why measure?	Planning	Innovation	Mission objectives
Measure for whom?	Accountability	Market orientation	Stakeholders

methodology, the remainder of this chapter uses an analysis of empirical survey data further to explore these research questions.

Methodology

This research combines theoretical models drawn from a range of literature with a mix of quantitative and qualitative data collected from the field. The data collection was based on a telephone questionnaire survey – carried out between March and July 2006 – of 41 socially entrepreneurial organizations based in Asia, Africa, North and South America, and Europe. An international sample was used to represent a sample frame of the field as a whole. The geographical distribution of the sample is set out below (see Table 13.2). Respondents represented a cross-section of socially entrepreneurial organizations already identified as leaders in the field by the four major network and grant-marking organizations for social entrepreneurship: Ashoka; the Schwab Foundation; the Skoll Foundation; UnLtd (see Table 13.3). Each of these four groups selects its fellows/grant awardees on the basis of their conformance to the key socially entrepreneurial qualities identified above, so it is reasonable to expect that they would support each of the four research questions considered in this chapter. None of the organizations was a recent start-up and all had been operational for at least five years.

The organizations operated across a variety of sectors including health, education, social services, advocacy and economic development (see Table 13.4). However, no sector-specific patterns appeared in the data. Similarly, despite the different cultural contexts of the sample organization, no local or regional patterns emerged from the data.

A mixed methodology approach was developed and pre-tested with five organizations. Data collected included quantitative and qualitative information. A mixture of quantitative and qualitative approaches was

Table 13.2   Regional distribution of sample organizations

Region	Number of organizations
Europe	14
Africa	8
Latin America	8
Asia	6
North America	5
	41

253

Table 13.3 Sample organization details

Sample number	Sector	Country
1	Environment	Bangladesh
2	Human rights	Cambodia
3	Economic development	Japan
4	Economic development	Pakistan
5	Environment	Singapore
6	Education	Afghanistan
7	Environment	Argentina
8	Economic development	Bolivia
9	Education	Brazil
10	Health	Brazil
11	Economic development	Chile
12	Education	Colombia
13	Environment	Peru
14	Environment	Mexico
15	Disability	USA
16	Environment	USA
17	Education	USA
18	Peace	USA
19	Economic development	USA
20	Environment	Egypt
21	Economic development	Mozambique
22	Economic development	Kenya
23	Economic development	Kenya
24	Health	South Africa
25	Health	South Africa
26	Economic development	Czech Republic
27	Economic development	Nigeria
28	Economic development	Nigeria
29	Education	Germany
30	Economic development	Hungary
31	Work integration	Netherlands
32	Work integration	Netherlands
33	Work integration	Spain
34	Economic development	UK
35	Environment	UK
36	Environment	UK
37	Environment	UK
38	Youth work	UK
39	Economic development	UK
40	Economic development	UK
41	Environment	UK

Table 13.4 Sectoral distribution of sample organizations

Sectoral focus	Number of organizations
Economic development	15
Environment	11
Education	5
Health	3
Work integration	3
Human rights	1
Peace	1
Disability	1
Youth	1
	41

adopted, given the nature of the research questions, which are concerned with both actual practices and the interpretive context of such action (Richie, 2003). Furthermore, the survey should be seen as reflecting the exploratory concerns of the research (Miles and Huberman, 1994; Ritchie, 2003): to analyse how social entrepreneurs conceive of – as well as use – different metrics in their organizations.

Interviewees were of CEO level or equivalent. A field researcher familiar with social entrepreneurship carried out the interviews either in English or Spanish. The main interviews were then organized around a telephone questionnaire comprising 26 open and closed questions.

All survey responses were recorded and transcribed. The data therefore comprised transcripts and additional explanatory written notes made by the researcher shortly after each interview. The analysis of the data involved three processes. First, data was entered into SPSS. Second, transcripts and notes were read and reread for familiarization with the qualitative data and to identify sub-themes and cross-sectional issues that were then coded. Third, SPSS was used to carry out the quantitative analysis of the data and to facilitate cross-tabulation.

Data analysis

The first two sections of the questionnaire were designed to explore the measurement context and strategic intent of the sample organizations' performance metrics. This corresponds to part of the main research question, namely to what extent social entrepreneurship can be characterized by its performance measurement in general. The remainder of the questionnaire then addresses the specific issues of performance measurement in the three defining characteristics of social entrepreneurship. Taken together this data will explore further the main research questions of to what extent is social entrepreneurship characterized by its performance measurement approaches to sociality, innovation and market orientation.

Measurement context and strategic intent

All respondents in the sample reported that they used some system of performance measurement, although two suggested that these were still under development. This is, perhaps, unsurprising given that all the organizations in the sample had already been identified as 'high performing' by third parties. Furthermore, over half of the sample (31 organizations) used multiple metrics in a 'dashboard' approach. Three broad categories of unit of measurement emerged (in order of popularity): non-financial output; financial output; non-financial outcome (see Table 13.5).

The most commonly mentioned category of unit of measurement was non-financial output (36 organizations), these included, amongst many others: staff satisfaction levels (Organization 38); number of user groups of a service (Organizations 7, 15); number of people trained (Organizations 4, 6, 12, 29); number of landmines cleared (Organization 18); greenhouse gas emissions (Organization 16, 41). This category typically reflected the social mission objectives of the organization and could be very diverse. The primary objective of this category was to assemble quantitative data to demonstrate mission effectiveness and a range of methodologies and data collection approaches were used. For example a Latin American youth environmental organization stated:

> We monitor the number of kilograms of sorted waste per municipality, the monthly exchange of paper and glass bottles for sapling and seeds, the number of trees planted each year, and the number of families that are visited to monitor the absence of dengue fever mosquitoes.
>
> (Organization 7)

Such non-financial output measures typically focused on impacts that were both easily measurable and fairly short term, based on a return on investment efficiency logic (though see below for the very limited use of social return on investment methods). Externalities and long-term changes and impacts were not considered within this category.

Table 13.5   Categories of performance measurement unit

Unit of measurement	Number of organizations
Non-financial output	36
Financial output	19
Non-financial outcome	17

The second most popular category of unit of measurement was financial data (19 organizations), these included, for example: 'resource diversification and financial sustainability' (Organization 11); 'revenue, expenses, and net income' (Organization 17); 'the number of new customers, market share, margins, profitability, efficiency, productivity, and added value' (Organization 21). The organizations that focussed primarily on financial data collection fell into three sectoral groups: economic development (15); work integration (3); environment (1). The choice of unit of measurement was consistent with these organizations main mission objectives that generally rely on market-based models.

The third – and least popular – category of unit of measurement was non-financial outcome, including a range of difficult to measure externalities, intangibles, and longer term impacts such as value-added over time (Organizations 3, 8), macro-level societal changes (Organizations 20, 23), individual psychological issues (Organization 34). A Latin American ecological organization was typical of this group:

> We focus on strengthening infrastructure; growth in information and research; better law enforcement of conservation ... alternative productive activities for the population; environmental education.
>
> (Organization 14)

Beyond the organizations that attempted to capture non-financial outcomes, there was some evidence of others who recognized the value of such analysis desirable (for example, evidence of the long-term impact of knowledge transfer) but found it too resource intensive and difficult to justify operationally, for example:

> We would like to do follow-ups on how people do after our work, but we just can't.
>
> (Organization 29)

Another organization explicitly mentioned that 'social impact' and 'effectiveness in achieving a social mission' were both subject to some measurement, but conceded that 'not every aspect is measured with the same rigour' (Organization 31).

The survey revealed a range of methods used to capture performance data, including (see Table 13.6): baseline surveys; questionnaires; social audit; focus groups; social return on investment (SROI); the Balanced Scorecard; benchmarking; use of proxies; key performance indicators (KPIs).

The most popular method for collecting data was through a baseline survey followed up by repeat data collection at regular intervals and subsequent comparative analysis. Such data was collected in two forms, sometimes combined: questionnaires; other primary and secondary data. Baseline data analysis was used to assess performance against all three categories of unit of measurement noted above. For example, non-financial outputs and outcomes are addressed by a Latin American health organization as follows:

> We conduct a baseline interview with each family in their home concerning data on their health, education, citizenship, income and housing to define a Family Action Plan; then there is a monthly progress review to monitor and adjust the Plan; when the family is discharged there is a final evaluation form to measure the total impact to family life. Families also complete an annual survey. All of this information is then published in our annual report.
>
> (Organization 10)

Table 13.6 Performance measurement methods

Methodology	Number of organizations
Baseline survey	22
Questionnaire	18
Social audit	5
Focus group	4
SROI	3
Balanced scorecard	2
Benchmarking	2
Use of proxies	2
KPIs	1

Alternatively, an African economic development organization focused on financial data collection:

> We set up three visits over time: the first is three to four weeks after purchase and uses a semi-structured interview to establish the individual's socio-economic profile; the second 12–18 months later to monitor progress in the profile; the third after a further 15–18 months completes the data collection process.
>
> (Organization 24)

An Eastern European training organization used a baseline approach to capture trainees' progress as a key outcome of its work:

> When young learners enter a course, we take a baseline survey of their reading, writing, comprehension and articulation skills. Then they undergo a documented course of training … at the end of each stage, their skills are measured against the baseline' (Organization 4). In cases where the mission concerned community or societal issues (for example the environment) baseline data was typically developed from other primary or secondary sources.

Whilst the questionnaire format was the most popular method of collecting baseline data in the sample (15 organizations), elsewhere questionnaires were used outside of baseline surveys to give shorter-term snapshots of output performance. For example, a fair trade organization noted:

> There are specific indicators for each stakeholder group, who answer questionnaires rating their indicators from 1–5.
>
> (Organization 3)

Five organizations within the sample mentioned that they used 'social audit' methods to capture their performance (Organizations 3, 15, 22, 35, 39). Whilst the term was not clearly defined by any of the respondents it appears to represent a largely qualitative approach to represent stakeholder judgements of organizational performance in a structured way, typically as an annual report. Focus groups were used by four organizations to collect performance data (Organizations 1, 25, 26, 41) and also represented attempts better to integrate stakeholders into performance assessment and planning.

Perhaps surprisingly, well-established models of performance measurement – social return on investment (Organizations 13, 15, 36), the Balanced Scorecard (Organizations 17, 35), KPIs (Organization 21) – were not widely used, largely because they were perceived as being costly and of little strategic value in terms of resource acquisition (see further below). However, when such methods were used they were seen as offering holistic solutions to accounting for complex performance objectives, for example:

> We measure social return on investment by city using a monthly evaluation by project. We aim to measure impact on economic development according to a set of themes: employment created and how that translates into additional income; poverty compared against a baseline measurement; health, illness, and domestic violence; how much waste has been treated; how many trees are being cut down.
>
> (Organization 13)

A small number of organizations within the sample suggested that they used benchmarking (Organizations 2, 39) as a baseline methodology, for example:

> We hired a sociology student to set up a social audit programme including benchmarking our outputs and testing with follow-up questionnaires.
>
> (Organization 39)

Finally, two organizations (Organizations 2, 31) explicitly mentioned using proxies to help them collect performance data on impacts that were otherwise difficult to capture. For example, a human rights organization reported:

> Human rights is a sensitive area since governments don't give statistics on torture. So, other indicators are used to compare against baseline measurements, for example: are there rights to have a lawyer; are there human rights laws; at what stage was a lawyer allowed to be present; how many lawyers are there in the country?
>
> (Organization 2)

Some 34 of the sample organizations indicated that performance measurement was important to support management action and organizational success. The same number agreed that performance measurement

Table 13.7 Performance measurement and strategy

Response	Number of organizations
Performance measurement is part of strategy	20
Performance measurement drives strategy	10
Both	4
Neither	3
No response	4
Total	41

systems were directly related to strategic planning (see Table 13.7). Another 20 stated that is what part of strategy whilst ten suggested that metrics drove strategy (four cited both), for example:

> The information derived from SROI provides vital input when determining strategy.
>
> (Organization 15)

Another organization used measurement systems as a strategy development tool,

> Interviews are conducted by special teams and successfully determine socio-economic return on investment; thus the results inform the technology development plan of the organisation, and also its marketing strategy.
>
> (Organization 24)

The majority of organizations within the sample had only recently (within the past one to two years) introduced the performance measurement systems that they described (see Table 13.8), most some time after they had started operations. This suggests that there were external factors that effected the introduction of such metrics and is considered further in the next section.

Table 13.8 When performance metrics were introduced

Time since metrics were introduced	Number of organizations
1–2 years	18
3–5 years	8
>5 years	10
From start (not defined)	5

Performance measurement: sociality

Having established that the majority of the sample use performance measurement as part of their strategic planning, the next section will explore how control metrics are used to legitimate the organization's social mission.

Control metrics are used to assess operational effectiveness: the 'what' of performance measurement and reporting. In social entrepreneurship this means measuring the deadweight impact of organizational action in terms of its public benefit context, process and outputs (sociality). Because of both the complexity of measuring such performance and the potential opportunity for moral hazard presented by the legitimacy surplus noted above, the credibility of the measurement process is of particular importance here, as is identifying the key stakeholders.

Of the sample organizations, 14 directly linked their social performance measurement with their operational effectiveness, for example:

> We use social performance measurement as a management tool … it acts as a health check for the organization.
>
> (Organization 3)

There was also evidence that performance measurement supported social mission objectives,

> Our mission and values require social goals and we want to know if we are achieving them.
>
> (Organization 34)

Measurement was also seen as important for growth and ongoing success by two organizations (26, 31):

> Data helps us to create a replicable model for the developing world.
>
> (Organization 26)

Elsewhere control metrics were cited as contributing to: 'improving motivation and confidence' (Organization 21; and 22); 'helping reorganize our priorities and fine tuning the allocation of resources' (Organization 24); 'allowing our management practices to be informed by a common language' (Organization 34). The deadweight issue was also acknowledged explicitly 'to understand if a difference is really being made' (Organization 27).

The significance of the context of performance was acknowledged in the survey by seven organizations that recognized the need to demonstrate mission impact both to internal (staff) and external (beneficiaries, investors, government etc) 'because stakeholders wanted it' (Organization 20), for example:

> We do it for shareholders and also government.
>
> (Organization 32)

Social enterprises typically saw this in business terms ('We're like a start-up that needs to show itself and the outside world its potential', Organization 17), whereas elsewhere the focus was on less commercial factors ('We want to perceive which of our actions were effective in improving the quality of life of our beneficiaries', Organization 10). Some 13 organizations suggested that performance measurement data (and processes) were important to get and maintain funding and financial support. Two organizations specifically linked accountability and performance measurement (see further below) as a legitimating process, for example:

> Metrics show that you are fulfilling your goals and gives you credibility and builds your accountability.
>
> (Organization 13)

In terms of the processes of performance measurement, the sample demonstrates an understanding of the importance of using appropriate methodologies as well as the significance of the audit context of data reporting. Examples of the former are the use of focus groups and stakeholder engagement mechanisms, whilst examples of the latter are third party verification and external audit. Both are present in the sample, for example:

> Stakeholders are included through focus group discussion and at community meetings at different stages of the project: design; implementation; and post-implementation.
>
> (Organization 1)

Seven other organizations specifically mentioned that a participatory process with key stakeholders shaped their performance measurement approach, for example:

> Representatives of all the stakeholder groups get together with investors for a half a day conference and discussion once a year to pool information and generate feedback.
>
> (Organization 3)

In terms of the reliability of data, external audit was also cited by seven organizations as being important in validating their performance measurement, as Organization 15 noted:

> External auditors measure our performance annually. They measure number of users of books and groups of users. They analyse the social return on investment of each dollar spent and use benchmarks, for example. The Library of Congress spends US$5 for each book it adds to its library, it costs [organization] only US$2.
>
> (Organization 15)

An environmental organization combined the notions of audit and stakeholder engagement in a unique model:

> An annual audit brings the people together who are responsible for different areas. The system is based on trust – a social audit is too formulaic. But then a 'wise council' is brought in to see the results.
>
> (Organization 36)

Organization 22 summarized the legitimating importance of verifying reporting practices:

> External audit has improved our credibility.

In summary, there is evidence in the sample of social entrepreneurs grasping the value of control metrics being used to demonstrate social impact and report it to key stakeholders via credible processes. However, such evidence is present only in a minority of the overall sample.

Performance measurement: innovation

Planning metrics represent the 'why' of performance measurement and reporting – namely, the strategic rationale for the control data assembled elsewhere. They build a model through which diverse operational issues can be consolidated into a comparative analytic of the organizational now and future. As has already been suggested, in social entrepreneurship planning metrics would be expected to demonstrate innovation.

The sample evidence supports this assumption. Innovation was described as 'important' or 'very important' by all but two of the sample with 27 organizations reporting that measurement data had led directly to strategic change within their organisation, for ezample:

> A new position in the organization has been created especially to monitor performance and increase transparency.
>
> (Organization 1)

The types of innovation reported fell into three categories: product; process; market (see Table 13.9). Five organizations demonstrated evidence of a combination of at least two out of the three.

Product innovations tended to be incremental with some building upon existing technologies whilst others introduced existing technologies into new contexts. Organization 15 was explicit about the former (referring to its introduction of a water pump in East Africa):

> We aim to fill market gaps using an existing technology for a market that was not previously served.

Whereas an example of the latter is:

> We introduced organic cotton into Bangladesh.
>
> (Organization 3)

Four organizations specifically mentioned the importance of research and development as a planning metric for innovation (Organizations 3, 21, 22, 25).

Process innovation works at the institutional level to create new models of action, often by linking previously disparate elements, for example:

> It was important to us to link composting – as an emissions reduction strategy – to FDI [foreign direct investment] initiatives in developing countries.
>
> (Organization 1)

Table 13.9   Type of planning innovation

Type of innovation	Number of organizations
Product	12
Process	9
Market	6
Multiple	5

Three organizations highlighted how planning metrics helped innovate processes within their own management systems as part of a 'culture of change' (Organization 35). One organization explicitly structured innovation processes:

> Innovation is part of our culture and we have processes in place to foster it. For example, we have two days away each year when team leaders go to see other businesses to try to bring in freshness all the time...we count innovations through the value they create afterwards.
>
> (Organization 41)

There was some sense in three organizations that this was in response to the pressures of the commercial market:

> We have to keep pace with the market, so every quarter the company gets together to pool thoughts and generate new ideas.
>
> (Organization 39; and 8, 40)

The final type of innovation was at the market level and demonstrated a more disruptive set of changes, typically at the macro-societal level. Here social entrepreneurship works in a similar way to social movements – reframing conceptual categories and normative assumptions the better to address social or environmental issues:

> We want to change people's values, beliefs, and traditions.
>
> (Organization 4)

In summary, there is good evidence here of an important link between planning metrics and strategic innovation around mission objectives in social entrepreneurship.

Performance measurement: market orientation

Accountability metrics embed performance impact in their social context. For social entrepreneurship this means framing its market orientation in terms of a mission focus on beneficiaries, their needs, and the effectiveness of interventions to address these needs. Accountability metrics represent the 'for whom' of performance measurement, providing a justification for organizational action in terms of how answerable it is to its key stakeholders.

There is strong evidence in the sample of a focus on accountability to stakeholders as a dimension of performance. All organizations within

Table 13.10 Key stakeholders

Key stakeholder	Example	Number of organizations
Direct beneficiaries	Service recipients	28
Funders	Philanthropists	23
Indirect beneficiaries	Government	10
Customers	Ethical market	10
Externalities	The environment	9
Employees	Staff	7
Multiple	–	13

the sample identified their key stakeholders and recognized them as being 'important'. Six groups of stakeholders emerge from the survey data (see Table 13.10): direct beneficiaries; funders; indirect beneficiaries; customers (particularly for social enterprises); externalities (for instance more abstract stakeholder constructs such as the environment); employees. Some 13 organizations mentioned some combination of stakeholders as being important in their performance measurement.

Direct beneficiaries were clearly identified as the most important stakeholders in terms of accountability metrics, but it was, perhaps, surprising to find that funders were seen as almost as important within the sample (both by social enterprises and non-commercial organizations). Accountability metrics were seen as both a requirement of existing investment ('It was a condition of a loan from the IFC [International Finance Corporation], Organization 23) and as a method to attract new capital, for example:

> Performance data makes us more attractive to investors and markets . . . and enables our business to globalize.
>
> (Organization 8)

As has been noted elsewhere, the process of developing performance measurement methodologies, as well as the mechanisms actually used to collect data, also reflected a focus on stakeholder voice and organizational accountability. Twenty-seven organizations involved stakeholders in the design of accountability metrics and planning, for example:

> We interview all key stakeholders and give them a voice in our strategic planning.
>
> (Organization 17)

Employees were also part of the development process of accountability metrics:

> Employees are involved in all our target-setting with indicators developed from a group of two hundred and fifty employees plus a pool of customers, NGOs, and public officials.
>
> (Organization 26)

Organization 17 reported the strategic effect of enhanced accountability metrics:

> Improved accountability has brought about behavioural change in our organization. We now have monthly performance scorecards and bonuses based on performance.
>
> (Organization 17)

In summary, the findings from the survey indicate that organizations used accountability metrics to bring stakeholders into the strategic assessment and planning of their social mission. However, the focus on funders as a key stakeholder group suggests some possible conflicts of interest in fulfilling all mission objectives: this is considered further below.

Conclusion

The data analysis above suggests that social entrepreneurship uses accountability metrics to legitimize, to innovate, as well as to embed beneficiaries into the mission.

As a consequence, we can conclude that, as a whole, the sample of socially entrepreneurial organizations surveyed here demonstrate some, if not all, of the unique performance measurement approaches that are consistent with sociality, innovation and market orientation as defining features of this phenomenon.

However, a number of issues emerge from the survey data. First, although performance measurement is clearly seen as strategic and important, the majority of the sample have only recognized this some time after start-up. Furthermore, there is some evidence that the driver behind the adoption of new metrics was not mission-driven, but resource-driven: namely that they were required by funders. The focus on funders as the key stakeholder in the design and reporting of performance measurement has inherent dangers. For example, the mission of the organization may become distorted by the influence, via imposed measurement systems, of the funders' own mission objectives. This can create a dysfunctional principal–agent relationship where the organization responds to the needs of its funders ahead of the needs of its beneficiaries and other key stakeholders, causing mission drift. Indeed, to some extent, the venture philanthropy model is largely founded upon this concept (albeit with positive intentions: John, 2007).

Second, only a minority of the sample assessed outcomes as well as – or instead of – outputs. This may well reflect the difficulty and resource intensiveness of measuring the latter, but it also has strategic implications for the wider narrative that such impact measurement creates. Output data is typically short term and reflects a managerialist mindset when compared to outcome data that is often longitudinal, nuanced, contingent and more socially embedded. The preference for output data suggests a transactional view of organizational action, perhaps driven by funder agendas rather than mission objectives. The lack of adoption of social return on investment methodologies – that do offer a structured approach to capturing outcomes as well as outputs – supports this point.

Finally, the relatively weak evidence of innovation at the market/systems level (as opposed to products and processes) suggests that the social entrepreneurs in this sample were more interested in alleviating immediate problems rather than addressing their underlying causes. Social movements have demonstrated over the years that fundamental, systemic change only comes about through political processes and disruptive normative and cognitive innovation. Social entrepreneurs profess to a desire to change the world – to do so they will need more than product and process innovation alone.

This chapter has used data from an ideal-type sample of social entrepreneurial organizations from around the world to explore the functions of performance metrics in this sector. It has demonstrated that social entrepreneurship is characterized by its use of control, planning and accountability metrics across its defining elements of sociality, innovation and market orientation. Whilst the survey cannot claim to be exhaustive or even, perhaps, fully representative of a movement that is growing fast and adapting as it goes, what it has shown is that social entrepreneurs are serious about proving their impact both to themselves and to world at large.

Acknowledgement

I acknowledge the important work of Jeremy Nicholls and Maria Fernanda Diez within the research project that informed the background to this contribution.

References

Alvord, S., Brown, L. and Letts, C. 2004. Social Entrepreneurship and Societal Transformation: An Exploratory Study. *Journal of Applied Behavioral Science*, **40**(3): 260–83.

Arrow, K. 1951. *Social Choice and Individual Values*. New Haven: Yale University Press.

Austin, R. 1996. *Measuring and Managing Performance in Organisations*. New York: Dorset House.

Beck, U. 1992. *Risk Society: Towards a New Modernity*. London: Sage.

Bevan, C. and Hood, C. 2006. What's Measured is What Matters: Targets and Gaming in the English Public Health Care System. *Public Administration*, **84**(3): 517–38.

BOND – British Overseas NGOs for Development 2006. *A BOND Approach to Quality in Non-Governmental Organization: Putting Beneficiaries First*. A report by Keystone and AccountAbility for BOND, London.

Boschee, J. and McClurg, D. 2003. *Toward a Better Understanding of Social Entrepreneurship: Some Important Distinctions*. Minnesota: Institute for Social Entrepreneurs.

Chipman, J. and Moore, J. 1978. The New Welfare Economics 1939–1974. *International Economic Review*, **19**(3): 547–84.

Clotfelter, C. 1992. The Distributional Consequences of Nonprofit Activities. In Clotfelter, C. (ed), *Who Benefits From The Nonprofit Sector?*: 1–23, Chicago: University of Chicago Press.

Connolly, C. and Hyndman, N. 2000. Charity Accounting: An Empirical Analysis of the Impact of Recent Changes. *The British Accounting Review*, **32**(1): 77–100.

Dart, R. 2004. The Legitimacy of Social Enterprise. *Nonprofit Management and Leadership*, **14**(4): 411–24.

Dees, J. G. 1994. *Social Enterprise: Private Initiatives for Common Good*. Harvard: Harvard Business School Press.

Dees, J. G. 1998a. *The Meaning of Social Entrepreneurship*. Available at http://faculty.fuqua.duke.edu/centers/case/files/dees-SE.pdf.

Dees, J. G. 1998b. Enterprising Nonprofits. *Harvard Business Review*, **76**(1): 54–67.

Dees, J. G. 2003. Social Entrepreneurship Is about Innovation and Impact, Not Income. Discussion paper on Social Edge (www.socialedge.org), Skoll Center for Social Entrepreneurship, Saïd Business School, University of Oxford.

DiMaggio, P. and Anheier, H. 1990. The Sociology of Nonprofit Organizations and Sectors. *Annual Review of Sociology*, **16**(1): 137–59. Discussion paper available at CASE website, Duke University: http://www.caseatduke.org/articles/1004/corner.htm.

Edwards, M. and Hulme, D. 1995. Introduction: NGO Performance and Accountability. In Edwards, M., and Hulme, D. (eds), *Beyond the Magic Bullet: NGO Performance and Accountability in the Post Cold War World*: 1–20. London: Earthscan.

Edwards, M. and Hulme, D. 1996. Too Close For Comfort: The Impact of Official Aid on Non-Governmental Organisations. *World Development*, **24**(6): 961–73.

Elkington, J. 1997. *Cannibals with Forks: The Triple Bottom Line of 21st Century Business*. London: Capstone.

Emerson, J. 1999. *Social Return on Investment: Exploring Aspects of Value Creation*. *REDF box set*, 2, ch. 8. San Francisco: Roberts Enterprise Development Foundation.

Emerson, J. 2003. The Blended Value Proposition: Integrating Social and Financial Returns. *California Management Review*, **45**(4): 35–51.

Etzioni, A., Cantor, R., Henry, S., and Rayner, S. 1992. *Making Markets: Interdisciplinary Perspective on Economic Exchange*. Westport, CT: Greenwood Press.

Feldman, A. 1980. *Welfare Economics and Social Choice Theory*. Boston: Martinus Press.

Forbes, D. 1998. Measuring the Unmeasurable. *Nonprofit and Voluntary Sector Quarterly*, **27**(2): 183–202.

Giddens, A. 1990. *The Consequences of Modernity*. Cambridge: Polity Press.

Gray, R. 2002. The Social Accounting Project and Accounting Organizations and Society: Privileging Engagement, Imaginings, New Accountings And Pragmatism Over Critique?, *Accounting Organizations and Society*, **27**(7): 687–708.

Haakonssen, K. (ed) 2002. *Adam Smith: The Theory of Moral Sentiments*. Cambridge Texts in the History of Philosophy. Cambridge: Cambridge University Press.

Harvey, D. 2007. *A Brief History of Neo-Liberalism*. Oxford: Oxford University Press.

Hood, C. 1991. A Public Management for All Seasons. *Public Administration*, **69**(1): 3–19.

Hopwood, A. 1978. Towards an Organizational Perspective for the Study of Accounting and Information Systems. *Accounting, Organizations and Society*, **3**(1): 3–13.

Hopwood, A. 1983. On Trying to Study Accounting in the Contexts in which it Operates. *Accounting, Organizations and Society*, **8**(3): 287–305.

Hopwood, A. and Miller, P. 1994. *Accounting as Social and Institutional Practice*. Cambridge: Cambridge Studies in Management.

Hopwood, A., Burchell, S., and Clubb, C. 1994. Value-Added Accounting and National Economic Policy. In Hopwood. and Miller, *Accounting As Social And Institutional Practice*: 211–336.

Jacobs, A. 2006. Helping People is Difficult: Growth and Performance in Social Enterprises Working for International Relief and Development. In Nicholls, *Social Entrepreneurship*: 247–70.

Jepson, P. 2005. Governance and accountability of Environmental NGOs. *Environmental Science and Policy*, **8**(5): 515–24.

John, R. 2007. *Beyond The Cheque: How Venture Philanthropists Add Value*. Skoll Centre for Social Entrepreneurship, available at: http://www.sbs.ox.ac.uk/skoll/research/Short+papers/Short+papers.htm.

Kendall, J. and Knapp, M. 2000. Measuring the Performance of Voluntary Organizations. *Public Management*, **2**(1): 105–32.

Leadbeater, C. 1997. *The Rise of the Social Entrepreneur*. London: Demos.

LeGrand, J. 2003. *Motivation, Agency, and Public Policy: Of Knights and Knaves, Pawns and Queens*. Oxford: Oxford University Press.

LeGrand, J. and Bartlett, W. (eds) 1993. *Quasi-Markets and Social Policy*. Basingstoke: Palgrave Macmillan.

Light, P. 2008. *The Search for Social Entrepreneurship*. Washington, DC: Brookings Institute.

Lister, S. 2003. NGO legitimacy – Technical Issue or Social Construct. *Critique of Anthropology*, **23**(2): 175–92.

Little, I. 1950. *A Critique of Welfare Economics*. Oxford: Clarendon Press.

Loft, A. 1994. Accountancy and the First World War. In Hopwood. and Miller, *Accounting as Social and Institutional Practice*: 116–37.

Miles, M. and Huberman, A. 1994. *Qualitative Data Analysis: An Expanded Sourcebook* (2nd edn). Thousand Oaks, CA: Sage.

Miller, P. 1994. Accounting As Social And Institutional Practice: An Introduction. In Hopwood. and Miller, *Accounting as Social and Institutional Practice*: 1–39.

Mulgan. G. 2007. *Social Innovation*. Skoll Centre for Social Entrepreneurship, available at: http://www.sbs.ox.ac.uk/skoll/research/Short+papers/Short+papers.htm.

Nicholls, A. 2004. Social Entrepreneurship: The Emerging Landscape. In Crainer, S. and Dearlove, D. (eds), *The Financial Times Handbook of Management* (third edn): 636–43. Harlow: FT Prentice Hall.

Nicholls, A. 2006. Social Entrepreneurship. In Jones-Evans, D. and Carter, S. (eds), *Enterprise and Small Business: Principles, Practice and Policy* (second edn): 220–42. Harlow: FT Prentice Hall.

Nicholls, A. (ed) 2008a. *Social Entrepreneurship: New Models of Sustainable Social Change* (paperback edn). Oxford: Oxford University Press.

Nicholls, A. 2008b. Capturing the Performance of the Socially Entrepreneurial Organisation (SEO): An Organisational Legitimacy Approach. In Robinson, J., Mair, J. and Hockerts, K. (eds), *International Perspectives on Social Entrepreneurship Research*: 27–74. Basingstoke: Palgrave Macmillan.

Nicholls, A. 2009, "We Do Good Things, Don't We?": "Blended Value Accounting" in Social Entrepreneurship, *Accounting, Organizations, and Society*, **34**(6/7): 755–69.

Nicholls, A. and Opal, C. 2005. *Fair Trade: Market-Driven Ethical Consumption*. London: Sage.

Nicholls, A. and Cho, A. 2006. Social Entrepreneurship: The Structuration of a Field. In Nicholls, A. (ed.), *Social Entrepreneurship: New Paradigms of Sustainable Social Change*: 99–118. Oxford: Oxford University Press.

Nicholls, A. and Young, R. 2008. Introduction: The Changing Landscape of Social Entrepreneurship; vii–xxiii, In Nicholls, *Social Entrepreneurship*.

O'Connell, J. 1982. *Welfare Economic Theory*. Boston: Auburn House Publishing.

Offer, A. 2007. *The Challenge of Affluence*. Oxford: Oxford University Press.

Osbourne, D. and Gaebler, T. 1992. *Reinventing Government*. Reading, MA: Addison-Wesley.

Paton, R. 2003. *Managing and Measuring Social Enterprises*. London: Sage.

Power, M. 1994a. The Audit Society. In Hopwoodand Miller, *Accounting As Social and Institutional Practice*: 299–316. Power, M., 1994b. *The Audit Explosion*. London: Demos.

Power, M. 2003. Auditing and The Production of Legitimacy. *Accounting, Organizations and Society*, **28**(4): 379–94.

Ritchie, J. 2003. The Applications of Qualitative Methods to Social Research. In Ritchie, J. and Lewis, J. (eds), *Qualitative Research Practice: A Guide for Social Science Students and Researchers*: 24–46. London: Sage.

REDF – Roberts Enterprise Development Foundation 2000. *SROI Methodology*, Roberts Enterprise Development Foundation. San Francisco.

Rousseau, D. 2006. Is There Such a Thing as "Evidenced-Based Management"? *Academy of Management Review*, **31**(2): 256–69.

Suchman, M. 1995. Managing Legitimacy: Strategic and Institutional Approaches. *Academy of Management Review*, **20**(3): 517–610.

Taylor-Gooby, P. 2004. *New Risks, New Welfare: The Transformation of the European Welfare State.* Oxford: Oxford University Press.

Taylor-Gooby, P. 2006. New Approaches to Expert and Institutional Risk. *Journal of Risk Research*, **9**(1): 79–95.

Young. R. 2006. For What It's Worth: Social Value and the Future of Social Entrepreneurship. In Nicholls, *Social Entrepreneurship*: 56–73.

14
Is It Ever Better to Lend Than to Give? A Social Embeddedness View of Alternative Approaches to Poverty Alleviation

Bart Victor and Woodrow Lucas

Introduction

Recently a promising new practice of promoting economic growth and opportunity for the poor, micro-lending, has emerged in global efforts to alleviate the conditions of poverty. In this chapter we examine micro-lending as an activity that potentially can help reduce the vulnerability and isolation of the poor. Controversially, the basis of micro-lending is debt financing for the poor. Traditional charity or public welfare generally employs non-contingent gifts to the poor. That is, charity provides direct assistance to poor through wealth transfers without explicit expectation or terms of repayment. From a purely economic perspective, charity would always be preferred over loans by poor recipients. In this contribution we explore an apparent paradox: that lending might actually be preferable to charity when the intention is the permanent alleviation of poverty. By viewing the problem of poverty alleviation through the perspective of embeddedness we reveal a complex story of the social meaning of charity and lending (Gouldner, 1960; Mauss, 1923), and their impact on poverty (Afrane, 2002; Granovetter, 1973, 1985). From this view we offer propositions about when and how direct lending might be a more effective practice for poverty alleviation than charity.

In the starkest of definitions, poverty can be described as an absolute or relative absence of wealth. This is the definition that underlies most of the measures of poverty used in public policy and development research. For example, the World Bank defines *extreme poverty* as living on less than US$1 per day, and *moderate poverty* as less than $2 a day (in purchasing power parity). In the US, poverty is officially measured in terms of income sufficiency to purchase basic goods and services. In the Organisation for Economic Co-operation and Development (OECD) the poverty line is based on a measure of 'economic distance', a level of income set at 50% of the median household income. Thus, poverty as we commonly understand it is an economic condition.[1]

However, the lack of income, relative or absolute, has shown itself to be an inadequate operational definition when applied to the challenge of poverty alleviation (Kozel and Parker, 2000; Narayan, 1997). The relationship between deprivation and suffering has proven far more complex than the economic measurement of poverty might indicate. In this contribution we first develop a social embeddedness view of poverty (Briggs, 1998; Granovetter, 1973). Applying this view we analyze the potential relative impacts of charity and loan-based aid on poverty. We develop a model which proposes that, for relief from the immediate conditions of poverty, charity is more effective than lending. However, when the intention of the aid is the permanent alleviation of poverty, charity may be less effective and even unintentionally generative of the conditions of poverty. For the purposes of permanent poverty alleviation, direct, loan-based aid may be more effective.

Poverty is a condition of unfreedom

Poverty is a condition of real human suffering and as such is a shared concern across countries and cultures. Who exactly is in poverty, how it is measured and what constitutes the alleviation of poverty, though, remain highly controversial (Sen, 1981). In general poverty is understood as a condition of economic deficit absolutely or relative to the condition of the non-poor. Such deficits are marked by the association between the deficit and suffering. However, that association has proven to be complex. Development researchers such as Amartya Sen have demonstrated that income insufficiency is only loosely related to the experience of poverty in terms of human suffering (Sen, 1981, 1999). In Sen's research, the quality of life, indicated by such measures as life expectancy, health, physical security, hunger and homelessness is associated but not directly caused by income insufficiency (Sen, 1984, 1999). Instead, factors such as race, gender, age, class, political conditions, geography and the environment all interact to create the condition of poverty. As a consequence the simple redistribution of wealth has a frustratingly weak impact on the alleviation of poverty. Sen's work is mirrored by other research on poverty which uncovers similar complex dynamics both creating poverty and resisting its alleviation (e.g. Briggs, 1998; Minear and Weiss, 1995; Seccombe, 2000).

Collectively, the recent study of poverty reveals that being poor involves more than simply having a low income (Drèze and Sen, 1995). To capture this complexity a more nuanced definition of poverty is increasingly being employed. The United Nations Committee on Economic, Social and Cultural Rights defines poverty as 'a human condition characterized by the sustained or chronic deprivation of the resources, capabilities, choices, security and power necessary for the enjoyment of an adequate standard of living and other civil, cultural, economic, political and social rights. Employing this definition of poverty we turn to understanding its causes and subsequently the impact of forms of charity and loans on its alleviation.

An embeddedness view of the causes of poverty

Sen (1999) coined the phrase 'unfreedom' to describe the conditions of the world's impoverished majority. In Sen's construction of the condition of poverty, income provides a degree of freedom of choice. However, this freedom of choice can only be activated to enhance the quality of life through the effective or substantive freedom to choose. Critical capabilities which can constitute substantive freedoms include political and economic participation, social opportunities, security, and liberties of voice, faith, and movement (Sen, 1999).

We propose applying a socio-economic embeddedness view to describe the conditions which promote or limit substantive freedom. A primary contribution of the embeddedness view has been to describe economic relations between individuals in actual social networks rather than in abstract idealized markets. This view characterizes social processes as a 'fluid' and complex mixing of economic and non-economic factors (Polanyi, 1957; White, 1981). A social embeddedness view of the condition of poverty highlights the structure and prevalence of the ties amongst the poor and between the poor and the non-poor (Granovetter, 1973, 1985). The view also reveals the political, social and cultural meaning of the transactions carried by such ties (Zukin and Dimaggio, 1990). From an embeddedness perspective, poverty can be described as a condition of relative or absolute isolation between the social networks of the poor and non-poor (Stack, 1974). Embeddedness further characterizes the condition of poverty as a preponderance of strong ties amongst the poor and a dearth of weak ties between the poor and non-poor (Granovetter, 1973, 1985). Such isolated strong tie networks can account for the persistent vulnerability and resource scarcity observed in communities of poverty (Venkatesh, 2006). As Granovetter (1973: 213) notes 'the heavy concentration of social energy in strong ties has the impact of fragmenting communities of the poor into encapsulated networks with poor connections between these units; individuals so encapsulated may then lose some of the advantages associated with the outreach of weak ties. This may be one more reason why poverty is self-perpetuating'.

From this view, like that of Sen; the alleviation of poverty would require more than simply the transfer of wealth. 'The options that a person has depend greatly on the relations with others . . .' (Drèze and Sen, 1995: 6). The view of poverty as an 'embedded' condition then offers a perspective to investigate both the failures of traditional approaches to poverty alleviation and to provide some hope for the apparent potential success of alternative approaches. Alleviating the causes of poverty requires transforming the socio-economic conditions in which the poor are embedded (Figure 14.1). Specifically, alleviating poverty requires: (a) linking the poor into the larger economy (Burt, 1992); (b) enhancing the mutuality of interests between the poor and the non-poor (Granovetter, 1973, 1985); and (c) enriching the social and reputation capital of the poor (Granovetter, 2005; Putnam, 1993).

Recent history has revealed a complex picture of global progress towards the alleviation of poverty. On many measures, including income, life expectancy, literacy, childhood mortality and hunger global progress against poverty has been startling. According to the World Bank, the proportion of the developing world's population living in extreme economic poverty (i.e. incomes of less than $1 PPP/day) has declined from 28% in 1990 to 21% in 2001. However, the vast majority of that improvement has occurred in East and South Asia (importantly

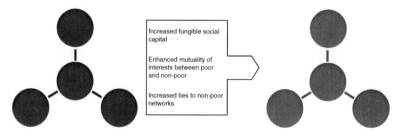

Figure 14.1   A social embeddedness model of poverty alleviation

China and India). In Sub-Saharan Africa extreme poverty increased from 41% in 1981 to 46% in 2001. In Russia and the former Soviet Union poverty rates rose to 6% at the end of the 1990s before beginning to recede more recently. Over the same period poverty remains at the same or even slightly higher levels in the Americas (including the US).

As positive as much of this progress appears, poverty remains an enormous global challenge. The movement from poverty described by the World Bank is from extreme to moderate poverty. Most of the world's population (as much as 80% by some estimates) lives in conditions of significant unfreedom. That is, they lack the substantive freedom to create and sustain an acceptable quality of life. The lives of the poor remain precarious, dangerous, and disadvantaged. Thus, while general economic development is critically important, more targeted, intentional responses are still required to truly alleviate poverty. That poverty persists for so many in even the wealthiest nations argues powerfully for such intended action.

It is against this evidence of progress and frustration that a critical reassessment of the programmatic global efforts to alleviate poverty is underway. In particular, the global approach to both public and private aid has come under serious criticism. By most estimates, aid directed at poverty alleviation is extremely inefficient, dubiously effective and, arguably, counter-productive (Easterly, 2006; Sachs, 2005).

A central feature of the criticisms of traditional approaches to poverty alleviation has been the evidence that their effects are not only inefficient, but also ephemeral. Charity works well to temporarily ameliorate the conditions of poverty by providing food, shelter and security. Charity also functions well to restore what the poor may lose as a result of crisis or catastrophe. However, charity has been criticized for failing to transform the conditions that create and maintain poverty (Easterly, 2006; Sachs, 2005).

There continues to be a call for new approaches and methods to effectively address poverty. Amongst these new approaches are those which attempt to alleviate poverty through direct lending. Notably, the Nobel Peace Prize was recently awarded to one of the early exemplars of this approach, Mohammed Yunus and his organization, the Grameen Bank.

Micro-lending

Lasting peace cannot be achieved unless large population groups find ways in which to break out of poverty. Micro-credit is one such means. Development from below also serves to advance democracy and human rights.

(Mjøs, 2006: 2)

While there are numerous variations and innovations on the theme of micro-lending, most institutions share the basic features found in the efforts of Mohammed Yunus and the Grameen Bank. These common features include (a) small interest bearing loans (typically less than $1000) for the capitalization of productive or entrepreneurial activities, (b) borrowers who because of their poverty have not had access to traditional banking, (c) loan collateral is provided by shared small group commitments and (d) loans are made for working capital or other commercial purposes. In recent years, micro-lending has expanded exponentially (Armendariz, and Morduch, 2000). Today the Grameen Bank itself lends to more than 2 million people. Around the world some 9000 additional microfinance institutions (MFI) have been organized (UNITUS.com). Benefits attributed to micro-lending include direct improvements to small-scale enterprises, increased personal income, increased personal spending on children's education, improved housing and better nutrition. Repayment rates for microfinance are typically between 95 and 100%. (Brau and Woller, 2004; Khandker, 1998). There have been claims of other social benefits such as opportunity for political empowerment and choices of public versus private schooling for children. Finally there are claims of psychological benefits from micro-lending such as increases in self-confidence and self-esteem (Afrane, 2002; Brau and Woller, 2004; Sebstad and Chen, 1996). These benefits are illustrated in the following example:

> With her first loan of $125, Wilma (an impoverished woman in the Philippines) bought another sewing machine and some high-quality material. The resulting products were easy to sell because they were attractive and stylish. Wilma hired a friend to work for her. Production increased, and Wilma's customers expanded beyond door to door. She met women who liked her products enough to buy them in larger quantities, so they could resell them in other neighborhoods. With each successive loan, Wilma bought another machine and hired another neighbor to work with her to meet the increasing demand. Three of her seamstresses and two cutters work on-site, and three more seamstresses work from home on a piece-by-piece basis. She hopes to rent space at a nearby market and open a boutique to sell her own products as well as other inventory (http://www.opportunity.org).

Such claims are not without controversy, and the extent and persistence of the impact of micro-lending on the alleviation of poverty remains controversial (Brau and Woller, 2004). However, the practice of lending-based poverty alleviation has emerged as a popular alternative to the traditional charitable gift based approaches.

Charity or loans? Alternatives for the alleviation of poverty

> Yunus believes firmly that alms destroy the initiative and creativity of poor people.
>
> (Mjøs, 2006: 2)

Charity is often society's choice of intervention to alleviate the conditions of poverty. Every day, all over the world, private charity and public welfare relieve the immediate experience of poverty. They relieve hunger, provide shelter, protect health and provide access to positive experiences. Similarly, around the world the poor are preyed upon by lenders who offer debt that tightens the grip of poverty (Stegman, 2001). On the surface, charity would appear preferable to lending simply because the poor are by definition severely resource limited. The debt associated with a loan, even if that debt is limited to the principle, would apparently disadvantage lending based-aid to the poor in comparison with charity. Are there conditions when this might not be true? That is, are there conditions when, towards the objective of alleviating poverty, lending might be preferable to charity?

We will argue that while it will provide relief from the immediate suffering from poverty, the giving and receiving of charity does not necessarily improve the embedded conditions of poverty. We will further argue that, unlike charity, the process of lending and repayment may function to fundamentally alleviate poverty.

Charity and loans: comparisons

When comparing loans and charity we begin with the observation that both are forms of the transfer of wealth between the non-poor and the poor. For this analysis we further specify that the transfer is between relative strangers (for example through a weak tie). Both the charitable gift and the loan share two critical features: the transfer creates obligations from the poor to the non-poor, and the created obligation carries expectations between the poor and non-poor for repayment, the contingencies for default and the basis for future interactions. While, structurally, charity and loans might be comparable, the embedded meanings of these common features are very distinct. These distinctions in turn may have different consequences.

Debts of gratitude or money: comparing the obligations created by charity versus loans

... A gift necessarily implies the notion of credit (Mauss, 1923: 35).

In his landmark study of primitive cultures, Mauss (1923) described the often complex terms of reciprocity embedded in 'non-contingent' gift exchanges. While such terms varied extensively between cultures, from the annual potlatch rituals in the Pacific Northwest to the 'voluntary/obligatory' fetes and fairs of the Pygmies, gift exchange is always associated with the creation and/or expiation of some debt (Mauss, 1923). It is inherent in all gift-giving that a particular form of indebtedness for the receiver is created. The debt created by offering a gift is implicit and importantly social, even between strangers (Komter, 2004; Kopytoff, 1988). Further, gift debts are truly aversive and motivating (Gouldner, 1960; Mauss, 1923). In contrast, loans are defined by their explicit and commoditized terms of repayment (Kopytoff, 1988). The granting and accepting of a loan incorporates the sharing of expectations for the time and amount of return from the borrower to the lender. Such terms may or may not include money interest and may or may not be secured with collateral. The debt, like that created from the receipt of a gift, is averse and motivating (Stegman, 2001).

Thus there is no difference between a gift and a loan in the sense they both create a debt which must be repaid or defaulted. However, the critical difference between the social or affective debt created by the gift and the commoditized debt created by loans may differentially affect the impact of the debt on the conditions of poverty.

Even within a culture and between social equals, the receiving of a gift debt can be seen as burdensome. Ruth Benedict, in her landmark study of Japan, described how gift-giving was a central feature of the relationship between persons, between individuals and the state, and between the living and their ancestors. Benedict notes that even the simple expressions of thanks, *arigato (this difficult thing)*, carries recognition of the weight of the debt taken when but the smallest of courtesies are extended (Benedict, 1946).

In the case of the poor, the 'balance of debt' created by charitable gift giving can exacerbate the status differences between the poor and non-poor (Schwartz, 1967). The sociologist Alvin Gouldner (1960) described how charitable gift transactions establish or reinforce the status differences between giver and recipient. The charitable gift is always at the discretion of the non-poor. And such debt is uniquely borne by the poor. Thus, the charitable gift is embedded in the differential status identities of the giver and receiver (Schwartz, 1967). Effectively, accepting charity reconfirms the social status of the receiver as 'poor' (Bougheas et al., 2005).

Not just unequal though, the poor are often strangers to the givers. This stranger-to-stranger exchange may heighten the debt burden of charity for the poor. The meaning and magnitude of gift debt is deeply embedded in the cultural context of the exchange (Mauss, 1923). The strength of the tie between giver and receiver has important consequences for whether the gift will be accepted, how the gift is given and received, and the weight of the debt created. The more distant the relationship between the giver and receiver, the more gratitude is expected (Bar-Tal et al., 1977). Further, between strangers, the felt weight of gift debt potentially might be even greater than intended by the giver. The misunderstanding of the meaning of gift debt is a recurring theme in studies of cross-cultural exchange (Fan, 2002; Hwang, 1987).

The impossibility and even the preference for non-reciprocal exchange in charitable giving has often perplexed economists. Why would anyone simply give to the poor without hope of repayment? This is particularly puzzling when the poor are strangers to the non-poor, and are socially, geographically and economically separated (Becker, 1974). The answer offered by economists is to locate the charitable motive in some direct or indirect benefit to the giver (Becker, 1974). Direct benefits might include a 'warm glow' acclaim, or alleviation of guilt (Andreoni, 1990). Indirect benefits include status effects (a socially acceptable way to signal wealth), or the advantages of inclusion in elite communities of fellow givers (Becker, 1974). Such benefits to the giver are enhanced in value when the poor recipient cannot explicitly 'repay' the debt of charity.

To the extent charitable giving is motivated by the desire to provide assistance to those in need (Bougheas et al., 2005), establishing that need is an essential and defining process in the making of a gift. That is, there is no direct benefit to charitable giving without its felt impact on poverty. The charitable gift then is given in response to the giver's perception of the needs of the poor. If the receiver turns out to not be 'needy' the value to the giver is dramatically reduced (Lee and McKenzie, 1990). In a sense, what the poor have to offer the non-poor in exchange for the gift of charity is their suffering (Lee and McKenzie, 1990). The charitable gift feeds the child, builds a shelter, or bandages a wound. In this way the 'balance of debt' is maintained by the poor recipient and non-poor giver through a cycle of suffering and relief (Poppendieck, 1998).

Thus, when the debt of the gift is extended to the poor by the non-poor, the value to the giver is heightened by the extent of the evidence of suffering and the improbability of repayment. Further, the non-poor may prefer conditions of exchange which further limit or even bar the poor from repaying the debt. Anonymous giving and refusal to accept explicit thanks are frequently characteristic of charitable exchanges (Becker, 1974). Studies show that individuals who anticipate being unable to return a favor are less willing to ask for and receive needed help than individuals who anticipate being able to reciprocate (Greenberg and Shapiro, 1971). The combination of the difficulty and ambiguity of the terms of repayment of the gift and the limitations on repayment opportunity make the charitable gift to the poor particularly burdensome. Perhaps unsurprisingly, the poor often loathe accepting gift charity and express a preference for other types of aid (Godelier, 1999; Seccombe, 2000).

In contrast, the debt created by lending may be comparatively less burdensome and less directly reinforcing of status differences between the poor and non-poor. The explicit and commoditized nature of loan debt limits the intended and unintended weight of the debt created. Loan debts are expressed in monetized terms. While money certainly has deep and important social meaning (Baker and Jimerson, 1992; Zelizer, 1994), it is first and foremost a medium of exchange between strangers. The objective, physical and routinized nature of money-based exchanges make loan debt far less subject to misunderstanding than gift debt (Mauss, 1923).

Unlike charitable gifts, loan debts are exchanged between persons of equal as well as un-equal status. Thus the identity exchanged in lending does not necessarily exacerbate social differences or label the borrower as poor (Keister, 2001). The lender and the borrower must agree upon how much capital is transferred. In determining eligibility for a loan, the lender considers amount of capital the borrower might be expected to repay. The poor then can explicitly and fully repay (or default on) the loan. The 'balance of debt' in the case of loans is maintained by the poor through a cycle of lending and repayment.

Relieving the suffering of the poor: gifts or loans?

It has long been posited that aid to the poor might be distinguished into two broad categories

- relief: aid to remove the immediate suffering caused by poverty; and
- development: aid to alleviate the conditions of poverty permanently. (Ball and Halevy, 1996; Minear and Weiss, 1995)[2]

In this chapter, this distinction is drawn to permit an analysis of the impact of the two distinct types or forms of aid described above: charity and loans. Relief includes both emergency aid in response to disaster and recurring aid directed at persistent sufferings. This form of aid is motivated by the evidence of suffering and its use or effectiveness is measured by the relief of suffering. In contrast, development aid has as its intent the uplifting of the poor who, while they are certainly found suffering from the ill effects of poverty, seek an enduring change from the conditions that create the suffering. The question raised here is, given a particular aid intention, does it matter how aid is provided (Figure 14.2)?

The suffering that marks poverty can include the desperate need for food, shelter, potable water, physical security, advocacy for justice, and

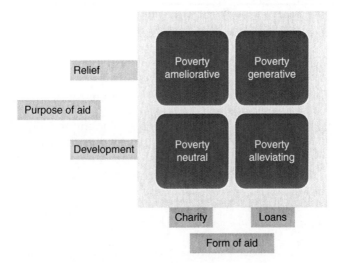

Figure 14.2   Differential impacts on poverty by form and purpose of aid

more. To relieve suffering, charity must supply the poor with what they lack. Relief must deliver the food, shelter, security, or justice to the poor. Such needs might be chronically associated with physical or mental disability or acutely caused by disaster or misfortune. 'The basic impetus of relief is one of unconditional humanity: everything must be tried to reach those in need'(de Waal, 2004). This criterion would require that not only is the relief aid provided, but that it is accepted and used by the poor to relieve their suffering. It might be further specified that accepting such relief would not deepen or extend the suffering of the poor. That is, while that the provision of relief is intended to reduce the suffering created by the conditions of poverty, relief ought never to cause greater poverty (Poppendieck, 1998).

The poor and non-poor are often brought together over suffering. For the non-poor, it is the potential to eliminate specific suffering through relief aid that brings them into the relationship with the poor (Lee and McKenzie, 1990). What the poor have to 'offer' the non-poor is their suffering and the gratitude for being relieved of it. From the social embeddedness view, the impact of applying the form of aid to poverty relief might be understood in terms of how a given form of aid impacts (a) the links or ties between the poor and non-poor, (b) the mutuality of interests between the poor and non-poor, and (c) the social and reputation capital of the poor. From this view charity may well be better suited to relief than loans.

Paradoxically perhaps, to the extent that it is motivated by the non-poor's desire to relieve suffering, the more the poor suffer, the more capable they may be of satisfying the debt of charity. The content or meaning of the social capital of the poor in need of relief from suffering is the trust they can create in their worthiness for charity. That is, are they 'truly' needy? The more difficult to measure this need becomes, the more critical it becomes for the poor to establish the *bono fides* of their need to receive a gift (Lee and McKenzie, 1990). However, if such trust can be maintained, the poor can display the relief from suffering required to expiate the debt of gift charity (Lee and McKenzie, 1990).

As a consequence of this exchange of gift for gratitude, the poor might be no better off, but their situation might not be expected to necessarily worsen. That is, the exchange of gift charity for relief may be expected to leave unchanged the low and different status of the poor (Poppendieck, 1998).

A loan for relief would create a different kind of debt obligation than charity and may be expected to have different consequences for the poor. When received in relief, the value of a loan, like that of a gift, would be immediately consumed to relieve suffering. While such 'consumption' would be of real benefit to the poor, it would not necessarily enhance the poor's capabilities. That is, relief aid is intended to restore the poor to their conditions prior to the emergency or recurring circumstances that create the suffering. Relief does not prevent crisis or transform chronic conditions; it is instead intended to ameliorate the suffering that ensues. In the wake of the relief of suffering, the poor may not be expected to have created a surplus of value which could be used to repay a debt (Ball and Halevy, 1996; Minear and Weiss, 1995).

The tragic experience of the poor with the consequences of consumption lending is the foundation of the indictment of fringe banking noted above. A common source of consumption loans for the poor in urban America is 'payday' lending and pawn shops (Stegman, 2001). Such providers of loans to the poor claim to offer a source of needed resources for those outside the traditional banking system. These loans are generally of short maturity and interest-bearing. In this way, the payday and pawnshop loans superficially appear structurally identical to the loans of the micro-lenders. However, the impact of payday and pawnshop loans on poverty is far different.

The kind of debt offered by payday and pawnshop lenders is justified by its relief function according to the Deputy Banking Commissioner of the State of North Carolina: 'Say you have someone in your family who is ill and all of a sudden you have a $100 bill from the doctor and medicine that will cost another $100. What cost are you willing to pay to obtain that $200?' (quoted in Stegman, 2001: 19). These 'fringe' bankers offer consumer credit to isolated, needy individuals on explicit, monetized terms (Caskey and Zikmund, 1990; Stegman, 2001).

It is perhaps not surprising that the debt created by relief lending like payday or pawnshop loans is frequently defaulted. 'Payday borrowers tend to be repeat customers, with 48% taking out seven or more total advances in a year, and 22% taking 14 or more. Borrowers also tend to roll over or renew the same loan, postponing final payment and accruing significant interest charges; about 40% had renewed loans five times or more' (Stegman, 2001). The combination of the consumption use and high default rates associated with relief lending leads to the expectation that this form of aid may deepen the conditions of poverty. Defaulting on a commoditized debt reduces the tradable social capital of the poor. Not only is the debt not repaid to the lender but failure to repay the loan becomes a visible stain on the reputation of the borrower. This further isolates the poor from the non-poor by reinforcing the identity of being a bad risk, unable or unwilling to repay a debt.

Additionally, the tie between the relief lender and the poor can evolve into one in which the interests of the non-poor being becomes the perpetuation of the conditions of poverty. In the case of lenders like those described above, the high default rates and concomitantly high costs of the loans exacerbate the asymmetry of interests between the poor and non-poor. For pawnbrokers the prior possession and a high collateral value to loan value ratio creates an interest for the lender in default (Caskey and Zikmund, 1990). In the case 'fringe' banking, often the fees, pre-paid interest and high interest rates create an interest for the lender in 'rolling over' the debt. A study by the state of Indiana estimated that '77 percent of payday loans are rollovers, with the average payday customer averaging more than ten loans per year' (Stegman, 2001: 19) With such rollovers, effective annual percentage interest rates can readily exceed 400%.

> It'd be great if it was the middle class and it was just the plumber and all they need is $200 this one time to get them by. But that's just not the reality. These are people who are really not making it.... They're not fixing a blown tire or a pipe—they're paying the rent. "[Payday lenders are] taking advantage of people in time of need.... We've got to get some controls on the interest rates. Three, four hundred percent? There ought to be a law.
>
>   (Consumer credit counselor quoted in Stegman, 2001: 16)

In the context of the alleviation of poverty, these types of debt can be seen as undermining the foundation for future ties between the poor and non-poor, the potential for the destruction of social capital, and the reduction of 'substantive freedom' of the poor. In contrast, charity can relieve suffering without substantially worsening the underlying conditions of poverty. Thus for relief intentions, the form of aid utilized may have critical implications on the conditions of poverty:

Proposition 1: Relief aid in the form of a charitable gift will be more effective for the relief of suffering than relief aid in the form of loans.

Proposition 2: Relief aid in the form of a charitable gift will be less generative of the conditions of poverty than relief aid in the form of loans.

Proposition 2a: Relief aid in the form of a loan will increase the social isolation of the poor more than relief aid in the form of a gift.

Proposition 2b: Relief aid in the form of a loan will increase the asymmetry of interests between the poor and non-poor more than relief aid in the form of a gift.

Proposition 2c: Relief aid in the form of a loan will decrease the social and reputation capital of the poor more than relief aid in the form of a gift.

Alleviating poverty through development: charity or loans?

Ultimately it is the ambition of all concerned about poverty to eliminate it entirely and permanently. To accomplish this goal, the underlying conditions that create and perpetuate the suffering must be transformed. Aid from the poor to the non-poor with this intention is generally called development. As described above, to accomplish its intent, development aid must generate substantive freedom for the poor (Sen, 1999). From the embeddedness point of view, development aid must result in (a) more effective integration of the poor into the larger economy; (b) greater mutuality of interests between the poor and the non-poor; and (c) sufficient increases in social and reputation capital of the poor to enable sustainable increases in capabilities and income. Given this view we can compare the differential impacts of the form of aid on the aims of development.

The implicit debt created by the gift would appear, other things being equal, to be less burdensome for development purposes than loans. Unlike relief, development is intended to increase the capacity of the poor to produce value, whether through their labor, the utilization of their real property, or as entrepreneurs. The principal repayment and any interest or fees on a loan would be a tax on this value. However, considering the additional consequences of charitable gift debt and the potential development generative effects of the loan debt cycle, loans might, under certain conditions, be expected to be more beneficial than charity for development purposes.

What the poor have to offer from development is the change in their status and the value generated from the economic activity. Successful development leaves the poor increasingly non-poor. To the extent that this is the case, they are increasingly capable of participating in economic life on the same terms as the non-poor. The promise of development is that the poor can climb up on the ladder of economic development to be integrated into the larger economy (Sachs, 2005).

For these gains from development to persist; for poverty to be truly ended, the underlying causes of poverty must be changed. The form of aid for development might well make a difference on these terms. The initiation and completion of the debt creation-satisfaction cycle from charity and loans could be more or less generative of tradable social capital, access to new and valuable resources, and mutually beneficial exchange ties for the poor. In particular, 'bridging' ties are critical for development (Narayan, 1999; Woolcock and Narayan, 2000). That is, increasing the relationships that link the poor to the non-poor world outside and endowing the poor with the reputation capital that is commonly leveraged in economic exchange are key to sustainable economic development. The advantages of such ties are clearly visible in non-poor financial markets where firms with such linkages are more likely to get a loan, with lower interest rates, and have less collateral required for security (Uzzi, 1999).

Successfully initiating and completing the loan cycle can both provide the poor with the capital necessary for development and with the foundations of a credit-worthy reputation, more economic transaction ties and mutually beneficial relationships on which to build further. The successful completion of the loan debt cycle for development also directly benefits the lender. The lender accomplishes their social and economic purpose, receives a return on capital, and gains a usable tie to a productive, credit-worthy borrower (or group of borrowers). The small size of the loans, the riskiness of the projects, and the costs of the lending itself do not erode all these benefits for the micro-lender. The recent experience of micro-lenders has demonstrated that it is possible to grow a micro-lending institution to significant size and that even a secondary market for the loans can be developed and operated profitably (UNITUS.com). The potential for success for the borrowers is also high. Micro-lenders routinely report repayment rates that rival and often exceed comparable rates amongst the non-poor (Brau and Woller, 2004).

In contrast, completing the charity cycle expends the capital of the non-poor source and does not necessarily build the reputation, ties or mutual benefit relationships for the poor. Further, the charity cycle confirms the status of the poor. One of the critical factors maintaining the isolation and unfreedom of the poor is the indignity of poverty (Poppendieck, 1998). This indignity is felt by the poor themselves and inherent in the relative position of the poor to the non-poor. For development to be effective, for the isolation of the poor to be reduced, this indignity must be overcome. The explicit, public, and definitive satisfaction of the debt possible with loan can be a means to this end.

At the initiation of the development cycle, the need for capital must be established regardless of whether the intent is to give or lend. However, lending further requires explicit agreement between lender and borrower on the amount and terms for the loan. With this explicit prior contract, the borrower can demonstrate, on the same criteria as the non-poor, their creditworthiness. Such a demonstration has value in banking and capital markets (Keister, 2001). Proof of credit-worthiness is essential for both participation in formal banking and to securing favorable terms and conditions for future financing. Attaining this reputation for creditworthiness is also of direct value for the poor for themselves. Debt repayment may be a form of mastery for borrowers which results in increased self efficacy and subsequent agency (Gecas, 1989).

These impacts are not limited to the dyad of the borrower and the lender. The reputation capital accrued and the economic ties created can benefit the close network of relationship between the poor. 'Due to the network effects, improving the status of a given agent also improves the outlook for that agent's connections. This is the contagion effect ... ' (Calvó-Armengol and Jackson, 2004: 428). The common practice of group based lending by micro-finance institutions can promote the benefits of this contagion effect even further (Armendariz, and Morduch, 2000). An example from on micro-lender in India (Spandana) illustrates these impacts.

> In 1998 Sivamma received a loan in the amount of US$85 (4000 Rupees) from Spandana, a microfinance institution in her city. Initially her business was collecting human hair. Sivamma used her ingenuity and decided to use the loan money to buy trinkets with which to pay children to collect the hair from their mothers' brushes. Now Sivamma has hundreds of women working for her. They also pay the children trinkets in exchange for hair and then sell the hair to Sivamma, who in turn sells it to those who use the oil from the hair follicles to manufacture medicinal products. Previously she could only borrow from unscrupulous money lenders at a very exorbitant interest rate. Today she can receive from Spandana both short-term loans without any collateral and long-term loans because she has become credit worthy.
>
> (www.kbyutv.org/programs/smallfortunes/borrowers/)

Thus, the creation of the indebtedness of loan aid establishes a mutual interest between lender and borrower, enhances the borrower's self esteem, and the repayment of creates fungible social capital. In contrast, the creation of the indebtedness of charity aide exacerbates status differentials between giver and receiver and can undermine self-esteem. Satisfaction of the debt of a gift is ambiguous and creates no valuable 'social' capital.

For development intentions, the form of aid utilized may have critical implications on the conditions of poverty:

Proposition 3: Development aid in the form of a loan will be more effective for the alleviation of poverty than aid in the form of gifts.

Proposition 3a: Relief aid in the form of a loan will increase the social integration of the poor more than relief aid in the form of a charitable gift.

Proposition 3b: Relief aid in the form of a loan will increase the mutuality of interests between the poor and non-poor more than relief aid in the form of a charitable gift.

Proposition 3c: Relief aid in the form of a loan will increase the social and reputation capital of the poor more than relief aid in the form of a charitable gift.

Implications for poverty alleviation and social entrepreneurship

An apparent paradox motivated this study. In the world of business, lenders to the poor have traditionally occupied a marginal and morally suspect place. Pawnshops, payday lenders and other 'fringe' bankers were considered predatory at worst and vaguely unsavory at best. Yet in 2006, the Grameen Bank, a lender to the poor, was selected for the Nobel Peace Prize. Even before this singular recognition, lending to the poor was becoming a regular and generally accepted feature of the global effort to end poverty (Armendariz and Morduch, 2000). There were no simple distinctions between micro-lenders like the Grameen Bank and 'fringe' bankers. Both groups of lenders made interest-bearing loans; all required some form of collateral or joint guarantee; all actively 'sold' their loans; all sought sustainability and growth for their banks.

At the foundation of this paradox is a crucial question inherent in every effort to apply business models to the problem of poverty alleviation. Lending models are potentially extraordinarily effective, but only when they are used well and for the right intent. So can business models be used to directly and effectively alleviate poverty?

To seek a part of the answer, we first established that less poverty must mean more substantive freedom. Sen's analysis requires we understand that simply increasing income does not necessarily alleviate poverty (1999). Instead we are drawn to a complex of factors dynamically interacting to create and maintain poverty. It is the transformation of those interactions that alleviates poverty. We viewed these interactions in the terms of social and economic embeddedness to describe contrast how lending could be compared with charity in terms of its impact on poverty.

The analysis revealed an interaction of a kind. Loans are indeed different from charity, and that difference matters, depending on what the poor and the non-poor need and desire. When the need is immediate and relief from suffering is the goal, charity seems best. Unlike a lender, the charitable giver expects in return that which someone relieved of a suffering can offer. But charity only can be expected to provide relief. By giving charity, the non-poor do not join in partnership, they do not share a mutual interest, and they do not see the poor as equals. As a result, charity leaves the poor isolated and lacking substantive freedom.

But when the need goal is to lift the poor from poverty, loans may well have a role. Lenders expect borrowers to repay, not in gratitude, but in kind. Unlike the gift giver, until they are repaid, lenders *need* the borrowers to be productive. When repaid, the lender has an interest in renewing the tie with a creditworthy partner. And not just the lender, but the borrowers themselves gain from the transaction. Before and after receiving a gift of charity, the poor remain *the poor*. But the poor borrower gains both the new capabilities developed to meet the demands of repayment and the reputation as someone with whom others can do business. That is, when it all works, the poor become more like the non-poor. Of course it doesn't always work. And not everyone desires or can make the changes required for development. But among the billions of poor in our world, there are many who desire something more – something better (Fischer and Benson, 2006). Loans may have a distinct role to play in their futures.

Notes

1. There are many forms of poverty such as spiritual, emotional or moral poverty which are not necessarily economic in any sense. However, for the purposes of this essay, we will concern ourselves solely with poverty which is importantly economic.

2. There is controversy about how these two kinds of aid are related (e.g. whether they are elements of a single continuum of aid), whether they should be provided in some sort of sequence, and how each type of aid might interact, the distinction between them remains important (Smillie, 1998).

References

Afrane, S. 2002. Impact Assessment of Microfinance Interventions in Ghana and South Africa: A Synthesis of Major Impacts and Lessons. *Journal of Microfinance*, 4(1): 37–58.

Andreoni, J. 1990. Impure Altruism and Donations to Public Goods: A Theory of Warm Glow Giving? *Economic Journal*, 100(401): 464–77.

Armendariz, de Aghion, B. and Morduch, J. 2000. Microfinance Beyond Group Lending. *The Economics of Transition*, 8(2): 401–20.

Baker, W. E.,and Jimerson, J. B. 1992. The Sociology of Money. *American Behavioral Science*, 35(6): 678–93.

Becker, G. S. 1974. A Theory of Social Interactions. *Journal of Political Economics*, 82(6): 1063–93.

Ball, N., and Halevy, T. 1996. *Making Peace Work: The Role of the International Development Community*. Washington, DC: Overseas Development Council.

Bar-Tal, D., Bar-Zohar Y., Greenberg, M. and Hermon, M. 1977. Reciprocity Behavior in the Relationship Between Donor and Recipient and Between Harm-Doer and Victim. *Sociometry*, 40(3): 293–98.

Benedict, R. 1946. *The Chrysanthemum and the Sword: Patterns of Japanese Culture*. Boston: Houghton Mifflin.

Bougheas, S., Dasgupta, I. and Morrissey, O. 2005. Tough Love or Unconditional Charity? CREDIT Research Paper. Centre for Research in Economic Development and International Trade, School of Economics, University of Nottingham, UK.

Brau, J. and Woller, G. 2004. Microfinance: A Comprehensive Review of the Existing Literature and an Outline for Future Financial Research. *Journal of Entrepreneurial Finance and Business Ventures*, 9: 1–26.

Briggs, X. d. S. 1998. Brown Kids in White Suburbs: Housing Mobility and the Multiple Faces of Social Capital. *Housing Policy Debate*, 9(1): 177–221.

Burt, R. 1992. *Structural Holes: The Social Structure of Competition*. Cambridge, MA: Harvard University Press.

Calvó-Armengol, A. and Jackson, M. O. 2004. The Effects of Social Networks on Employment and Inequality. *American Economic Review*, 94(3): 426–54.

Caskey, J. P., and Zikmund, B. J. 1990. Pawnshops: The Consumer's Lender of Last Resort. *Economic Review – Federal Reserve Bank of Kansas City*. 75(2): 5–18.

de Waal, A. 2004. Rethinking Aid. Developing a Human Security Package for Africa. *New Economy*, 11(3): 158–63.

Drèze, J. and Sen, A. 1995. *India: Economic Development and Social Opportunity*. Oxford: Clarendon Press.

Easterly, W. 2006. *The White Man's Burden*. New York: Penguin.

Fan, Y. 2002. Ganxi's Consequences: Personal Gains at Social Cost. *Journal of Business Ethics*, 38(4): 371–80.

Fischer, E. F. and Benson. 2006. *Broccoli and Desire: Global Connections and Maya Struggles in Post-war Guatemala*. Palo Alto, CA: Stanford University Press.

Gecas, V. 1989. The Social Psychology of Self-Efficacy. *Annual Review of Sociology*, 15: 291–316.

Godelier, M. 1999. *The Enigma of the Gift*. Cambridge: Polity Press.

Gouldner, A.H. 1960. The Norm of Reciprocity: A Preliminary Statement. *American Sociological Review*, 25(2): 161–78.

Granovetter, M. 1973. The Strength of' Weak Ties. *American Journal of Sociology*, 78(6): 1360–80.

Granovetter, M. 1985. Economic Action and Social Structure: The Problem of Embeddedness. *American Journal of Sociology*, 91(3): 481–510.

Granovetter, M. 2005. The Impact of Social Structure on Economic Outcomes. *Journal of Economic Perspectives*, 19(1): 33–50.

Greenberg, M. S. and Shapiro, S. P. 1971. Indebtedness: An Adverse Aspect of Asking for and Receiving Help. *Sociometry*, 34(2): 290–301.

Hwang, K. 1987. Face and Favour: The Chinese Power Game. *American Journal of Sociology*, 92(4): 944–74.

Keister, L. A. 2001. Exchange Structures in Transition: A Longitudinal Study of Lending and Trade Relations in Chinese Business Groups. *American Sociological Review*, 66(3): 336–60.

Khandker, S. 1998. *Fighting Poverty with Microcredit: Experience in Bangladesh*. New York: Oxford University Press for the World Bank.

Komter, A. E. 2004. Gratitude and Gift Exchange. In Emmons R. A., McCullough M. E. (eds.), *Psychology of Gratitude*: 195–212. New York: Oxford University Press.

Kopytoff, I. 1988. The Cultural Biography of Things. In Appadurai, A. (ed.), *The Social Life of Things: Commodities in Cultural Perspective*: 64–91. Cambridge: Cambridge University Press.

Kozel, V. and Parker, B. 2000. Integrated Approaches to Poverty Assessment in India. In Bamberger, M. (ed.), *Integrating Quantitative and Qualitative Research in Development Projects*. Washington, DC: World Bank.

Lee, D. and McKenzie, R. 1990. Second Thoughts on the Public-Good Justification for Government Poverty Programs. *The Journal of Legal Studies*, 19(1): 189–202.

Mauss, M. 1950/1923. *The Gift: The Form and Reason for Exchange in Archaic Societies*. London: Routledge.

Minear, L. and Weiss, T. 1995. *Mercy Under Fire: 20–21*. Boulder, CO: Westview Press.

Mjøs, O. D. 2006. *Presentation Speech for the Nobel Peace Prize 2006 by Chairman of the Norwegian Nobel Committee*. Oslo, December 10, 2006.

Narayan, D. 1997. *Voices of the Poor. Poverty and Social Capital in Tanzania. Environmentally Sustainable Development Monograph 20*. Washington, DC: World Bank.

Narayan, D. 1999. *Bonds and Bridges: Social Capital and Poverty. Policy Research Working Paper 2167*. World Bank, Poverty Reduction and Economic Management Network. Washington, DC: World Bank.

Polanyi, K. 1957. The Economy as Institute Process. In Dalton, G. (ed.), *Primitive, Archaic, and Modern Economies: Essays of Karl Polanyi*. Boston, Beacon, 1968: 139–74.

Poppendieck, J. 1998. *Sweet Charity: Emergency Food and the End of Entitlement*. New York: Penguin.

Putnam, R. 1993. *Making Democracy Work: Civic Traditions in Modern Italy*. Princeton, NJ: Princeton University Press.

Sachs, J. 2005. *The End of Poverty: Economic Possibilities for Our Time*. New York: Penguin.

Schwartz, B. 1967. The Social Psychology of the Gift. *American Journal of Sociology*, **73**(1): 1–11.

Sebstad, J. and Chen, G. 1996. *Overview of Studies on the Impact of Microenterprise Credit*. Assessing the Impact of Microenterprise Services. Washington, DC: AIMS.

Seccombe, K. 2000. Families in Poverty in the 1990s: Trends, Causes, Consequences, and Lessons Learned. *Journal of Marriage and Family*, **62**(4): 1094–113.

Sen, A. 1981. *Poverty and Famines: An Essay on Entitlement and Deprivation*. Oxford: Clarendon Press.

Sen, A. 1984. *Resources, Values, and Development*. Oxford: Basil Blackwell.

Sen, A. 1999. *Development as Freedom*. New York: Knopf.

Smillie, I. 1998. Relief and Development: The Struggle for Synergy. Providence, Humanitarianism and War Project Occasional paper no. 33, Providence: Thomas J. Watson Jr. Institute for International Studies, Brown University.

Stack, C. 1974. *All Our Kin*. New York: Harper & Row.

Stegman, M. 2001. The Public Policy Challenges of Payday Lending. *Popular Government*, **66**(3), 16–22.

United Nations High Commissioner of Human Rights, Human Rights in Development, "What is Poverty?" available online: http://www.unhchr.ch/development/poverty-02.html.

UNITUS, Innovative Solutions to Global Poverty, http://www.unitus.com/.

Uzzi, B. 1999. Social Relations and Networks in the Making of Financial Capital. *American Social Review*, **64**: 481–505.

Venkatesh, S. 2006. *Off the Books: The Underground Economy of the Urban Poor*. Cambridge, MA: Harvard University Press.

White, H. C. 1981. Where Do Markets Come From? *American Journal Sociol*, **87**(3): 517–47.

Woolcock, M. and Narayan, D. 2000. Social Capital: Implications for Development Theory, Research, and Policy. *World Bank Research Observer*, **15**(2): 225–49.

Zelizer, V. 1994. *The Social Meaning of Money*. New York: Basic Books.

Zukin, S. and DiMaggio, P. 1990. *Structures of Capital: The Social Organization of the Economy*. New York: Cambridge University Press.

Index